THE REPUBLIC OF PLATO

Benjamin Jowett's
'Introduction and Analysis'

Based on his 1888 translation

Stew Hanley

Book Cover by Stew Hanley

First edition 2025

Contents

Introduction & Analysis
Background & Overview

The Republic of Plato is the longest of his works with the exception of the Laws, and is certainly the greatest of them. There are nearer approaches to modern metaphysics in the Philebus and in the Sophist; the Politicus or Statesman is more ideal; the form and institutions of the State are more clearly drawn out in the Laws; as works of art, the Symposium and the Protagoras are of higher excellence. But no other Dialogue of Plato has the same largeness of view and the same perfection of style; no other shows an equal knowledge of the world, or contains more of those thoughts which are new as well as old, and not of one age only but of all. Nowhere in Plato is there a deeper irony or a greater wealth of humour or imagery, or more dramatic power. Nor in any other of his writings is the attempt made to interweave life and speculation, or to connect politics with philosophy. The Republic is the centre around which the other Dialogues may be grouped; here philosophy reaches the highest point (cp, especially in Books V, VI, VII) to which ancient thinkers ever attained. Plato among the Greeks, like Bacon among the moderns, was the first who conceived a method of knowledge, although neither of them always distinguished the bare outline or form from the substance of truth; and both of them had to be content with an abstraction of science which was not yet realized. He was the greatest metaphysical genius whom the world has seen; and in him, more than in any other ancient thinker, the germs of future knowledge are contained. The sciences of logic and psychology, which have supplied so many instruments of thought to after-ages, are based upon the analyses of Socrates and Plato. The principles of definition, the law of contradiction, the fallacy of arguing in a circle, the distinction between the essence and accidents of a thing or notion, between means and ends, between causes and conditions; also the division of the mind into the rational, concupiscent, and irascible elements, or of pleasures and desires into necessary and unnecessary—these and other great forms of thought are all of them to be found in the Republic, and were probably first invented by Plato. The greatest of all logical truths, and the one of which writers on philosophy are most apt to lose sight, the difference between words and things, has been most strenuously insisted on by him (cp. Rep.; Polit.; Cratyl. 435, 436 ff), although he has not always avoided the confusion of them in his own writings (e.g. Rep.). But he does not bind up truth in logical formulae,—logic is still veiled in metaphysics; and the science which he imagines to 'contemplate all truth and all existence' is very unlike the doctrine of the syllogism which Aristotle claims to have discovered (Soph. Elenchi, 33. 18).

Neither must we forget that the Republic is but the third part of a still larger design which was to have included an ideal history of Athens, as well as a political and physical philosophy. The fragment of the Critias has given birth to a world-famous fiction, second only in importance to the tale of Troy and the legend of Arthur; and is said as a fact to have inspired some of the early navigators of the sixteenth century. This mythical tale, of which the subject was a history of the wars of the Athenians against the Island of Atlantis, is supposed to be founded upon an unfinished poem of Solon, to which it would have stood in the same relation as the writings of the logographers to the poems of Homer. It would have told of a struggle for Liberty (cp. Tim. 25 C), intended to represent the conflict of Persia and Hellas. We may judge from the noble commencement of the Timaeus, from the fragment of the Critias itself, and from the third book of the Laws, in what manner Plato would have treated this high argument. We can only guess why the great design was abandoned; perhaps because Plato became sensible of some incongruity in a fictitious history, or because he had lost his interest in it, or because advancing years forbade the completion of it; and we may please ourselves with the fancy that had this imaginary narrative ever been finished, we should have found Plato himself sympathising with the struggle for Hellenic independence (cp. Laws, iii. 698 ff.), singing a hymn of triumph over Marathon and Salamis, perhaps making the reflection of Herodotus (v. 78) where he contemplates the growth of the Athenian empire—'How brave a thing is freedom of speech, which has made the Athenians so far exceed every other state of Hellas in greatness!' or, more probably, attributing the victory to the ancient good order of Athens and to the favor of Apollo and Athene (cp. Introd. to Critias).

Again, Plato may be regarded as the 'captain' ('arhchegoz') or leader of a goodly band of followers; for in the Republic is to be found the original of Cicero's De Republica, of St. Augustine's City of God, of the Utopia of Sir Thomas More, and of the numerous other imaginary States which are framed upon the same model. The extent to which Aristotle or the Aristotelian school were indebted to him in the Politics has been little recognised, and the recognition is the more necessary because it is not made by Aristotle himself. The two philosophers had more in common than they were conscious of; and probably some elements of Plato remain still undetected in Aristotle. In English philosophy too, many affinities may be traced, not only in the works of the Cambridge Platonists, but in great original writers like Berkeley or Coleridge, to Plato and his ideas. That there is a truth higher than experience, of which the mind bears witness to herself, is a conviction which in our own generation has been enthusiastically asserted, and is perhaps gaining ground. Of the Greek authors who at the Renaissance brought a new life into the world Plato has had the greatest influence. The Republic of Plato is also the first treatise upon education, of which the writings of Milton and Locke, Rousseau, Jean Paul, and Goethe are the legitimate descendants. Like Dante or Bunyan, he has a revelation of another life; like Bacon, he is profoundly impressed with the unity of knowledge; in the early Church he exercised a real influence on theology, and at the Revival of Literature on politics. Even the fragments of his words when 'repeated at second-hand' (Symp. 215 D) have in all ages ravished the hearts of men, who have seen reflected in them their own higher nature. He is the father of idealism in philosophy, in politics, in literature. And many of the latest conceptions of modern thinkers and statesmen, such as the unity of knowledge, the reign of law, and the equality of the sexes, have been anticipated in a dream by him.

The argument of the Republic is the search after Justice, the nature of which is first hinted at by Cephalus, the just and blameless old man—then discussed on the basis of proverbial morality by Socrates and Polemarchus—then caricatured by Thrasymachus and partially explained by Socrates—reduced to an abstraction by Glaucon and Adeimantus, and having become invisible in the individual reappears at length in the ideal State which is constructed by Socrates. The first care of the rulers is to be education, of which an outline is drawn after the old Hellenic model, providing only for an improved religion and morality, and more simplicity in music and gymnastic, a manlier strain of poetry, and greater harmony of the individual and the State. We are thus led on to the conception of a higher State, in which 'no man calls anything his own,' and in which there is neither 'marrying nor giving in marriage,' and 'kings are philosophers' and 'philosophers are kings;' and there is another and higher education, intellectual as well as moral and religious, of science as well as of art, and not of youth only but of the whole of life. Such a State is hardly to be realized in this world and quickly degenerates. To the perfect ideal succeeds the government of the soldier and the lover of honour, this again declining into democracy, and democracy into tyranny, in an imaginary but regular order having not much resemblance to the actual facts. When 'the wheel has come full circle' we do not begin again with a new period of human life; but we have passed from the best to the worst, and there we end. The subject is then changed and the old quarrel of poetry and philosophy which had been more lightly treated in the earlier books of the Republic is now resumed and fought out to a conclusion. Poetry is discovered to be an imitation thrice removed from the truth, and Homer, as well as the dramatic poets, having been condemned as an imitator, is sent into banishment along with them. And the idea of the State is supplemented by the revelation of a future life.

The division into books, like all similar divisions (Cp. Sir G.C. Lewis in the Classical Museum, vol. ii. p 1.), is probably later than the age of Plato. The natural divisions are five in number;—(1) Book I and the first half of Book II down to the paragraph beginning, 'I had always admired the genius of Glaucon and Adeimantus,' which is introductory; the first book containing a refutation of the popular and sophistical notions of justice, and concluding, like some of the earlier Dialogues, without arriving at any definite result. To this is appended a restatement of the nature of justice according to common opinion, and an answer is demanded to the question—What is justice, stripped of appearances? The second division (2) includes the remainder of the second and the whole of the third and fourth books, which are mainly occupied with the construction of the first State and the first education. The third division (3) consists of the fifth, sixth, and seventh books, in which philosophy rather than justice is the subject of enquiry, and the second State is constructed on principles of communism and ruled by philosophers, and the contemplation of the idea of good takes the place of the social and political virtues. In the eighth and ninth books (4) the perversions of States and of the individuals who correspond to them are reviewed in succession; and the nature of pleasure and the principle of tyranny are further analysed in the individual man. The tenth book (5) is the conclusion of the whole, in which the relations of philosophy to poetry are finally determined, and the happiness of the citizens in this life, which has now been assured, is crowned by the vision of another.

Or a more general division into two parts may be adopted; the first (Books I - IV) containing the description of a State framed generally in accordance with Hellenic notions of religion and morality, while in the second (Books V - X) the Hellenic State is transformed into an ideal kingdom of philosophy, of which all other governments are the perversions. These two points of view are really opposed, and the opposition is only veiled by the genius of Plato. The Republic, like the Phaedrus (see Introduction to Phaedrus), is an imperfect whole; the higher light of philosophy breaks through the regularity of the Hellenic temple, which at last fades away into the heavens. Whether this imperfection of structure arises from an enlargement of the plan; or from the imperfect reconcilement in the writer's own mind of the struggling elements of thought which are now first brought together by him; or, perhaps, from the composition of the work at different times—are questions, like the similar question about the Iliad and the Odyssey, which are worth asking, but which cannot have a distinct answer. In the age of Plato there was no regular mode of publication, and an author would have the less scruple in altering or adding to a work which was known only to a few of his friends. There is no absurdity in supposing that he may have laid his labours aside for a time, or turned from one work to another; and such interruptions would be more likely to occur in the case of a long than of a short writing. In all attempts to determine the chronological order of the Platonic writings on internal evidence, this uncertainty about any single Dialogue being composed at one time is a disturbing element, which must be admitted to affect longer works, such as the Republic and the Laws, more than shorter ones. But, on the other hand, the seeming discrepancies of the Republic may only arise out of the discordant elements which the philosopher has attempted to unite in a single whole, perhaps without being himself able to recognise the inconsistency which is obvious to us. For there is a judgment of after ages which few great writers have ever been able to anticipate for themselves. They do not perceive the want of connexion in their own writings, or the gaps in their systems which are visible enough to those who come after them. In the beginnings of literature and philosophy, amid the first efforts of thought and language, more inconsistencies occur than now, when the paths of speculation are well worn and the meaning of words precisely defined. For consistency, too, is the growth of time; and some of the greatest creations of the human mind have been wanting in unity. Tried by this test, several of the Platonic Dialogues, according to our modern ideas, appear to be defective, but the deficiency is no proof that they were composed at different times or by different hands. And the supposition that the Republic was written uninterruptedly and by a continuous effort is in some degree confirmed by the numerous references from one part of the work to another.

The second title, 'Concerning Justice,' is not the one by which the Republic is quoted, either by Aristotle or generally in antiquity, and, like the other second titles of the Platonic Dialogues, may therefore be assumed to be of later date. Morgenstern and others have asked whether the definition of justice, which is the professed aim, or the construction of the State is the principal argument of the work. The answer is, that the two blend in one, and are two faces of the same truth; for justice is the order of the State, and the State is the visible embodiment of justice under the conditions of human society. The one is the soul and the other is the body, and the Greek ideal of the State, as of the individual, is a fair mind in a fair body. In Hegelian phraseology the state is the reality of which justice is the idea. Or, described in Christian language, the kingdom of God is within, and yet developes into a Church or external kingdom; 'the house not made with hands, eternal in the heavens,' is reduced to the proportions of an earthly building. Or, to use a Platonic image, justice and the State are the warp and the woof which run through the whole texture. And when the constitution of the State is completed, the conception of justice is not dismissed, but reappears under the same or different names throughout the work, both as the inner law of the individual soul, and finally as the principle of rewards and punishments in another life. The virtues are based on justice, of which common honesty in buying and selling is the shadow, and justice is based on the idea of good, which is the harmony of the world, and is reflected both in the institutions of states and in motions of the heavenly bodies (cp. Tim. 47). The Timaeus, which takes up the political rather than the ethical side of the Republic, and is chiefly occupied with hypotheses concerning the outward world, yet contains many indications that the same law is supposed to reign over the State, over nature, and over man.

Too much, however, has been made of this question both in ancient and modern times. There is a stage of criticism in which all works, whether of nature or of art, are referred to design. Now in ancient writings, and indeed in literature generally, there remains often a large element which was not comprehended in the original design. For the plan grows under the author's hand; new thoughts occur to him in the act of writing; he has not worked out the argument to the end before he begins. The reader who seeks to find some one idea under which the whole may be conceived, must necessarily seize on the vaguest and most general. Thus Stallbaum, who is dissatisfied with the ordinary explanations of the argument of the Republic, imagines himself to have found the true argument 'in the representation of human life in a State perfected by justice, and governed according to the idea of good.' There may be some use in such general descriptions, but they can hardly be said to express the design of the writer. The truth is, that we may as well speak of many designs as of one; nor need anything be excluded from the plan of a great work to which the mind is naturally led by the association of ideas, and which does not interfere with the general purpose. What kind or degree of unity is to be sought after in a building, in the plastic arts, in poetry, in prose, is a problem which has to be determined relatively to the subject-matter. To Plato himself, the enquiry 'what was the intention of the writer,' or 'what was the principal argument of the Republic' would have been hardly intelligible, and therefore had better be at once dismissed (cp. the Introduction to the Phaedrus).

Is not the Republic the vehicle of three or four great truths which, to Plato's own mind, are most naturally represented in the form of the State? Just as in the Jewish prophets the reign of Messiah, or 'the day of the Lord,' or the suffering Servant or people of God, or the 'Sun of righteousness with healing in his wings' only convey, to us at least, their great spiritual ideals, so through the Greek State Plato reveals to us his own thoughts about divine perfection, which is the idea of good—like the sun in the visible world;—about human perfection, which is justice—about education beginning in youth and continuing in later years—about poets and sophists and tyrants who are the false teachers and evil rulers of mankind—about 'the world' which is the embodiment of them—about a kingdom which exists nowhere upon earth but is laid up in heaven to be the pattern and rule of human life. No such inspired creation is at unity with itself, any more than the clouds of heaven when the sun pierces through them. Every shade of light and dark, of truth, and of fiction which is the veil of truth, is allowable in a work of philosophical imagination. It is not all on the same plane; it easily passes from ideas to myths and fancies, from facts to figures of speech. It is not prose but poetry, at least a great part of it, and ought not to be judged by the rules of logic or the probabilities of history. The writer is not fashioning his ideas into an artistic whole; they take possession of him and are too much for him. We have no need therefore to discuss whether a State such as Plato has conceived is practicable or not, or whether the outward form or the inward life came first into the mind of the writer. For the practicability of his ideas has nothing to do with their truth; and the highest thoughts to which he attains may be truly said to bear the greatest 'marks of design'—justice more than the external frame-work of the State, the idea of good more than justice. The great science of dialectic or the organisation of ideas has no real content; but is only a type of the method or spirit in which the higher knowledge is to be pursued by the spectator of all time and all existence. It is in the fifth, sixth, and seventh books that Plato reaches the 'summit of speculation,' and these, although they fail to satisfy the requirements of a modern thinker, may therefore be regarded as the most important, as they are also the most original, portions of the work.

It is not necessary to discuss at length a minor question which has been raised by Boeckh, respecting the imaginary date at which the conversation was held (the year 411 B.C. which is proposed by him will do as well as any other); for a writer of fiction, and especially a writer who, like Plato, is notoriously careless of chronology (cp. Rep., Symp., 193 A, etc.), only aims at general probability. Whether all the persons mentioned in the Republic could ever have met at any one time is not a difficulty which would have occurred to an Athenian reading the work forty years later, or to Plato himself at the time of writing (any more than to Shakespeare respecting one of his own dramas); and need not greatly trouble us now. Yet this may be a question having no answer 'which is still worth asking,' because the investigation shows that we cannot argue historically from the dates in Plato; it would be useless therefore to waste time in inventing far-fetched reconcilements of them in order to avoid chronological difficulties, such, for example, as the conjecture of C.F. Hermann, that Glaucon and Adeimantus are not the brothers but the uncles of Plato (cp. Apol. 34 A), or the fancy of Stallbaum that Plato intentionally left anachronisms indicating the dates at which some of his Dialogues were written.

The principal characters in the Republic are Cephalus, Polemarchus, Thrasymachus, Socrates, Glaucon, and Adeimantus. Cephalus appears in the introduction only, Polemarchus drops at the end of the first argument, and Thrasymachus is reduced to silence at the close of the first book. The main discussion is carried on by Socrates, Glaucon, and Adeimantus. Among the company are Lysias (the orator) and Euthydemus, the sons of Cephalus and brothers of Polemarchus, an unknown Charmantides—these are mute auditors; also there is Cleitophon, who once interrupts, where, as in the Dialogue which bears his name, he appears as the friend and ally of Thrasymachus.

Cephalus, the patriarch of the house, has been appropriately engaged in offering a sacrifice. He is the pattern of an old man who has almost done with life, and is at peace with himself and with all mankind. He feels that he is drawing nearer to the world below, and seems to linger around the memory of the past. He is eager that Socrates should come to visit him, fond of the poetry of the last generation, happy in the consciousness of a well-spent life, glad at having escaped from the tyranny of youthful lusts. His love of conversation, his affection, his indifference to riches, even his garrulity, are interesting traits of character. He is not one of those who have nothing to say, because their whole mind has been absorbed in making money. Yet he acknowledges that riches have the advantage of placing men above the temptation to dishonesty or falsehood. The respectful attention shown to him by Socrates, whose love of conversation, no less than the mission imposed upon him by the Oracle, leads him to ask questions of all men, young and old alike, should also be noted. Who better suited to raise the question of justice than Cephalus, whose life might seem to be the expression of it? The moderation with which old age is pictured by Cephalus as a very tolerable portion of existence is characteristic, not only of him, but of Greek feeling generally, and contrasts with the exaggeration of Cicero in the De Senectute. The evening of life is described by Plato in the most expressive manner, yet with the fewest possible touches. As Cicero remarks (Ep. ad Attic. iv. 16), the aged Cephalus would have been out of place in the discussion which follows, and which he could neither have understood nor taken part in without a violation of dramatic propriety (cp. Lysimachus in the Laches).

His 'son and heir' Polemarchus has the frankness and impetuousness of youth; he is for detaining Socrates by force in the opening scene, and will not 'let him off' on the subject of women and children. Like Cephalus, he is limited in his point of view, and represents the proverbial stage of morality which has rules of life rather than principles; and he quotes Simonides (cp. Aristoph. Clouds) as his father had quoted Pindar. But after this he has no more to say; the answers which he makes are only elicited from him by the dialectic of Socrates. He has not yet experienced the influence of the Sophists like Glaucon and Adeimantus, nor is he sensible of the necessity of refuting them; he belongs to the pre-Socratic or pre-dialectical age. He is incapable of arguing, and is bewildered by Socrates to such a degree that he does not know what he is saying. He is made to admit that justice is a thief, and that the virtues follow the analogy of the arts. From his brother Lysias (contra Eratosth.) we learn that he fell a victim to the Thirty Tyrants, but no allusion is here made to his fate, nor to the circumstance that Cephalus and his family were of Syracusan origin, and had migrated from Thurii to Athens.

The 'Chalcedonian giant,' Thrasymachus, of whom we have already heard in the Phaedrus, is the personification of the Sophists, according to Plato's conception of them, in some of their worst characteristics. He is vain and blustering, refusing to discourse unless he is paid, fond of making an oration, and hoping thereby to escape the inevitable Socrates; but a mere child in argument, and unable to foresee that the next 'move' (to use a Platonic expression) will 'shut him up.' He has reached the stage of framing general notions, and in this respect is in advance of Cephalus and Polemarchus. But he is incapable of defending them in a discussion, and vainly tries to cover his confusion with banter and insolence. Whether such doctrines as are attributed to him by Plato were really held either by him or by any other Sophist is uncertain; in the infancy of philosophy serious errors about morality might easily grow up—they are certainly put into the mouths of speakers in Thucydides; but we are concerned at present with Plato's description of him, and not with the historical reality. The inequality of the contest adds greatly to the humour of the scene. The pompous and empty Sophist is utterly helpless in the hands of the great master of dialectic, who knows how to touch all the springs of vanity and weakness in him. He is greatly irritated by the irony of Socrates, but his noisy and imbecile rage only lays him more and more open to the thrusts of his assailant. His determination to cram down their throats, or put 'bodily into their souls' his own words, elicits a cry of horror from Socrates. The state of his temper is quite as worthy of remark as the process of the argument. Nothing is more amusing than his complete submission when he has been once thoroughly beaten. At first he seems to continue the discussion with reluctance, but soon with apparent good-will, and he even testifies his interest at a later stage by one or two occasional remarks. When attacked by Glaucon he is humorously protected by Socrates 'as one who has never been his enemy and is now his friend.' From Cicero and Quintilian and from Aristotle's Rhetoric we learn that the Sophist whom Plato has made so ridiculous was a man of note whose writings were preserved in later ages. The play on his name which was made by his contemporary Herodicus (Aris. Rhet.), 'thou wast ever bold in battle,' seems to show that the description of him is not devoid of verisimilitude.

When Thrasymachus has been silenced, the two principal respondents, Glaucon and Adeimantus, appear on the scene: here, as in Greek tragedy (cp. Introd. to Phaedo), three actors are introduced. At first sight the two sons of Ariston may seem to wear a family likeness, like the two

friends Simmias and Cebes in the Phaedo. But on a nearer examination of
them the similarity vanishes, and they are seen to be distinct characters.
Glaucon is the impetuous youth who can 'just never have enough of
fechting' (cp. the character of him in Xen. Mem. iii. 6); the man of pleasure
who is acquainted with the mysteries of love; the 'juvenis qui gaudet
canibus,' and who improves the breed of animals; the lover of art and music
who has all the experiences of youthful life. He is full of quickness and
penetration, piercing easily below the clumsy platitudes of Thrasymachus
to the real difficulty; he turns out to the light the seamy side of human
life, and yet does not lose faith in the just and true. It is Glaucon who
seizes what may be termed the ludicrous relation of the philosopher to
the world, to whom a state of simplicity is 'a city of pigs,' who is always
prepared with a jest when the argument offers him an opportunity, and
who is ever ready to second the humour of Socrates and to appreciate
the ridiculous, whether in the connoisseurs of music, or in the lovers of
theatricals, or in the fantastic behaviour of the citizens of democracy. His
weaknesses are several times alluded to by Socrates, who, however, will
not allow him to be attacked by his brother Adeimantus. He is a soldier,
and, like Adeimantus, has been distinguished at the battle of Megara
(anno 456?)...The character of Adeimantus is deeper and graver, and the
profounder objections are commonly put into his mouth. Glaucon is more
demonstrative, and generally opens the game. Adeimantus pursues the
argument further. Glaucon has more of the liveliness and quick sympathy
of youth; Adeimantus has the maturer judgment of a grown-up man of the
world. In the second book, when Glaucon insists that justice and injustice
shall be considered without regard to their consequences, Adeimantus
remarks that they are regarded by mankind in general only for the sake
of their consequences; and in a similar vein of reflection he urges at the
beginning of the fourth book that Socrates fails in making his citizens
happy, and is answered that happiness is not the first but the second thing,
not the direct aim but the indirect consequence of the good government
of a State. In the discussion about religion and mythology, Adeimantus
is the respondent, but Glaucon breaks in with a slight jest, and carries

on the conversation in a lighter tone about music and gymnastic to the
end of the book. It is Adeimantus again who volunteers the criticism of
common sense on the Socratic method of argument, and who refuses
to let Socrates pass lightly over the question of women and children.
It is Adeimantus who is the respondent in the more argumentative, as
Glaucon in the lighter and more imaginative portions of the Dialogue.
For example, throughout the greater part of the sixth book, the causes
of the corruption of philosophy and the conception of the idea of good
are discussed with Adeimantus. Glaucon resumes his place of principal
respondent; but he has a difficulty in apprehending the higher education
of Socrates, and makes some false hits in the course of the discussion.
Once more Adeimantus returns with the allusion to his brother Glaucon
whom he compares to the contentious State; in the next book he is again
superseded, and Glaucon continues to the end.

  Thus in a succession of characters Plato represents the successive stages
of morality, beginning with the Athenian gentleman of the olden time,
who is followed by the practical man of that day regulating his life by
proverbs and saws; to him succeeds the wild generalization of the Sophists,
and lastly come the young disciples of the great teacher, who know the
sophistical arguments but will not be convinced by them, and desire to go
deeper into the nature of things. These too, like Cephalus, Polemarchus,
Thrasymachus, are clearly distinguished from one another. Neither in the
Republic, nor in any other Dialogue of Plato, is a single character repeated.

  The delineation of Socrates in the Republic is not wholly consistent.
In the first book we have more of the real Socrates, such as he is depicted
in the Memorabilia of Xenophon, in the earliest Dialogues of Plato, and
in the Apology. He is ironical, provoking, questioning, the old enemy
of the Sophists, ready to put on the mask of Silenus as well as to argue
seriously. But in the sixth book his enmity towards the Sophists abates; he
acknowledges that they are the representatives rather than the corrupters
of the world. He also becomes more dogmatic and constructive, passing
beyond the range either of the political or the speculative ideas of the real
Socrates. In one passage Plato himself seems to intimate that the time had

now come for Socrates, who had passed his whole life in philosophy, to give his own opinion and not to be always repeating the notions of other men. There is no evidence that either the idea of good or the conception of a perfect state were comprehended in the Socratic teaching, though he certainly dwelt on the nature of the universal and of final causes (cp. Xen. Mem.; Phaedo); and a deep thinker like him, in his thirty or forty years of public teaching, could hardly have failed to touch on the nature of family relations, for which there is also some positive evidence in the Memorabilia (Mem.) The Socratic method is nominally retained; and every inference is either put into the mouth of the respondent or represented as the common discovery of him and Socrates. But any one can see that this is a mere form, of which the affectation grows wearisome as the work advances. The method of enquiry has passed into a method of teaching in which by the help of interlocutors the same thesis is looked at from various points of view. The nature of the process is truly characterized by Glaucon, when he describes himself as a companion who is not good for much in an investigation, but can see what he is shown, and may, perhaps, give the answer to a question more fluently than another.

Neither can we be absolutely certain that Socrates himself taught the immortality of the soul, which is unknown to his disciple Glaucon in the Republic (cp. Apol.); nor is there any reason to suppose that he used myths or revelations of another world as a vehicle of instruction, or that he would have banished poetry or have denounced the Greek mythology. His favorite oath is retained, and a slight mention is made of the daemonium, or internal sign, which is alluded to by Socrates as a phenomenon peculiar to himself. A real element of Socratic teaching, which is more prominent in the Republic than in any of the other Dialogues of Plato, is the use of example and illustration τὰ φορτικὰ αὐτῷ προσφέροντες, 'Let us apply the test of common instances.' 'You,' says Adeimantus, ironically, in the sixth book, 'are so unaccustomed to speak in images.' And this use of examples or images, though truly Socratic in origin, is enlarged by the genius of Plato into the form of an allegory or parable, which embodies in the concrete what has been already described, or is about to be described, in the abstract.

Thus the figure of the cave in Book VII is a recapitulation of the divisions of knowledge in Book VI. The composite animal in Book IX is an allegory of the parts of the soul. The noble captain and the ship and the true pilot in Book VI are a figure of the relation of the people to the philosophers in the State which has been described. Other figures, such as the dog, or the marriage of the portionless maiden, or the drones and wasps in the eighth and ninth books, also form links of connexion in long passages, or are used to recall previous discussions.

Plato is most true to the character of his master when he describes him as 'not of this world.' And with this representation of him the ideal state and the other paradoxes of the Republic are quite in accordance, though they cannot be shown to have been speculations of Socrates. To him, as to other great teachers both philosophical and religious, when they looked upward, the world seemed to be the embodiment of error and evil. The common sense of mankind has revolted against this view, or has only partially admitted it. And even in Socrates himself the sterner judgement of the multitude at times passes into a sort of ironical pity or love. Men in general are incapable of philosophy, and are therefore at enmity with the philosopher; but their misunderstanding of him is unavoidable: for they have never seen him as he truly is in his own image; they are only acquainted with artificial systems possessing no native force of truth—words which admit of many applications. Their leaders have nothing to measure with, and are therefore ignorant of their own stature. But they are to be pitied or laughed at, not to be quarrelled with; they mean well with their nostrums, if they could only learn that they are cutting off a Hydra's head. This moderation towards those who are in error is one of the most characteristic features of Socrates in the Republic. In all the different representations of Socrates, whether of Xenophon or Plato, and amid the differences of the earlier or later Dialogues, he always retains the character of the unwearied and disinterested seeker after truth, without which he would have ceased to be Socrates.

Leaving the characters we may now analyse the contents of the Republic, and then proceed to consider (1) The general aspects of this

Hellenic ideal of the State, (2) The modern lights in which the thoughts of Plato may be read.

Book I - Introduction & Analysis
Wealth, Justice, Moderation & their Opposites

The Republic opens with a truly Greek scene—a festival in honour of the goddess Bendis which is held in the Piraeus; to this is added the promise of an equestrian torch-race in the evening. The whole work is supposed to be recited by Socrates on the day after the festival to a small party, consisting of Critias, Timaeus, Hermocrates, and another; this we learn from the first words of the Timaeus.

When the rhetorical advantage of reciting the Dialogue has been gained, the attention is not distracted by any reference to the audience; nor is the reader further reminded of the extraordinary length of the narrative. Of the numerous company, three only take any serious part in the discussion; nor are we informed whether in the evening they went to the torch-race, or talked, as in the Symposium, through the night. The manner in which the conversation has arisen is described as follows:—Socrates and his companion Glaucon are about to leave the festival when they are detained by a message from Polemarchus, who speedily appears accompanied by Adeimantus, the brother of Glaucon, and with playful violence compels them to remain, promising them not only the torch-race, but the pleasure of conversation with the young, which to Socrates is a far greater attraction. They return to the house of Cephalus, Polemarchus' father, now in extreme old age, who is found sitting upon a cushioned seat crowned for a sacrifice. 'You should come to me oftener, Socrates, for I am too old to go to you; and at my time of life, having lost other pleasures, I care the more for conversation.' Socrates asks him what he thinks of age, to which the old man replies, that the sorrows and discontents of age are to be attributed to the tempers of men, and that age is a time of peace in which the tyranny of the passions is no longer felt. Yes, replies Socrates, but the world will say, Cephalus, that you are happy in old age because you are rich. 'And there is something in what they say, Socrates, but not so much as they imagine—as Themistocles replied to the Seriphian, "Neither you, if you had been an Athenian, nor I, if I had been a Seriphian, would ever have been famous," I might in like manner reply to you, Neither a good poor man can be happy in age, nor yet a bad rich man.' Socrates remarks that Cephalus appears not to care about riches, a quality which he ascribes to his having inherited, not acquired them, and would like to know what he considers to be the chief advantage of them. Cephalus answers that when you are old the belief in the world below grows upon you, and then to have done justice and never to have been compelled to do injustice through poverty, and never to have deceived anyone, are felt to be unspeakable blessings. Socrates, who is evidently preparing for an argument, next asks, What is the meaning of the word justice? To tell the truth and pay your debts? No more than this? Or must we admit exceptions? Ought I, for example, to put back into the hands of my friend, who has gone mad, the sword which I borrowed of him when he was in his right mind? 'There must be exceptions.' 'And yet,' says Polemarchus, 'the definition which has been given has the authority of Simonides.' Here Cephalus retires to look after the sacrifices, and bequeaths, as Socrates facetiously remarks, the possession of the argument to his heir, Polemarchus...

The description of old age is finished, and Plato, as his manner is, has touched the key-note of the whole work in asking for the definition of justice, first suggesting the question which Glaucon afterwards pursues respecting external goods, and preparing for the concluding mythus of the world below in the slight allusion of Cephalus. The portrait of the just man is a natural frontispiece or introduction to the long discourse which follows, and may perhaps imply that in all our perplexity about the nature of justice, there is no difficulty in discerning 'who is a just man.' The first explanation has been supported by a saying of Simonides; and now Socrates has a mind to show that the resolution of justice into two unconnected precepts, which have no common principle, fails to satisfy the demands of dialectic.

...He proceeds: What did Simonides mean by this saying of his? Did he mean that I was to give back arms to a madman? 'No, not in that case, not if the parties are friends, and evil would result. He meant that you were to do what was proper, good to friends and harm to enemies.' Every act does something to somebody; and following this analogy, Socrates asks, What is this due and proper thing which justice does, and to whom? He is answered that justice does good to friends and harm to enemies. But in what way good or harm? 'In making alliances with the one, and going to war with the other.' Then in time of peace what is the good of justice? The answer is that justice is of use in contracts, and contracts are money partnerships. Yes; but how in such partnerships is the just man of more use than any other man? 'When you want to have money safely kept and not used.' Then justice will be useful when money is useless. And there is another difficulty: justice, like the art of war or any other art, must be of opposites, good at attack as well as at defence, at stealing as well as at guarding. But then justice is a thief, though a hero notwithstanding, like Autolycus, the Homeric hero, who was 'excellent above all men in theft and perjury'—to such a pass have you and Homer and Simonides brought us; though I do not forget that the thieving must be for the good of friends and the harm of enemies. And still there arises another question: Are friends to be interpreted as real or seeming; enemies as real or seeming? And are our friends to be only the good, and our enemies to be the evil? The answer is, that we must do good to our seeming and real good friends, and evil to our seeming and real evil enemies—good to the good, evil to the evil. But ought we to render evil for evil at all, when to do so will only make men more evil? Can justice produce injustice any more than the art of horsemanship can make bad horsemen, or heat produce cold? The final conclusion is, that no sage or poet ever said that the just return evil for evil; this was a maxim of some rich and mighty man, Periander, Perdiccas, or Ismenias the Theban (about B.C. 398-381)...

Thus the first stage of aphoristic or unconscious morality is shown to be inadequate to the wants of the age; the authority of the poets is set aside, and through the winding mazes of dialectic we make an approach to the Christian precept of forgiveness of injuries. Similar words are applied by the Persian mystic poet to the Divine being when the questioning spirit is stirred within him:—'If because I do evil, Thou punishest me by evil, what is the difference between Thee and me?' In this both Plato and Kheyam rise above the level of many Christian (?) theologians. The first definition of justice easily passes into the second; for the simple words 'to speak the truth and pay your debts' is substituted the more abstract 'to do good to your friends and harm to your enemies.' Either of these explanations gives a sufficient rule of life for plain men, but they both fall short of the precision of philosophy. We may note in passing the antiquity of casuistry, which not only arises out of the conflict of established principles in particular cases, but also out of the effort to attain them, and is prior as well as posterior to our fundamental notions of morality. The 'interrogation' of moral ideas; the appeal to the authority of Homer; the conclusion that the maxim, 'Do good to your friends and harm to your enemies,' being erroneous, could not have been the word of any great man, are all of them very characteristic of the Platonic Socrates.

...Here Thrasymachus, who has made several attempts to interrupt, but has hitherto been kept in order by the company, takes advantage of a pause and rushes into the arena, beginning, like a savage animal, with a roar. 'Socrates,' he says, 'what folly is this?—Why do you agree to be vanquished by one another in a pretended argument?' He then prohibits all the ordinary definitions of justice; to which Socrates replies that he cannot tell how many twelve is, if he is forbidden to say 2 x 6, or 3 x 4, or 6 x 2, or 4 x 3. At first Thrasymachus is reluctant to argue; but at length, with a promise of payment on the part of the company and of praise from Socrates, he is induced to open the game. 'Listen,' he says, 'my answer is that might is right, justice the interest of the stronger: now praise me.' Let me understand you first. Do you mean that because Polydamas the wrestler, who is stronger than we are, finds the eating of beef for his interest, the eating of beef is also for our interest, who are not so strong? Thrasymachus is indignant at the illustration, and in pompous words, apparently intended to restore dignity to the argument, he explains his meaning to be that the rulers make laws for their own interests. But suppose, says Socrates, that the ruler or stronger makes a mistake—then the interest of the stronger is not his interest. Thrasymachus is saved from this speedy downfall by his disciple Cleitophon, who introduces the word 'thinks;'—not the actual interest of the ruler, but what he thinks or what seems to be his interest, is justice. The contradiction is escaped by the unmeaning evasion: for though his real and apparent interests may differ, what the ruler thinks to be his interest will always remain what he thinks to be his interest.

Of course this was not the original assertion, nor is the new interpretation accepted by Thrasymachus himself. But Socrates is not disposed to quarrel about words, if, as he significantly insinuates, his adversary has changed his mind. In what follows Thrasymachus does in fact withdraw his admission that the ruler may make a mistake, for he affirms that the ruler as a ruler is infallible. Socrates is quite ready to accept the new position, which he equally turns against Thrasymachus by the help of the analogy of the arts. Every art or science has an interest, but this interest is to be distinguished from the accidental interest of the artist, and is only concerned with the good of the things or persons which come under the art. And justice has an interest which is the interest not of the ruler or judge, but of those who come under his sway.

Thrasymachus is on the brink of the inevitable conclusion, when he makes a bold diversion. 'Tell me, Socrates,' he says, 'have you a nurse?' What a question! Why do you ask? 'Because, if you have, she neglects you and lets you go about drivelling, and has not even taught you to know the shepherd from the sheep. For you fancy that shepherds and rulers never think of their own interest, but only of their sheep or subjects, whereas the truth is that they fatten them for their use, sheep and subjects alike. And experience proves that in every relation of life the just man is the loser and the unjust the gainer, especially where injustice is on the grand scale, which is quite another thing from the petty rogueries of swindlers and burglars and robbers of temples. The language of men proves this—our 'gracious' and 'blessed' tyrant and the like—all which tends to show (1) that justice is the interest of the stronger; and (2) that injustice is more profitable and also stronger than justice.'

Thrasymachus, who is better at a speech than at a close argument, having deluged the company with words, has a mind to escape. But the others will not let him go, and Socrates adds a humble but earnest request that he will not desert them at such a crisis of their fate. 'And what can I do more for you?' he says; 'would you have me put the words bodily into your souls?' God forbid! replies Socrates; but we want you to be consistent in the use of terms, and not to employ 'physician' in an exact sense, and then again 'shepherd' or 'ruler' in an inexact,—if the words are strictly taken, the ruler and the shepherd look only to the good of their people or flocks and not to their own: whereas you insist that rulers are solely actuated by love of office. 'No doubt about it,' replies Thrasymachus. Then why are they paid? Is not the reason, that their interest is not comprehended in their art, and is therefore the concern of another art, the art of pay, which is common to the arts in general, and therefore not identical with any one of them? Nor would any man be a ruler unless he were induced by the hope of reward or the fear of punishment;—the reward is money or honour, the punishment is the necessity of being ruled by a man worse than himself. And if a State (or Church) were composed entirely of good men, they would be affected by the last motive only; and there would be as much 'nolo episcopari' as there is at present of the opposite...

The satire on existing governments is heightened by the simple and apparently incidental manner in which the last remark is introduced. There is a similar irony in the argument that the governors of mankind do not like being in office, and that therefore they demand pay.

...Enough of this: the other assertion of Thrasymachus is far more important—that the unjust life is more gainful than the just. Now, as you and I, Glaucon, are not convinced by him, we must reply to him; but if we try to compare their respective gains we shall want a judge to decide for us; we had better therefore proceed by making mutual admissions of the truth to one another.

Thrasymachus had asserted that perfect injustice was more gainful than perfect justice, and after a little hesitation he is induced by Socrates to admit the still greater paradox that injustice is virtue and justice vice. Socrates praises his frankness, and assumes the attitude of one whose only wish is to understand the meaning of his opponents. At the same time he is weaving a net in which Thrasymachus is finally enclosed. The admission is elicited from him that the just man seeks to gain an advantage over the unjust only, but not over the just, while the unjust would gain an advantage over either. Socrates, in order to test this statement, employs once more the favourite analogy of the arts. The musician, doctor, skilled artist of any sort, does not seek to gain more than the skilled, but only more than the unskilled (that is to say, he works up to a rule, standard, law, and does not exceed it), whereas the unskilled makes random efforts at excess. Thus the skilled falls on the side of the good, and the unskilled on the side of the evil, and the just is the skilled, and the unjust is the unskilled.

There was great difficulty in bringing Thrasymachus to the point; the day was hot and he was streaming with perspiration, and for the first time in his life he was seen to blush. But his other thesis that injustice was stronger than justice has not yet been refuted, and Socrates now proceeds to the consideration of this, which, with the assistance of Thrasymachus, he hopes to clear up; the latter is at first churlish, but in the judicious hands of Socrates is soon restored to good-humour: Is there not honour among thieves? Is not the strength of injustice only a remnant of justice? Is not absolute injustice absolute weakness also? A house that is divided against itself cannot stand; two men who quarrel detract from one another's strength, and he who is at war with himself is the enemy of himself and the gods. Not wickedness therefore, but semi-wickedness flourishes in states,—a remnant of good is needed in order to make union in action possible,—there is no kingdom of evil in this world.

Another question has not been answered: Is the just or the unjust the happier? To this we reply, that every art has an end and an excellence or virtue by which the end is accomplished. And is not the end of the soul happiness, and justice the excellence of the soul by which happiness is attained? Justice and happiness being thus shown to be inseparable, the question whether the just or the unjust is the happier has disappeared.

Thrasymachus replies: 'Let this be your entertainment, Socrates, at the festival of Bendis.' Yes; and a very good entertainment with which your kindness has supplied me, now that you have left off scolding. And yet not a good entertainment—but that was my own fault, for I tasted of too many things. First of all the nature of justice was the subject of our enquiry, and then whether justice is virtue and wisdom, or evil and folly; and then the comparative advantages of just and unjust: and the sum of all is that I know not what justice is; how then shall I know whether the just is happy or not?...

Thus the sophistical fabric has been demolished, chiefly by appealing to the analogy of the arts. 'Justice is like the arts (1) in having no external interest, and (2) in not aiming at excess, and (3) justice is to happiness what the implement of the workman is to his work.' At this the modern reader is apt to stumble, because he forgets that Plato is writing in an age when the arts and the virtues, like the moral and intellectual faculties, were still undistinguished. Among early enquirers into the nature of human action the arts helped to fill up the void of speculation; and at first the comparison of the arts and the virtues was not perceived by them to be fallacious. They only saw the points of agreement in them and not the points of difference. Virtue, like art, must take means to an end; good manners are both an art and a virtue; character is naturally described under the image of a statue; and there are many other figures of speech which are readily transferred from art to morals. The next generation cleared up these perplexities; or at least supplied after ages with a further analysis of them. The contemporaries of Plato were in a state of transition, and had not yet fully realized the common-sense distinction of Aristotle, that 'virtue is concerned with action, art with production' (Nic. Eth.), or that 'virtue implies intention and constancy of purpose,' whereas 'art requires knowledge only'. And yet in the absurdities which follow from some uses of the analogy, there seems to be an intimation conveyed that virtue is more than art. This is implied in the reductio ad absurdum that 'justice is a thief,' and in the dissatisfaction which Socrates expresses at the final result.

The expression 'an art of pay' which is described as 'common to all the arts' is not in accordance with the ordinary use of language. Nor is it employed elsewhere either by Plato or by any other Greek writer. It is suggested by the argument, and seems to extend the conception of art to doing as well as making. Another flaw or inaccuracy of language may be noted in the words 'men who are injured are made more unjust.' For those who are injured are not necessarily made worse, but only harmed or ill-treated.

The second of the three arguments, 'that the just does not aim at excess,' has a real meaning, though wrapped up in an enigmatical form. That the good is of the nature of the finite is a peculiarly Hellenic sentiment, which may be compared with the language of those modern writers who speak of virtue as fitness, and of freedom as obedience to law. The mathematical or logical notion of limit easily passes into an ethical one, and even finds a mythological expression in the conception of envy (Greek). Ideas of measure, equality, order, unity, proportion, still linger in the writings of moralists; and the true spirit of the fine arts is better conveyed by such terms than by superlatives.

'When workmen strive to do better than well, They do confound their skill in covetousness.'
(King John. Act. iv. Sc. 2.)

The harmony of the soul and body, and of the parts of the soul with one another, a harmony 'fairer than that of musical notes,' is the true Hellenic mode of conceiving the perfection of human nature.

In what may be called the epilogue of the discussion with Thrasymachus, Plato argues that evil is not a principle of strength, but of discord and dissolution, just touching the question which has been often treated in modern times by theologians and philosophers, of the negative nature of evil. In the last argument we trace the germ of the Aristotelian doctrine of an end and a virtue directed towards the end, which again is suggested by the arts. The final reconcilement of justice and happiness and the identity of the individual and the State are also intimated. Socrates reassumes the character of a 'know-nothing;' at the same time he appears to be not wholly satisfied with the manner in which the argument has been conducted. Nothing is concluded; but the tendency of the dialectical process, here as always, is to enlarge our conception of ideas, and to widen their application to human life.

Book II - Introduction & Analysis
Individuals, the State & Education

Thrasymachus is pacified, but the intrepid Glaucon insists on continuing the argument. He is not satisfied with the indirect manner in which, at the end of the last book, Socrates had disposed of the question 'Whether the just or the unjust is the happier.' He begins by dividing goods into three classes:—first, goods desirable in themselves; secondly, goods desirable in themselves and for their results; thirdly, goods desirable for their results only. He then asks Socrates in which of the three classes he would place justice. In the second class, replies Socrates, among goods desirable for themselves and also for their results. 'Then the world in general are of another mind, for they say that justice belongs to the troublesome class of goods which are desirable for their results only. Socrates answers that this is the doctrine of Thrasymachus which he rejects. Glaucon thinks that Thrasymachus was too ready to listen to the voice of the charmer, and proposes to consider the nature of justice and injustice in themselves and apart from the results and rewards of them which the world is always dinning in his ears. He will first of all speak of the nature and origin of justice; secondly, of the manner in which men view justice as a necessity and not a good; and thirdly, he will prove the reasonableness of this view.

'To do injustice is said to be a good; to suffer injustice an evil. As the evil is discovered by experience to be greater than the good, the sufferers, who cannot also be doers, make a compact that they will have neither, and this compact or mean is called justice, but is really the impossibility of doing injustice. No one would observe such a compact if he were not obliged. Let us suppose that the just and unjust have two rings, like that of Gyges in the well-known story, which make them invisible, and then no difference will appear in them, for every one will do evil if he can. And he who abstains will be regarded by the world as a fool for his pains. Men may praise him in public out of fear for themselves, but they will laugh at him in their hearts (Cp. Gorgias.)

'And now let us frame an ideal of the just and unjust. Imagine the unjust man to be master of his craft, seldom making mistakes and easily correcting them; having gifts of money, speech, strength—the greatest villain bearing the highest character: and at his side let us place the just in his nobleness and simplicity—being, not seeming—without name or reward—clothed in his justice only—the best of men who is thought to be the worst, and let him die as he has lived. I might add (but I would rather put the rest into the mouth of the panegyrists of injustice—they will tell you) that the just man will be scourged, racked, bound, will have his eyes put out, and will at last be crucified (literally impaled)—and all this because he ought to have preferred seeming to being. How different is the case of the unjust who clings to appearance as the true reality! His high character makes him a ruler; he can marry where he likes, trade where he likes, help his friends and hurt his enemies; having got rich by dishonesty he can worship the gods better, and will therefore be more loved by them than the just.'

I was thinking what to answer, when Adeimantus joined in the already unequal fray. He considered that the most important point of all had been omitted:—'Men are taught to be just for the sake of rewards; parents and guardians make reputation the incentive to virtue. And other advantages are promised by them of a more solid kind, such as wealthy marriages and high offices. There are the pictures in Homer and Hesiod of fat sheep and heavy fleeces, rich corn-fields and trees toppling with fruit, which the gods provide in this life for the just. And the Orphic poets add a similar picture of another. The heroes of Musaeus and Eumolpus lie on couches at a festival, with garlands on their heads, enjoying as the meed of virtue a paradise of immortal drunkenness. Some go further, and speak of a fair posterity in the third and fourth generation. But the wicked they bury in a slough and make them carry water in a sieve: and in this life they attribute to them the infamy which Glaucon was assuming to be the lot of the just who are supposed to be unjust.

'Take another kind of argument which is found both in poetry and prose:—"Virtue," as Hesiod says, "is honourable but difficult, vice is easy and profitable." You may often see the wicked in great prosperity and the righteous afflicted by the will of heaven. And mendicant prophets knock at rich men's doors, promising to atone for the sins of themselves or their fathers in an easy fashion with sacrifices and festive games, or with charms and invocations to get rid of an enemy good or bad by divine help and at a small charge;—they appeal to books professing to be written by Musaeus and Orpheus, and carry away the minds of whole cities, and promise to "get souls out of purgatory;" and if we refuse to listen to them, no one knows what will happen to us.

'When a lively-minded ingenuous youth hears all this, what will be his conclusion? "Will he," in the language of Pindar, "make justice his high tower, or fortify himself with crooked deceit?" Justice, he reflects, without the appearance of justice, is misery and ruin; injustice has the promise of a glorious life. Appearance is master of truth and lord of happiness. To appearance then I will turn,—I will put on the show of virtue and trail behind me the fox of Archilochus. I hear some one saying that "wickedness is not easily concealed," to which I reply that "nothing great is easy." Union and force and rhetoric will do much; and if men say that they cannot prevail over the gods, still how do we know that there are gods? Only from the poets, who acknowledge that they may be appeased by sacrifices. Then why not sin and pay for indulgences out of your sin? For if the righteous are only unpunished, still they have no further reward, while the wicked may be unpunished and have the pleasure of sinning too. But what of the world below? Nay, says the argument, there are atoning powers who will set that matter right, as the poets, who are the sons of the gods, tell us; and this is confirmed by the authority of the State.

'How can we resist such arguments in favour of injustice? Add good
manners, and, as the wise tell us, we shall make the best of both worlds.
Who that is not a miserable caitiff will refrain from smiling at the praises
of justice? Even if a man knows the better part he will not be angry with
others; for he knows also that more than human virtue is needed to save a
man, and that he only praises justice who is incapable of injustice.

'The origin of the evil is that all men from the beginning, heroes, poets,
instructors of youth, have always asserted "the temporal dispensation,"
the honours and profits of justice. Had we been taught in early youth
the power of justice and injustice inherent in the soul, and unseen by
any human or divine eye, we should not have needed others to be our
guardians, but every one would have been the guardian of himself. This
is what I want you to show, Socrates;—other men use arguments which
rather tend to strengthen the position of Thrasymachus that "might is
right;" but from you I expect better things. And please, as Glaucon said, to
exclude reputation; let the just be thought unjust and the unjust just, and
do you still prove to us the superiority of justice'...

The thesis, which for the sake of argument has been maintained by
Glaucon, is the converse of that of Thrasymachus—not right is the interest
of the stronger, but right is the necessity of the weaker. Starting from the
same premises he carries the analysis of society a step further back;—might
is still right, but the might is the weakness of the many combined against
the strength of the few.

There have been theories in modern as well as in ancient times which
have a family likeness to the speculations of Glaucon; e.g. that power is
the foundation of right; or that a monarch has a divine right to govern
well or ill; or that virtue is self-love or the love of power; or that war
is the natural state of man; or that private vices are public benefits. All
such theories have a kind of plausibility from their partial agreement with
experience. For human nature oscillates between good and evil, and the
motives of actions and the origin of institutions may be explained to a
certain extent on either hypothesis according to the character or point
of view of a particular thinker. The obligation of maintaining authority

under all circumstances and sometimes by rather questionable means is felt strongly and has become a sort of instinct among civilized men. The divine right of kings, or more generally of governments, is one of the forms under which this natural feeling is expressed. Nor again is there any evil which has not some accompaniment of good or pleasure; nor any good which is free from some alloy of evil; nor any noble or generous thought which may not be attended by a shadow or the ghost of a shadow of self-interest or of self-love. We know that all human actions are imperfect; but we do not therefore attribute them to the worse rather than to the better motive or principle. Such a philosophy is both foolish and false, like that opinion of the clever rogue who assumes all other men to be like himself. And theories of this sort do not represent the real nature of the State, which is based on a vague sense of right gradually corrected and enlarged by custom and law (although capable also of perversion), any more than they describe the origin of society, which is to be sought in the family and in the social and religious feelings of man. Nor do they represent the average character of individuals, which cannot be explained simply on a theory of evil, but has always a counteracting element of good. And as men become better such theories appear more and more untruthful to them, because they are more conscious of their own disinterestedness. A little experience may make a man a cynic; a great deal will bring him back to a truer and kindlier view of the mixed nature of himself and his fellow men.

The two brothers ask Socrates to prove to them that the just is happy when they have taken from him all that in which happiness is ordinarily supposed to consist. Not that there is (1) any absurdity in the attempt to frame a notion of justice apart from circumstances. For the ideal must always be a paradox when compared with the ordinary conditions of human life. Neither the Stoical ideal nor the Christian ideal is true as a fact, but they may serve as a basis of education, and may exercise an ennobling influence. An ideal is none the worse because 'some one has made the discovery' that no such ideal was ever realized. And in a few exceptional individuals who are raised above the ordinary level of humanity, the ideal of happiness may be realized in death and misery. This may be the state which the reason deliberately approves, and which the utilitarian as well as every other moralist may be bound in certain cases to prefer.

Nor again, (2) must we forget that Plato, though he agrees generally with the view implied in the argument of the two brothers, is not expressing his own final conclusion, but rather seeking to dramatize one of the aspects of ethical truth. He is developing his idea gradually in a series of positions or situations. He is exhibiting Socrates for the first time undergoing the Socratic interrogation. Lastly, (3) the word 'happiness' involves some degree of confusion because associated in the language of modern philosophy with conscious pleasure or satisfaction, which was not equally present to his mind.

Glaucon has been drawing a picture of the misery of the just and the happiness of the unjust, to which the misery of the tyrant in Book IX is the answer and parallel. And still the unjust must appear just; that is 'the homage which vice pays to virtue.' But now Adeimantus, taking up the hint which had been already given by Glaucon, proceeds to show that in the opinion of mankind justice is regarded only for the sake of rewards and reputation, and points out the advantage which is given to such arguments as those of Thrasymachus and Glaucon by the conventional morality of mankind. He seems to feel the difficulty of 'justifying the ways of God to man.' Both the brothers touch upon the question, whether the morality of actions is determined by their consequences; and both of them go beyond the position of Socrates, that justice belongs to the class of goods not desirable for themselves only, but desirable for themselves and for their results, to which he recalls them. In their attempt to view justice as an internal principle, and in their condemnation of the poets, they anticipate him. The common life of Greece is not enough for them; they must penetrate deeper into the nature of things.

It has been objected that justice is honesty in the sense of Glaucon and Adeimantus, but is taken by Socrates to mean all virtue. May we not more truly say that the old-fashioned notion of justice is enlarged by Socrates, and becomes equivalent to universal order or well-being, first in the State, and secondly in the individual? He has found a new answer to his old

question (Protag.), 'whether the virtues are one or many,' viz. that one
is the ordering principle of the three others. In seeking to establish the
purely internal nature of justice, he is met by the fact that man is a social
being, and he tries to harmonise the two opposite theses as well as he
can. There is no more inconsistency in this than was inevitable in his
age and country; there is no use in turning upon him the cross lights
of modern philosophy, which, from some other point of view, would
appear equally inconsistent. Plato does not give the final solution of
philosophical questions for us; nor can he be judged of by our standard.

The remainder of the Republic is developed out of the question
of the sons of Ariston. Three points are deserving of remark in what
immediately follows:—First, that the answer of Socrates is altogether
indirect. He does not say that happiness consists in the contemplation
of the idea of justice, and still less will he be tempted to affirm the Stoical
paradox that the just man can be happy on the rack. But first he dwells
on the difficulty of the problem and insists on restoring man to his
natural condition, before he will answer the question at all. He too will
frame an ideal, but his ideal comprehends not only abstract justice, but
the whole relations of man. Under the fanciful illustration of the large
letters he implies that he will only look for justice in society, and that
from the State he will proceed to the individual. His answer in substance
amounts to this,—that under favourable conditions, i.e. in the perfect
State, justice and happiness will coincide, and that when justice has been
once found, happiness may be left to take care of itself. That he falls into
some degree of inconsistency, when in the tenth book he claims to have
got rid of the rewards and honours of justice, may be admitted; for he
has left those which exist in the perfect State. And the philosopher 'who
retires under the shelter of a wall' can hardly have been esteemed happy
by him, at least not in this world. Still he maintains the true attitude of
moral action. Let a man do his duty first, without asking whether he will
be happy or not, and happiness will be the inseparable accident which
attends him. 'Seek ye first the kingdom of God and his righteousness,
and all these things shall be added unto you.'

Secondly, it may be remarked that Plato preserves the genuine character of Greek thought in beginning with the State and in going on to the individual. First ethics, then politics—this is the order of ideas to us; the reverse is the order of history. Only after many struggles of thought does the individual assert his right as a moral being. In early ages he is not ONE, but one of many, the citizen of a State which is prior to him; and he has no notion of good or evil apart from the law of his country or the creed of his church. And to this type he is constantly tending to revert, whenever the influence of custom, or of party spirit, or the recollection of the past becomes too strong for him.

Thirdly, we may observe the confusion or identification of the individual and the State, of ethics and politics, which pervades early Greek speculation, and even in modern times retains a certain degree of influence. The subtle difference between the collective and individual action of mankind seems to have escaped early thinkers, and we too are sometimes in danger of forgetting the conditions of united human action, whenever we either elevate politics into ethics, or lower ethics to the standard of politics. The good man and the good citizen only coincide in the perfect State; and this perfection cannot be attained by legislation acting upon them from without, but, if at all, by education fashioning them from within.

...Socrates praises the sons of Ariston, 'inspired offspring of the renowned hero,' as the elegiac poet terms them; but he does not understand how they can argue so eloquently on behalf of injustice while their character shows that they are uninfluenced by their own arguments. He knows not how to answer them, although he is afraid of deserting justice in the hour of need. He therefore makes a condition, that having weak eyes he shall be allowed to read the large letters first and then go on to the smaller, that is, he must look for justice in the State first, and will then proceed to the individual. Accordingly he begins to construct the State.

Society arises out of the wants of man. His first want is food; his second a house; his third a coat. The sense of these needs and the possibility of satisfying them by exchange, draw individuals together on the same spot; and this is the beginning of a State, which we take the liberty to invent, although necessity is the real inventor. There must be first a husbandman, secondly a builder, thirdly a weaver, to which may be added a cobbler. Four or five citizens at least are required to make a city. Now men have different natures, and one man will do one thing better than many; and business waits for no man. Hence there must be a division of labour into different employments; into wholesale and retail trade; into workers, and makers of workmen's tools; into shepherds and husbandmen. A city which includes all this will have far exceeded the limit of four or five, and yet not be very large. But then again imports will be required, and imports necessitate exports, and this implies variety of produce in order to attract the taste of purchasers; also merchants and ships. In the city too we must have a market and money and retail trades; otherwise buyers and sellers will never meet, and the valuable time of the producers will be wasted in vain efforts at exchange. If we add hired servants the State will be complete. And we may guess that somewhere in the intercourse of the citizens with one another justice and injustice will appear.

Here follows a rustic picture of their way of life. They spend their days in houses which they have built for themselves; they make their own clothes and produce their own corn and wine. Their principal food is meal and flour, and they drink in moderation. They live on the best of terms with each other, and take care not to have too many children. 'But,' said Glaucon, interposing, 'are they not to have a relish?' Certainly; they will have salt and olives and cheese, vegetables and fruits, and chestnuts to roast at the fire. ''Tis a city of pigs, Socrates.' Why, I replied, what do you want more? 'Only the comforts of life,—sofas and tables, also sauces and sweets.' I see; you want not only a State, but a luxurious State; and possibly in the more complex frame we may sooner find justice and injustice. Then the fine arts must go to work—every conceivable instrument and ornament of luxury will be wanted. There will be dancers, painters, sculptors, musicians, cooks, barbers, tire-women, nurses, artists; swineherds and neatherds too for the animals, and physicians to cure the disorders of which luxury is the source. To feed all these superfluous mouths we shall need a part of our neighbour's land, and they will want a part of ours. And this is the origin of war, which may be traced to the same causes as other political evils. Our city will now require the slight addition of a camp, and the citizen will be converted into a soldier. But then again our old doctrine of the division of labour must not be forgotten. The art of war cannot be learned in a day, and there must be a natural aptitude for military duties. There will be some warlike natures who have this aptitude—dogs keen of scent, swift of foot to pursue, and strong of limb to fight. And as spirit is the foundation of courage, such natures, whether of men or animals, will be full of spirit. But these spirited natures are apt to bite and devour one another; the union of gentleness to friends and fierceness against enemies appears to be an impossibility, and the guardian of a State requires both qualities. Who then can be a guardian? The image of the dog suggests an answer. For dogs are gentle to friends and fierce to strangers. Your dog is a philosopher who judges by the rule of knowing or not knowing; and philosophy, whether in man or beast, is the parent of gentleness. The human watchdogs must be philosophers or lovers of learning which will make them gentle. And how are they to be learned without education?

But what shall their education be? Is any better than the old-fashioned sort which is comprehended under the name of music and gymnastic? Music includes literature, and literature is of two kinds, true and false. 'What do you mean?' he said. I mean that children hear stories before they learn gymnastics, and that the stories are either untrue, or have at most one or two grains of truth in a bushel of falsehood. Now early life is very impressible, and children ought not to learn what they will have to unlearn when they grow up; we must therefore have a censorship of nursery tales, banishing some and keeping others. Some of them are very improper, as we may see in the great instances of Homer and Hesiod, who not only tell lies but bad lies; stories about Uranus and Saturn, which are immoral as well as false, and which should never be spoken of to young persons, or indeed at all; or, if at all, then in a mystery, after the sacrifice, not of an Eleusinian pig, but of some unprocurable animal. Shall our youth be encouraged to beat their fathers by the example of Zeus, or our citizens be incited to quarrel by hearing or seeing representations of strife among the gods? Shall they listen to the narrative of Hephaestus binding his mother, and of Zeus sending him flying for helping her when she was beaten? Such tales may possibly have a mystical interpretation, but the young are incapable of understanding allegory. If any one asks what tales are to be allowed, we will answer that we are legislators and not book-makers; we only lay down the principles according to which books are to be written; to write them is the duty of others.

And our first principle is, that God must be represented as he is; not as the author of all things, but of good only. We will not suffer the poets to say that he is the steward of good and evil, or that he has two casks full of destinies;—or that Athene and Zeus incited Pandarus to break the treaty; or that God caused the sufferings of Niobe, or of Pelops, or the Trojan war; or that he makes men sin when he wishes to destroy them. Either these were not the actions of the gods, or God was just, and men were the better for being punished. But that the deed was evil, and God the author, is a wicked, suicidal fiction which we will allow no one, old or young, to utter. This is our first and great principle—God is the author of good only.

And the second principle is like unto it:—With God is no variableness or change of form. Reason teaches us this; for if we suppose a change in God, he must be changed either by another or by himself. By another?—but the best works of nature and art and the noblest qualities of mind are least liable to be changed by any external force. By himself?—but he cannot change for the better; he will hardly change for the worse. He remains for ever fairest and best in his own image. Therefore we refuse to listen to the poets who tell us of Here begging in the likeness of a priestess or of other deities who prowl about at night in strange disguises; all that blasphemous nonsense with which mothers fool the manhood out of their children must be suppressed. But some one will say that God, who is himself unchangeable, may take a form in relation to us. Why should he? For gods as well as men hate the lie in the soul, or principle of falsehood; and as for any other form of lying which is used for a purpose and is regarded as innocent in certain exceptional cases—what need have the gods of this? For they are not ignorant of antiquity like the poets, nor are they afraid of their enemies, nor is any madman a friend of theirs. God then is true, he is absolutely true; he changes not, he deceives not, by day or night, by word or sign. This is our second great principle—God is true. Away with the lying dream of Agamemnon in Homer, and the accusation of Thetis against Apollo in Aeschylus...

In order to give clearness to his conception of the State, Plato proceeds to trace the first principles of mutual need and of division of labour in an imaginary community of four or five citizens. Gradually this community increases; the division of labour extends to countries; imports necessitate exports; a medium of exchange is required, and retailers sit in the market-place to save the time of the producers. These are the steps by which Plato constructs the first or primitive State, introducing the elements of political economy by the way. As he is going to frame a second or civilized State, the simple naturally comes before the complex. He indulges, like Rousseau, in a picture of primitive life—an idea which has indeed often had a powerful influence on the imagination of mankind, but he does not seriously mean to say that one is better than the other (Politicus); nor can any inference be drawn from the description of the first state taken apart from the second, such as Aristotle appears to draw in the Politics. We should not interpret a Platonic dialogue any more than a poem or a parable in too literal or matter-of-fact a style. On the other hand, when we compare the lively fancy of Plato with the dried-up abstractions of modern treatises on philosophy, we are compelled to say with Protagoras, that the 'mythus is more interesting' (Protag.)

Several interesting remarks which in modern times would have a place in a treatise on Political Economy are scattered up and down the writings of Plato: especially Laws, Population; Free Trade; Adulteration; Wills and Bequests; Begging; Eryxias, (though not Plato's), Value and Demand; Republic, Division of Labour. The last subject, and also the origin of Retail Trade, is treated with admirable lucidity in the second book of the Republic. But Plato never combined his economic ideas into a system, and never seems to have recognized that Trade is one of the great motive powers of the State and of the world. He would make retail traders only of the inferior sort of citizens (Rep., Laws), though he remarks, quaintly enough (Laws), that 'if only the best men and the best women everywhere were compelled to keep taverns for a time or to carry on retail trade, etc., then we should knew how pleasant and agreeable all these things are.'

The disappointment of Glaucon at the 'city of pigs,' the ludicrous description of the ministers of luxury in the more refined State, and the afterthought of the necessity of doctors, the illustration of the nature of the guardian taken from the dog, the desirableness of offering some almost unprocurable victim when impure mysteries are to be celebrated, the behaviour of Zeus to his father and of Hephaestus to his mother, are touches of humour which have also a serious meaning. In speaking of education Plato rather startles us by affirming that a child must be trained in falsehood first and in truth afterwards. Yet this is not very different from saying that children must be taught through the medium of imagination as well as reason; that their minds can only develope gradually, and that there is much which they must learn without understanding. This is also the substance of Plato's view, though he must be acknowledged to have drawn the line somewhat differently from modern ethical writers, respecting truth and falsehood. To us, economies or accommodations would not be allowable unless they were required by the human faculties or necessary for the communication of knowledge to the simple and ignorant. We should insist that the word was inseparable from the intention, and that we must not be 'falsely true,' i.e. speak or act falsely in support of what was right or true. But Plato would limit the use of fictions only by requiring that they should have a good moral effect, and that such a dangerous weapon as falsehood should be employed by the rulers alone and for great objects.

A Greek in the age of Plato attached no importance to the question whether his religion was an historical fact. He was just beginning to be conscious that the past had a history; but he could see nothing beyond Homer and Hesiod. Whether their narratives were true or false did not seriously affect the political or social life of Hellas. Men only began to suspect that they were fictions when they recognised them to be immoral.

And so in all religions: the consideration of their morality comes first, afterwards the truth of the documents in which they are recorded, or of the events natural or supernatural which are told of them. But in modern times, and in Protestant countries perhaps more than in Catholic, we have been too much inclined to identify the historical with the moral; and some have refused to believe in religion at all, unless a superhuman accuracy was discernible in every part of the record. The facts of an ancient or religious history are amongst the most important of all facts; but they are frequently uncertain, and we only learn the true lesson which is to be gathered from them when we place ourselves above them. These reflections tend to show that the difference between Plato and ourselves, though not unimportant, is not so great as might at first sight appear. For we should agree with him in placing the moral before the historical truth of religion; and, generally, in disregarding those errors or misstatements of fact which necessarily occur in the early stages of all religions. We know also that changes in the traditions of a country cannot be made in a day; and are therefore tolerant of many things which science and criticism would condemn.

We note in passing that the allegorical interpretation of mythology, said to have been first introduced as early as the sixth century before Christ by Theagenes of Rhegium, was well established in the age of Plato, and here, as in the Phaedrus, though for a different reason, was rejected by him. That anachronisms whether of religion or law, when men have reached another stage of civilization, should be got rid of by fictions is in accordance with universal experience. Great is the art of interpretation; and by a natural process, which when once discovered was always going on, what could not be altered was explained away. And so without any palpable inconsistency there existed side by side two forms of religion, the tradition inherited or invented by the poets and the customary worship of the temple; on the other hand, there was the religion of the philosopher, who was dwelling in the heaven of ideas, but did not therefore refuse to offer a cock to Aesculapius, or to be seen saying his prayers at the rising of the sun. At length the antagonism between the popular and philosophical religion, never so great among the Greeks as in our own age, disappeared, and was only felt like the difference between the religion of the educated and uneducated among ourselves. The Zeus of Homer and Hesiod easily passed into the 'royal mind' of Plato (Philebus); the giant Heracles became the knight-errant and benefactor of mankind. These and still more wonderful transformations were readily effected by the ingenuity of Stoics and neo-Platonists in the two or three centuries before and after Christ. The Greek and Roman religions were gradually permeated by the spirit of philosophy; having lost their ancient meaning, they were resolved into poetry and morality; and probably were never purer than at the time of their decay, when their influence over the world was waning.

A singular conception which occurs towards the end of the book is the lie in the soul; this is connected with the Platonic and Socratic doctrine that involuntary ignorance is worse than voluntary. The lie in the soul is a true lie, the corruption of the highest truth, the deception of the highest part of the soul, from which he who is deceived has no power of delivering himself. For example, to represent God as false or immoral, or, according to Plato, as deluding men with appearances or as the author of evil; or again, to affirm with Protagoras that 'knowledge is sensation,' or that 'being is becoming,' or with Thrasymachus 'that might is right,' would have been regarded by Plato as a lie of this hateful sort. The greatest unconsciousness of the greatest untruth, e.g. if, in the language of the Gospels (John), 'he who was blind' were to say 'I see,' is another aspect of the state of mind which Plato is describing. The lie in the soul may be further compared with the sin against the Holy Ghost (Luke), allowing for the difference between Greek and Christian modes of speaking. To this is opposed the lie in words, which is only such a deception as may occur in a play or poem, or allegory or figure of speech, or in any sort of accommodation,—which though useless to the gods may be useful to men in certain cases. Socrates is here answering the question which he had himself raised about the propriety of deceiving a madman; and he is also contrasting the nature of God and man. For God is Truth, but mankind can only be true by appearing sometimes to be partial, or false. Reserving for another place the greater questions of religion or education, we may note further, (1) the approval of the old traditional education of Greece; (2) the preparation which Plato is making for the attack on Homer and the poets; (3) the preparation which he is also making for the use of economies in the State; (4) the contemptuous and at the same time euphemistic manner in which here as below he alludes to the 'Chronique Scandaleuse' of the gods.

Book III - Introduction & Analysis
Arts in Education

There is another motive in purifying religion, which is to banish fear; for no man can be courageous who is afraid of death, or who believes the tales which are repeated by the poets concerning the world below. They must be gently requested not to abuse hell; they may be reminded that their stories are both untrue and discouraging. Nor must they be angry if we expunge obnoxious passages, such as the depressing words of Achilles—'I would rather be a serving-man than rule over all the dead;' and the verses which tell of the squalid mansions, the senseless shadows, the flitting soul mourning over lost strength and youth, the soul with a gibber going beneath the earth like smoke, or the souls of the suitors which flutter about like bats. The terrors and horrors of Cocytus and Styx, ghosts and sapless shades, and the rest of their Tartarean nomenclature, must vanish. Such tales may have their use; but they are not the proper food for soldiers. As little can we admit the sorrows and sympathies of the Homeric heroes:—Achilles, the son of Thetis, in tears, throwing ashes on his head, or pacing up and down the sea-shore in distraction; or Priam, the cousin of the gods, crying aloud, rolling in the mire. A good man is not prostrated at the loss of children or fortune. Neither is death terrible to him; and therefore lamentations over the dead should not be practised by men of note; they should be the concern of inferior persons only, whether women or men. Still worse is the attribution of such weakness to the gods;

as when the goddesses say, 'Alas! my travail!' and worst of all, when the king of heaven himself laments his inability to save Hector, or sorrows over the impending doom of his dear Sarpedon. Such a character of God, if not ridiculed by our young men, is likely to be imitated by them. Nor should our citizens be given to excess of laughter—'Such violent delights' are followed by a violent re-action. The description in the Iliad of the gods shaking their sides at the clumsiness of Hephaestus will not be admitted by us. 'Certainly not.'

Truth should have a high place among the virtues, for falsehood, as we were saying, is useless to the gods, and only useful to men as a medicine. But this employment of falsehood must remain a privilege of state; the common man must not in return tell a lie to the ruler; any more than the patient would tell a lie to his physician, or the sailor to his captain.

In the next place our youth must be temperate, and temperance consists in self-control and obedience to authority. That is a lesson which Homer teaches in some places: 'The Achaeans marched on breathing prowess, in silent awe of their leaders;'—but a very different one in other places: 'O heavy with wine, who hast the eyes of a dog, but the heart of a stag.' Language of the latter kind will not impress self-control on the minds of youth. The same may be said about his praises of eating and drinking and his dread of starvation; also about the verses in which he tells of the rapturous loves of Zeus and Here, or of how Hephaestus once detained Ares and Aphrodite in a net on a similar occasion. There is a nobler strain heard in the words:—'Endure, my soul, thou hast endured worse.' Nor must we allow our citizens to receive bribes, or to say, 'Gifts persuade the gods, gifts reverend kings;' or to applaud the ignoble advice of Phoenix to Achilles that he should get money out of the Greeks before he assisted them; or the meanness of Achilles himself in taking gifts from Agamemnon; or his requiring a ransom for the body of Hector; or his cursing of Apollo; or his insolence to the river-god Scamander; or his dedication to the dead Patroclus of his own hair which had been already dedicated to the other river-god Spercheius; or his cruelty in dragging the body of Hector round the walls, and slaying the captives at the pyre: such a combination of meanness and cruelty in Cheiron's pupil is inconceivable. The amatory exploits of Peirithous and Theseus are equally unworthy. Either these so-called sons of gods were not the sons of gods, or they were not such as the poets imagine them, any more than the gods themselves are the authors of evil. The youth who believes that such things are done by those who have the blood of heaven flowing in their veins will be too ready to imitate their example.

Enough of gods and heroes;—what shall we say about men? What the poets and story-tellers say—that the wicked prosper and the righteous are afflicted, or that justice is another's gain? Such misrepresentations cannot be allowed by us. But in this we are anticipating the definition of justice, and had therefore better defer the enquiry.

The subjects of poetry have been sufficiently treated; next follows style. Now all poetry is a narrative of events past, present, or to come; and narrative is of three kinds, the simple, the imitative, and a composition of the two. An instance will make my meaning clear. The first scene in Homer is of the last or mixed kind, being partly description and partly dialogue. But if you throw the dialogue into the 'oratio obliqua,' the passage will run thus: The priest came and prayed Apollo that the Achaeans might take Troy and have a safe return if Agamemnon would only give him back his daughter; and the other Greeks assented, but Agamemnon was wroth, and so on—The whole then becomes descriptive, and the poet is the only speaker left; or, if you omit the narrative, the whole becomes dialogue. These are the three styles—which of them is to be admitted into our State? 'Do you ask whether tragedy and comedy are to be admitted?' Yes, but also something more—Is it not doubtful whether our guardians are to be imitators at all? Or rather, has not the question been already answered, for we have decided that one man cannot in his life play many parts, any more than he can act both tragedy and comedy, or be rhapsodist and actor at once? Human nature is coined into very small pieces, and as our guardians have their own business already, which is the care of freedom, they will have enough to do without imitating. If they imitate they should imitate, not any meanness or baseness, but the good only; for the mask which the actor wears is apt to become his face. We cannot allow men to play the parts of women, quarrelling, weeping, scolding, or boasting against the gods,—least of all when making love or in labour. They must not represent slaves, or bullies, or cowards, drunkards, or madmen, or blacksmiths, or neighing horses, or bellowing bulls, or sounding rivers, or a raging sea. A good or wise man will be willing to perform good and wise actions, but he will be ashamed to play an inferior part which he has never practised; and he will prefer to employ the descriptive style with as little imitation as possible. The man who has no self-respect, on the contrary, will imitate anybody and anything; sounds of nature and cries of animals alike; his whole performance will be imitation of gesture and voice. Now in the descriptive style there are few changes, but in the dramatic there are a great many. Poets and musicians use either, or a compound of both, and this compound is very attractive to youth and their teachers as well as to the vulgar. But our State in which one man plays one part only is not adapted for complexity. And when one of these polyphonous pantomimic gentlemen offers to exhibit himself and his poetry we will show him every observance of respect, but at the same time tell him that there is no room for his kind in our State; we prefer the rough, honest poet, and will not depart from our original models (Laws).

Next as to the music. A song or ode has three parts,—the subject, the harmony, and the rhythm; of which the two last are dependent upon the first. As we banished strains of lamentation, so we may now banish the mixed Lydian harmonies, which are the harmonies of lamentation; and as our citizens are to be temperate, we may also banish convivial harmonies, such as the Ionian and pure Lydian. Two remain—the Dorian and Phrygian, the first for war, the second for peace; the one expressive of courage, the other of obedience or instruction or religious feeling. And as we reject varieties of harmony, we shall also reject the many-stringed, variously-shaped instruments which give utterance to them, and in particular the flute, which is more complex than any of them. The lyre and the harp may be permitted in the town, and the Pan's-pipe in the fields. Thus we have made a purgation of music, and will now make a purgation

of metres. These should be like the harmonies, simple and suitable to
the occasion. There are four notes of the tetrachord, and there are three
ratios of metre, 3/2, 2/2, 2/1, which have all their characteristics, and
the feet have different characteristics as well as the rhythms. But about
this you and I must ask Damon, the great musician, who speaks, if I
remember rightly, of a martial measure as well as of dactylic, trochaic,
and iambic rhythms, which he arranges so as to equalize the syllables
with one another, assigning to each the proper quantity. We only
venture to affirm the general principle that the style is to conform to the
subject and the metre to the style; and that the simplicity and harmony
of the soul should be reflected in them all. This principle of simplicity
has to be learnt by every one in the days of his youth, and may be
gathered anywhere, from the creative and constructive arts, as well as
from the forms of plants and animals.

Other artists as well as poets should be warned against meanness or
unseemliness. Sculpture and painting equally with music must conform to
the law of simplicity. He who violates it cannot be allowed to work in our
city, and to corrupt the taste of our citizens. For our guardians must grow
up, not amid images of deformity which will gradually poison and corrupt
their souls, but in a land of health and beauty where they will drink in from
every object sweet and harmonious influences. And of all these influences
the greatest is the education given by music, which finds a way into the
innermost soul and imparts to it the sense of beauty and of deformity.
At first the effect is unconscious; but when reason arrives, then he who
has been thus trained welcomes her as the friend whom he always knew.
As in learning to read, first we acquire the elements or letters separately,
and afterwards their combinations, and cannot recognize reflections of
them until we know the letters themselves;—in like manner we must first
attain the elements or essential forms of the virtues, and then trace their
combinations in life and experience. There is a music of the soul which
answers to the harmony of the world; and the fairest object of a musical
soul is the fair mind in the fair body. Some defect in the latter may be
excused, but not in the former. True love is the daughter of temperance,

and temperance is utterly opposed to the madness of bodily pleasure. Enough has been said of music, which makes a fair ending with love.

Next we pass on to gymnastics; about which I would remark, that the soul is related to the body as a cause to an effect, and therefore if we educate the mind we may leave the education of the body in her charge, and need only give a general outline of the course to be pursued. In the first place the guardians must abstain from strong drink, for they should be the last persons to lose their wits. Whether the habits of the palaestra are suitable to them is more doubtful, for the ordinary gymnastic is a sleepy sort of thing, and if left off suddenly is apt to endanger health. But our warrior athletes must be wide-awake dogs, and must also be inured to all changes of food and climate. Hence they will require a simpler kind of gymnastic, akin to their simple music; and for their diet a rule may be found in Homer, who feeds his heroes on roast meat only, and gives them no fish although they are living at the sea-side, nor boiled meats which involve an apparatus of pots and pans; and, if I am not mistaken, he nowhere mentions sweet sauces. Sicilian cookery and Attic confections and Corinthian courtezans, which are to gymnastic what Lydian and Ionian melodies are to music, must be forbidden. Where gluttony and intemperance prevail the town quickly fills with doctors and pleaders; and law and medicine give themselves airs as soon as the freemen of a State take an interest in them. But what can show a more disgraceful state of education than to have to go abroad for justice because you have none of your own at home? And yet there IS a worse stage of the same disease—when men have learned to take a pleasure and pride in the twists and turns of the law; not considering how much better it would be for them so to order their lives as to have no need of a nodding justice. And there is a like disgrace in employing a physician, not for the cure of wounds or epidemic disorders, but because a man has by laziness and luxury contracted diseases which were unknown in the days of Asclepius. How simple is the Homeric practice of medicine. Eurypylus after he has been wounded drinks a posset of Pramnian wine, which is of a heating nature; and yet the sons of Asclepius blame neither the damsel who gives him the drink, nor Patroclus who is attending on him. The truth is that this modern system of nursing diseases was introduced by Herodicus the trainer; who, being of a sickly constitution, by a compound of training and medicine tortured first himself and then a good many other people, and lived a great deal longer than he had any right. But Asclepius would not practise this art, because he knew that the citizens of a well-ordered State have no leisure to be ill, and therefore he adopted the 'kill or cure' method, which artisans and labourers employ. 'They must be at their business,' they say, 'and have no time for coddling: if they recover, well; if they don't, there is an end of them.' Whereas the rich man is supposed to be a gentleman who can afford to be ill. Do you know a maxim of Phocylides—that 'when a man begins to be rich' (or, perhaps, a little sooner) 'he should practise virtue'? But how can excessive care of health be inconsistent with an ordinary occupation, and yet consistent with that practice of virtue which Phocylides inculcates? When a student imagines that philosophy gives him a headache, he never does anything; he is always unwell. This was the reason why Asclepius and his sons practised no such art. They were acting in the interest of the public, and did not wish to preserve useless lives, or raise up a puny offspring to wretched sires. Honest diseases they honestly cured; and if a man was wounded, they applied the proper remedies, and then let him eat and drink what he liked. But they declined to treat intemperate and worthless subjects, even though they might have made large fortunes out of them. As to the story of Pindar, that Asclepius was slain by a thunderbolt for restoring a rich man to life, that is a lie—following our old rule we must say either that he did not take bribes, or that he was not the son of a god.

Glaucon then asks Socrates whether the best physicians and the best judges will not be those who have had severally the greatest experience of diseases and of crimes. Socrates draws a distinction between the two professions. The physician should have had experience of disease in his own body, for he cures with his mind and not with his body. But the judge controls mind by mind; and therefore his mind should not be corrupted by crime. Where then is he to gain experience? How is he to be wise and also innocent? When young a good man is apt to be deceived by evil-doers, because he has no pattern of evil in himself; and therefore the judge should be of a certain age; his youth should have been innocent, and he should have acquired insight into evil not by the practice of it, but by the observation of it in others. This is the ideal of a judge; the criminal turned detective is wonderfully suspicious, but when in company with good men who have experience, he is at fault, for he foolishly imagines that every one is as bad as himself. Vice may be known of virtue, but cannot know virtue. This is the sort of medicine and this the sort of law which will prevail in our State; they will be healing arts to better natures; but the evil body will be left to die by the one, and the evil soul will be put to death by the other. And the need of either will be greatly diminished by good music which will give harmony to the soul, and good gymnastic which will give health to the body. Not that this division of music and gymnastic really corresponds to soul and body; for they are both equally concerned with the soul, which is tamed by the one and aroused and sustained by the other. The two together supply our guardians with their twofold nature. The passionate disposition when it has too much gymnastic is hardened and brutalized, the gentle or philosophic temper which has too much music becomes enervated. While a man is allowing music to pour like water through the funnel of his ears, the edge of his soul gradually wears away, and the passionate or spirited element is melted out of him. Too little spirit is easily exhausted; too much quickly passes into nervous irritability. So, again, the athlete by feeding and training has his courage doubled, but he soon grows stupid; he is like a wild beast, ready to do everything by blows and nothing by counsel or policy. There are two principles in man, reason and passion, and to these, not to the soul and body, the two arts of music and gymnastic correspond. He who mingles them in harmonious concord is the true musician,—he shall be the presiding genius of our State.

The next question is, Who are to be our rulers? First, the elder must rule the younger; and the best of the elders will be the best guardians. Now they will be the best who love their subjects most, and think that they have a common interest with them in the welfare of the state. These we must select; but they must be watched at every epoch of life to see whether they have retained the same opinions and held out against force and enchantment. For time and persuasion and the love of pleasure may enchant a man into a change of purpose, and the force of grief and pain may compel him. And therefore our guardians must be men who have been tried by many tests, like gold in the refiner's fire, and have been passed first through danger, then through pleasure, and at every age have come out of such trials victorious and without stain, in full command of themselves and their principles; having all their faculties in harmonious exercise for their country's good. These shall receive the highest honours both in life and death. (It would perhaps be better to confine the term 'guardians' to this select class: the younger men may be called 'auxiliaries.')

And now for one magnificent lie, in the belief of which, Oh that we could train our rulers!—at any rate let us make the attempt with the rest of the world. What I am going to tell is only another version of the legend of Cadmus; but our unbelieving generation will be slow to accept such a story. The tale must be imparted, first to the rulers, then to the soldiers, lastly to the people. We will inform them that their youth was a dream, and that during the time when they seemed to be undergoing their education they were really being fashioned in the earth, who sent them up when they were ready; and that they must protect and cherish her whose children they are, and regard each other as brothers and sisters. 'I do not wonder at your being ashamed to propound such a fiction.' There is more behind. These brothers and sisters have different natures, and some of them God framed to rule, whom he fashioned of gold; others he made of silver, to be auxiliaries; others again to be husbandmen and craftsmen, and these were formed by him of brass and iron. But as they are all sprung from a common stock, a golden parent may have a silver son, or a silver parent a golden son, and then there must be a change of rank; the son of the rich must descend, and the child of the artisan rise, in the social scale; for an oracle says 'that the State will come to an end if governed by a man of brass or iron.' Will our citizens ever believe all this? 'Not in the present generation, but in the next, perhaps, Yes.'

Now let the earthborn men go forth under the command of their rulers, and look about and pitch their camp in a high place, which will be safe against enemies from without, and likewise against insurrections from within. There let them sacrifice and set up their tents; for soldiers they are to be and not shopkeepers, the watchdogs and guardians of the sheep; and luxury and avarice will turn them into wolves and tyrants. Their habits and their dwellings should correspond to their education. They should have no property; their pay should only meet their expenses; and they should have common meals. Gold and silver we will tell them that they have from God, and this divine gift in their souls they must not alloy with that earthly dross which passes under the name of gold. They only of the citizens may not touch it, or be under the same roof with it, or drink from it; it is the accursed thing. Should they ever acquire houses or lands or money of their own, they will become householders and tradesmen instead of guardians, enemies and tyrants instead of helpers, and the hour of ruin, both to themselves and the rest of the State, will be at hand.

The religious and ethical aspect of Plato's education will hereafter be considered under a separate head. Some lesser points may be more conveniently noticed in this place.

1. The constant appeal to the authority of Homer, whom, with grave irony, Plato, after the manner of his age, summons as a witness about ethics and psychology, as well as about diet and medicine; attempting to distinguish the better lesson from the worse, sometimes altering the text from design; more than once quoting or alluding to Homer inaccurately, after the manner of the early logographers turning the Iliad into prose, and delighting to draw far-fetched inferences from his words, or to make ludicrous applications of them. He does not, like Heracleitus, get into a rage with Homer and Archilochus (Heracl.), but uses their words and expressions as vehicles of a higher truth; not on a system like Theagenes of Rhegium or Metrodorus, or in later times the Stoics, but as fancy may dictate. And the conclusions drawn from them are sound, although the premises are fictitious. These fanciful appeals to Homer add a charm to Plato's style, and at the same time they have the effect of a satire on the follies of Homeric interpretation. To us (and probably to himself), although they take the form of arguments, they are really figures of speech.

They may be compared with modern citations from Scripture, which have often a great rhetorical power even when the original meaning of the words is entirely lost sight of. The real, like the Platonic Socrates, as we gather from the Memorabilia of Xenophon, was fond of making similar adaptations. Great in all ages and countries, in religion as well as in law and literature, has been the art of interpretation.

2. 'The style is to conform to the subject and the metre to the style.' Notwithstanding the fascination which the word 'classical' exercises over us, we can hardly maintain that this rule is observed in all the Greek poetry which has come down to us. We cannot deny that the thought often exceeds the power of lucid expression in Aeschylus and Pindar; or that rhetoric gets the better of the thought in the Sophist-poet Euripides. Only perhaps in Sophocles is there a perfect harmony of the two; in him alone do we find a grace of language like the beauty of a Greek statue, in which there is nothing to add or to take away; at least this is true of single plays or of large portions of them. The connection in the Tragic Choruses and in the Greek lyric poets is not unfrequently a tangled thread which in an age before logic the poet was unable to draw out. Many thoughts and feelings mingled in his mind, and he had no power of disengaging or arranging them. For there is a subtle influence of logic which requires to be transferred from prose to poetry, just as the music and perfection of language are infused by poetry into prose. In all ages the poet has been a bad judge of his own meaning (Apol.); for he does not see that the word which is full of associations to his own mind is difficult and unmeaning to that of another; or that the sequence which is clear to himself is puzzling to others. There are many passages in some of our greatest modern poets which are far too obscure; in which there is no proportion between style and subject, in which any half-expressed figure, any harsh construction, any distorted collocation of words, any remote sequence of ideas is admitted; and there is no voice 'coming sweetly from nature,' or music adding the expression of feeling to thought. As if there could be poetry without beauty, or beauty without ease and clearness. The obscurities of early Greek poets arose necessarily out of the state of language and logic which existed in their age.

They are not examples to be followed by us; for the use of language ought in every generation to become clearer and clearer. Like Shakespere, they were great in spite, not in consequence, of their imperfections of expression. But there is no reason for returning to the necessary obscurity which prevailed in the infancy of literature. The English poets of the last century were certainly not obscure; and we have no excuse for losing what they had gained, or for going back to the earlier or transitional age which preceded them. The thought of our own times has not out-stripped language; a want of Plato's 'art of measuring' is the rule cause of the disproportion between them.

3. In the third book of the Republic a nearer approach is made to a theory of art than anywhere else in Plato. His views may be summed up as follows:—True art is not fanciful and imitative, but simple and ideal,—the expression of the highest moral energy, whether in action or repose. To live among works of plastic art which are of this noble and simple character, or to listen to such strains, is the best of influences,—the true Greek atmosphere, in which youth should be brought up. That is the way to create in them a natural good taste, which will have a feeling of truth and beauty in all things. For though the poets are to be expelled, still art is recognized as another aspect of reason—like love in the Symposium, extending over the same sphere, but confined to the preliminary education, and acting through the power of habit; and this conception of art is not limited to strains of music or the forms of plastic art, but pervades all nature and has a wide kindred in the world. The Republic of Plato, like the Athens of Pericles, has an artistic as well as a political side.

There is hardly any mention in Plato of the creative arts; only in two or three passages does he even allude to them (Rep.; Soph.). He is not lost in rapture at the great works of Phidias, the Parthenon, the Propylea, the statues of Zeus or Athene. He would probably have regarded any abstract truth of number or figure as higher than the greatest of them. Yet it is hard to suppose that some influence, such as he hopes to inspire in youth, did not pass into his own mind from the works of art which he saw around him. We are living upon the fragments of them, and find in a few broken stones the standard of truth and beauty. But in Plato this feeling has no expression; he nowhere says that beauty is the object of art; he seems to deny that wisdom can take an external form (Phaedrus); he does not distinguish the fine from the mechanical arts. Whether or no, like some writers, he felt more than he expressed, it is at any rate remarkable that the greatest perfection of the fine arts should coincide with an almost entire silence about them. In one very striking passage he tells us that a work of art, like the State, is a whole; and this conception of a whole and the love of the newly-born mathematical sciences may be regarded, if not as the inspiring, at any rate as the regulating principles of Greek art (Xen. Mem.; and Sophist).

4. Plato makes the true and subtle remark that the physician had better not be in robust health; and should have known what illness is in his own person. But the judge ought to have had no similar experience of evil; he is to be a good man who, having passed his youth in innocence, became acquainted late in life with the vices of others. And therefore, according to Plato, a judge should not be young, just as a young man according to Aristotle is not fit to be a hearer of moral philosophy. The bad, on the other hand, have a knowledge of vice, but no knowledge of virtue. It may be doubted, however, whether this train of reflection is well founded. In a remarkable passage of the Laws it is acknowledged that the evil may form a correct estimate of the good. The union of gentleness and courage in Book ii. at first seemed to be a paradox, yet was afterwards ascertained to be a truth. And Plato might also have found that the intuition of evil may be consistent with the abhorrence of it. There is a directness of aim in virtue which gives an insight into vice. And the knowledge of character is in some degree a natural sense independent of any special experience of good or evil.

5. One of the most remarkable conceptions of Plato, because un-Greek and also very different from anything which existed at all in his age of the world, is the transposition of ranks. In the Spartan state there had been enfranchisement of Helots and degradation of citizens under special circumstances. And in the ancient Greek aristocracies, merit was certainly

recognized as one of the elements on which government was based. The
founders of states were supposed to be their benefactors, who were raised
by their great actions above the ordinary level of humanity; at a later period,
the services of warriors and legislators were held to entitle them and their
descendants to the privileges of citizenship and to the first rank in the state.
And although the existence of an ideal aristocracy is slenderly proven from
the remains of early Greek history, and we have a difficulty in ascribing
such a character, however the idea may be defined, to any actual Hellenic
state—or indeed to any state which has ever existed in the world—still
the rule of the best was certainly the aspiration of philosophers, who
probably accommodated a good deal their views of primitive history to
their own notions of good government. Plato further insists on applying
to the guardians of his state a series of tests by which all those who fell short
of a fixed standard were either removed from the governing body, or not
admitted to it; and this 'academic' discipline did to a certain extent prevail
in Greek states, especially in Sparta. He also indicates that the system of
caste, which existed in a great part of the ancient, and is by no means extinct
in the modern European world, should be set aside from time to time
in favour of merit. He is aware how deeply the greater part of mankind
resent any interference with the order of society, and therefore he proposes
his novel idea in the form of what he himself calls a 'monstrous fiction.'
(Compare the ceremony of preparation for the two 'great waves' in Book
v.) Two principles are indicated by him: first, that there is a distinction of
ranks dependent on circumstances prior to the individual: second, that
this distinction is and ought to be broken through by personal qualities.
He adapts mythology like the Homeric poems to the wants of the state,
making 'the Phoenician tale' the vehicle of his ideas. Every Greek state
had a myth respecting its own origin; the Platonic republic may also have
a tale of earthborn men. The gravity and verisimilitude with which the
tale is told, and the analogy of Greek tradition, are a sufficient verification
of the 'monstrous falsehood.' Ancient poetry had spoken of a gold and
silver and brass and iron age succeeding one another, but Plato supposes
these differences in the natures of men to exist together in a single state.

Mythology supplies a figure under which the lesson may be taught (as Protagoras says, 'the myth is more interesting'), and also enables Plato to touch lightly on new principles without going into details. In this passage he shadows forth a general truth, but he does not tell us by what steps the transposition of ranks is to be effected. Indeed throughout the Republic he allows the lower ranks to fade into the distance. We do not know whether they are to carry arms, and whether in the fifth book they are or are not included in the communistic regulations respecting property and marriage. Nor is there any use in arguing strictly either from a few chance words, or from the silence of Plato, or in drawing inferences which were beyond his vision. Aristotle, in his criticism on the position of the lower classes, does not perceive that the poetical creation is 'like the air, invulnerable,' and cannot be penetrated by the shafts of his logic (Pol.).

6. Two paradoxes which strike the modern reader as in the highest degree fanciful and ideal, and which suggest to him many reflections, are to be found in the third book of the Republic: first, the great power of music, so much beyond any influence which is experienced by us in modern times, when the art or science has been far more developed, and has found the secret of harmony, as well as of melody; secondly, the indefinite and almost absolute control which the soul is supposed to exercise over the body.

In the first we suspect some degree of exaggeration, such as we may also observe among certain masters of the art, not unknown to us, at the present day. With this natural enthusiasm, which is felt by a few only, there seems to mingle in Plato a sort of Pythagorean reverence for numbers and numerical proportion to which Aristotle is a stranger. Intervals of sound and number are to him sacred things which have a law of their own, not dependent on the variations of sense. They rise above sense, and become a connecting link with the world of ideas. But it is evident that Plato is describing what to him appears to be also a fact. The power of a simple and characteristic melody on the impressible mind of the Greek is more than we can easily appreciate. The effect of national airs may bear some comparison with it. And, besides all this, there is a confusion between the harmony of musical notes and the harmony of soul and body, which is so potently inspired by them.

The second paradox leads up to some curious and interesting questions—How far can the mind control the body? Is the relation between them one of mutual antagonism or of mutual harmony? Are they two or one, and is either of them the cause of the other? May we not at times drop the opposition between them, and the mode of describing them, which is so familiar to us, and yet hardly conveys any precise meaning, and try to view this composite creature, man, in a more simple manner? Must we not at any rate admit that there is in human nature a higher and a lower principle, divided by no distinct line, which at times break asunder and take up arms against one another? Or again, they are reconciled and move together, either unconsciously in the ordinary work of life, or consciously in the pursuit of some noble aim, to be attained not without an effort, and for which every thought and nerve are strained. And then the body becomes the good friend or ally, or servant or instrument of the mind. And the mind has often a wonderful and almost superhuman power of banishing disease and weakness and calling out a hidden strength. Reason and the desires, the intellect and the senses are brought into harmony and obedience so as to form a single human being. They are ever parting, ever meeting; and the identity or diversity of their tendencies or operations is for the most part unnoticed by us. When the mind touches the body through the appetites, we acknowledge the responsibility of the one to the other. There is a tendency in us which says 'Drink.' There is another which says, 'Do not drink; it is not good for you.' And we all of us know which is the rightful superior. We are also responsible for our health, although into this sphere there enter some elements of necessity which may be beyond our control. Still even in the management of health, care and thought, continued over many years, may make us almost free agents, if we do not exact too much of ourselves, and if we acknowledge that all human freedom is limited by the laws of nature and of mind.

We are disappointed to find that Plato, in the general condemnation which he passes on the practice of medicine prevailing in his own day, depreciates the effects of diet. He would like to have diseases of a definite character and capable of receiving a definite treatment. He is afraid of invalidism interfering with the business of life. He does not recognize that time is the great healer both of mental and bodily disorders; and that remedies which are gradual and proceed little by little are safer than those which produce a sudden catastrophe. Neither does he see that there is no way in which the mind can more surely influence the body than by the control of eating and drinking; or any other action or occasion of human life on which the higher freedom of the will can be more simple or truly asserted.

7. Lesser matters of style may be remarked.

(1) The affected ignorance of music, which is Plato's way of expressing that he is passing lightly over the subject.

(2) The tentative manner in which here, as in the second book, he proceeds with the construction of the State.

(3) The description of the State sometimes as a reality, and then again as a work of imagination only; these are the arts by which he sustains the reader's interest.

(4) Connecting links, or the preparation for the entire expulsion of the poets in Book X.

(5) The companion pictures of the lover of litigation and the valetudinarian, the satirical jest about the maxim of Phocylides, the manner in which the image of the gold and silver citizens is taken up into the subject, and the argument from the practice of Asclepius, should not escape notice.

Book IV - Introduction & Analysis
Wealth, Poverty & Virtue

Adeimantus said: 'Suppose a person to argue, Socrates, that you make your citizens miserable, and this by their own free-will; they are the lords of the city, and yet instead of having, like other men, lands and houses and money of their own, they live as mercenaries and are always mounting guard.' You may add, I replied, that they receive no pay but only their food, and have no money to spend on a journey or a mistress. 'Well, and what answer do you give?' My answer is, that our guardians may or may not be the happiest of men,—I should not be surprised to find in the long-run that they were,—but this is not the aim of our constitution, which was designed for the good of the whole and not of any one part. If I went to a sculptor and blamed him for having painted the eye, which is the noblest feature of the face, not purple but black, he would reply: 'The eye must be an eye, and you should look at the statue as a whole.' 'Now I can well imagine a fool's paradise, in which everybody is eating and drinking, clothed in purple and fine linen, and potters lie on sofas and have their wheel at hand, that they may work a little when they please; and cobblers and all the other classes of a State lose their distinctive character. And a State may get on without cobblers; but when the guardians degenerate into boon companions, then the ruin is complete. Remember that we are not talking of peasants keeping holiday, but of a State in which every man is expected to do his own work. The happiness resides not in this or that class, but in the State as a whole. I have another remark to make:—A middle condition is best for artisans; they should have money enough to buy tools, and not enough to be independent of business. And will not the same condition be best for our citizens? If they are poor, they will be mean; if rich, luxurious and lazy; and in neither case contented. 'But then how will our poor city be able to go to war against an enemy who has money?' There may be a difficulty in fighting against one enemy; against two there will be none. In the first place, the contest will be carried on by trained warriors against well-to-do citizens: and is not a regular athlete an easy match for two stout opponents at least? Suppose also, that before engaging we send ambassadors to one of the two cities, saying, 'Silver and gold we have not; do you help us and take our share of the spoil;'—who would fight against the lean, wiry dogs, when they might join with them in preying upon the fatted sheep? 'But if many states join their resources, shall we not be in danger?' I am amused to hear you use the word 'state' of any but our own State. They are 'states,' but not 'a state'—many in one. For in every state there are two hostile nations, rich and poor, which you may set one against the other. But our State, while she remains true to her principles, will be in very deed the mightiest of Hellenic states.

To the size of the state there is no limit but the necessity of unity; it must be neither too large nor too small to be one. This is a matter of secondary importance, like the principle of transposition which was intimated in the parable of the earthborn men. The meaning there implied was that every man should do that for which he was fitted, and be at one with himself, and then the whole city would be united. But all these things are secondary, if education, which is the great matter, be duly regarded. When the wheel has once been set in motion, the speed is always increasing; and each generation improves upon the preceding, both in physical and moral qualities. The care of the governors should be directed to preserve music and gymnastic from innovation; alter the songs of a country, Damon says, and you will soon end by altering its laws. The change appears innocent at first, and begins in play; but the evil soon becomes serious, working secretly upon the characters of individuals, then upon social and commercial relations, and lastly upon the institutions of a state; and there is ruin and confusion everywhere. But if education remains in the established form, there will be no danger. A restorative process will be always going on; the spirit of law and order will raise up what has fallen down. Nor will any regulations be needed for the lesser matters of life—rules of deportment or fashions of dress. Like invites like for good or for evil. Education will correct deficiencies and supply the power of self-government. Far be it from us to enter into the particulars of legislation; let the guardians take care of education, and education will take care of all other things.

But without education they may patch and mend as they please; they will make no progress, any more than a patient who thinks to cure himself by some favourite remedy and will not give up his luxurious mode of living. If you tell such persons that they must first alter their habits, then they grow angry; they are charming people. 'Charming,—nay, the very reverse.' Evidently these gentlemen are not in your good graces, nor the state which is like them. And such states there are which first ordain under penalty of death that no one shall alter the constitution, and then suffer themselves to be flattered into and out of anything; and he who indulges them and fawns upon them, is their leader and saviour. 'Yes, the men are as bad as the states.' But do you not admire their cleverness? 'Nay, some of them are stupid enough to believe what the people tell them.' And when all the world is telling a man that he is six feet high, and he has no measure, how can he believe anything else? But don't get into a passion: to see our statesmen trying their nostrums, and fancying that they can cut off at a blow the Hydra-like rogueries of mankind, is as good as a play. Minute enactments are superfluous in good states, and are useless in bad ones.

And now what remains of the work of legislation? Nothing for us; but to Apollo the god of Delphi we leave the ordering of the greatest of all things—that is to say, religion. Only our ancestral deity sitting upon the centre and navel of the earth will be trusted by us if we have any sense, in an affair of such magnitude. No foreign god shall be supreme in our realms...

Here, as Socrates would say, let us 'reflect on' (Greek) what has preceded: thus far we have spoken not of the happiness of the citizens, but only of the well-being of the State. They may be the happiest of men, but our principal aim in founding the State was not to make them happy. They were to be guardians, not holiday-makers. In this pleasant manner is presented to us the famous question both of ancient and modern philosophy, touching the relation of duty to happiness, of right to utility.

First duty, then happiness, is the natural order of our moral ideas. The utilitarian principle is valuable as a corrective of error, and shows to us a side of ethics which is apt to be neglected. It may be admitted further that right and utility are co-extensive, and that he who makes the happiness of mankind his object has one of the highest and noblest motives of human action. But utility is not the historical basis of morality; nor the aspect in which moral and religious ideas commonly occur to the mind. The greatest happiness of all is, as we believe, the far-off result of the divine government of the universe. The greatest happiness of the individual is certainly to be found in a life of virtue and goodness. But we seem to be more assured of a law of right than we can be of a divine purpose, that 'all mankind should be saved;' and we infer the one from the other. And the greatest happiness of the individual may be the reverse of the greatest happiness in the ordinary sense of the term, and may be realised in a life of pain, or in a voluntary death. Further, the word 'happiness' has several ambiguities; it may mean either pleasure or an ideal life, happiness subjective or objective, in this world or in another, of ourselves only or of our neighbours and of all men everywhere. By the modern founder of Utilitarianism the self-regarding and disinterested motives of action are included under the same term, although they are commonly opposed by us as benevolence and self-love. The word happiness has not the definiteness or the sacredness of 'truth' and 'right'; it does not equally appeal to our higher nature, and has not sunk into the conscience of mankind. It is associated too much with the comforts and conveniences of life; too little with 'the goods of the soul which we desire for their own sake.' In a great trial, or danger, or temptation, or in any great and heroic action, it is scarcely thought of. For these reasons 'the greatest happiness' principle is not the true foundation of ethics. But though not the first principle, it is the second, which is like unto it, and is often of easier application. For the larger part of human actions are neither right nor wrong, except in so far as they tend to the happiness of mankind (Introd. to Gorgias and Philebus).

The same question reappears in politics, where the useful or expedient seems to claim a larger sphere and to have a greater authority. For concerning political measures, we chiefly ask: How will they affect the happiness of mankind? Yet here too we may observe that what we term expediency is merely the law of right limited by the conditions of human society. Right and truth are the highest aims of government as well as of individuals; and we ought not to lose sight of them because we cannot directly enforce them. They appeal to the better mind of nations; and sometimes they are too much for merely temporal interests to resist. They are the watchwords which all men use in matters of public policy, as well as in their private dealings; the peace of Europe may be said to depend upon them. In the most commercial and utilitarian states of society the power of ideas remains. And all the higher class of statesmen have in them something of that idealism which Pericles is said to have gathered from the teaching of Anaxagoras. They recognise that the true leader of men must be above the motives of ambition, and that national character is of greater value than material comfort and prosperity. And this is the order of thought in Plato; first, he expects his citizens to do their duty, and then under favourable circumstances, that is to say, in a well-ordered State, their happiness is assured. That he was far from excluding the modern principle of utility in politics is sufficiently evident from other passages; in which 'the most beneficial is affirmed to be the most honourable', and also 'the most sacred'.

We may note

(1) The manner in which the objection of Adeimantus here, is designed to draw out and deepen the argument of Socrates.

(2) The conception of a whole as lying at the foundation both of politics and of art, in the latter supplying the only principle of criticism, which, under the various names of harmony, symmetry, measure, proportion, unity, the Greek seems to have applied to works of art.

(3) The requirement that the State should be limited in size, after the traditional model of a Greek state; as in the Politics of Aristotle, the fact that the cities of Hellas were small is converted into a principle.

(4) The humorous pictures of the lean dogs and the fatted sheep, of the light active boxer upsetting two stout gentlemen at least, of the 'charming' patients who are always making themselves worse; or again, the playful assumption that there is no State but our own; or the grave irony with which the statesman is excused who believes that he is six feet high because he is told so, and having nothing to measure with is to be pardoned for his ignorance—he is too amusing for us to be seriously angry with him.

(5) The light and superficial manner in which religion is passed over when provision has been made for two great principles,—first, that religion shall be based on the highest conception of the gods, secondly, that the true national or Hellenic type shall be maintained...

Socrates proceeds: But where amid all this is justice? Son of Ariston, tell me where. Light a candle and search the city, and get your brother and the rest of our friends to help in seeking for her. 'That won't do,' replied Glaucon, 'you yourself promised to make the search and talked about the impiety of deserting justice.' Well, I said, I will lead the way, but do you follow. My notion is, that our State being perfect will contain all the four virtues—wisdom, courage, temperance, justice. If we eliminate the three first, the unknown remainder will be justice.

First then, of wisdom: the State which we have called into being will be wise because politic. And policy is one among many kinds of skill,—not the skill of the carpenter, or of the worker in metal, or of the husbandman, but the skill of him who advises about the interests of the whole State. Of such a kind is the skill of the guardians, who are a small class in number, far smaller than the blacksmiths; but in them is concentrated the wisdom of the State. And if this small ruling class have wisdom, then the whole State will be wise.

Our second virtue is courage, which we have no difficulty in finding in another class—that of soldiers. Courage may be defined as a sort of salvation—the never-failing salvation of the opinions which law and education have prescribed concerning dangers. You know the way in which dyers first prepare the white ground and then lay on the dye of purple or of any other colour. Colours dyed in this way become fixed, and no soap or lye will ever wash them out. Now the ground is education, and the laws are the colours; and if the ground is properly laid, neither the soap of pleasure nor the lye of pain or fear will ever wash them out. This power which preserves right opinion about danger I would ask you to call 'courage,' adding the epithet 'political' or 'civilized' in order to distinguish it from mere animal courage and from a higher courage which may hereafter be discussed.

Two virtues remain; temperance and justice. More than the preceding virtues temperance suggests the idea of harmony. Some light is thrown upon the nature of this virtue by the popular description of a man as 'master of himself'—which has an absurd sound, because the master is also the servant. The expression really means that the better principle in a man masters the worse. There are in cities whole classes—women, slaves and the like—who correspond to the worse, and a few only to the better; and in our State the former class are held under control by the latter. Now to which of these classes does temperance belong? 'To both of them.' And our State if any will be the abode of temperance; and we were right in describing this virtue as a harmony which is diffused through the whole, making the dwellers in the city to be of one mind, and attuning the upper and middle and lower classes like the strings of an instrument, whether you suppose them to differ in wisdom, strength or wealth.

And now we are near the spot; let us draw in and surround the cover and watch with all our eyes, lest justice should slip away and escape. Tell me, if you see the thicket move first. 'Nay, I would have you lead.' Well then, offer up a prayer and follow. The way is dark and difficult; but we must push on. I begin to see a track. 'Good news.' Why, Glaucon, our dulness of scent is quite ludicrous! While we are straining our eyes into the distance, justice is tumbling out at our feet. We are as bad as people looking for a thing which they have in their hands. Have you forgotten our old principle of the division of labour, or of every man doing his own business, concerning which we spoke at the foundation of the State—what but this was justice? Is there any other virtue remaining which can compete with wisdom and temperance and courage in the scale of political virtue? For 'every one having his own' is the great object of government; and the great object of trade is that every man should do his own business. Not that there is much harm in a carpenter trying to be a cobbler, or a cobbler transforming himself into a carpenter; but great evil may arise from the cobbler leaving his last and turning into a guardian or legislator, or when a single individual is trainer, warrior, legislator, all in one. And this evil is injustice, or every man doing another's business. I do not say that as yet we are in a condition to arrive at a final conclusion. For the definition which we believe to hold good in states has still to be tested by the individual. Having read the large letters we will now come back to the small. From the two together a brilliant light may be struck out...

Socrates proceeds to discover the nature of justice by a method of residues. Each of the first three virtues corresponds to one of the three parts of the soul and one of the three classes in the State, although the third, temperance, has more of the nature of a harmony than the first two. If there be a fourth virtue, that can only be sought for in the relation of the three parts in the soul or classes in the State to one another. It is obvious and simple, and for that very reason has not been found out. The modern logician will be inclined to object that ideas cannot be separated like chemical substances, but that they run into one another and may be only different aspects or names of the same thing, and such in this instance appears to be the case. For the definition here given of justice is verbally the same as one of the definitions of temperance given by Socrates in the Charmides, which however is only provisional, and is afterwards rejected. And so far from justice remaining over when the other virtues are eliminated, the justice and temperance of the Republic can with difficulty be distinguished. Temperance appears to be the virtue of a part only, and one of three, whereas justice is a universal virtue of the whole soul. Yet on the other hand temperance is also described as a sort of harmony, and in this respect is akin to justice. Justice seems to differ from temperance in degree rather than in kind; whereas temperance is the harmony of discordant elements, justice is the perfect order by which all natures and classes do their own business, the right man in the right place, the division and co-operation of all the citizens. Justice, again, is a more abstract notion than the other virtues, and therefore, from Plato's point of view, the foundation of them, to which they are referred and which in idea precedes them. The proposal to omit temperance is a mere trick of style intended to avoid monotony.

There is a famous question discussed in one of the earlier Dialogues of Plato (Protagoras; Arist. Nic. Ethics), 'Whether the virtues are one or many?' This receives an answer which is to the effect that there are four cardinal virtues (now for the first time brought together in ethical philosophy), and one supreme over the rest, which is not like Aristotle's conception of universal justice, virtue relative to others, but the whole of virtue relative to the parts. To this universal conception of justice or order in the first education and in the moral nature of man, the still more universal conception of the good in the second education and in the sphere of speculative knowledge seems to succeed. Both might be equally described by the terms 'law,' 'order,' 'harmony;' but while the idea of good embraces 'all time and all existence,' the conception of justice is not extended beyond man.

...Socrates is now going to identify the individual and the State. But first he must prove that there are three parts of the individual soul. His argument is as follows:—Quantity makes no difference in quality. The word 'just,' whether applied to the individual or to the State, has the same meaning. And the term 'justice' implied that the same three principles in the State and in the individual were doing their own business. But are they really three or one? The question is difficult, and one which can hardly be solved by the methods which we are now using; but the truer and longer way would take up too much of our time. 'The shorter will satisfy me.' Well then, you would admit that the qualities of states mean the qualities of the individuals who compose them? The Scythians and Thracians are passionate, our own race intellectual, and the Egyptians and Phoenicians covetous, because the individual members of each have such and such a

character; the difficulty is to determine whether the several principles are
one or three; whether, that is to say, we reason with one part of our nature,
desire with another, are angry with another, or whether the whole soul
comes into play in each sort of action. This enquiry, however, requires
a very exact definition of terms. The same thing in the same relation
cannot be affected in two opposite ways. But there is no impossibility in
a man standing still, yet moving his arms, or in a top which is fixed on
one spot going round upon its axis. There is no necessity to mention all
the possible exceptions; let us provisionally assume that opposites cannot
do or be or suffer opposites in the same relation. And to the class of
opposites belong assent and dissent, desire and avoidance. And one form
of desire is thirst and hunger: and here arises a new point—thirst is thirst
of drink, hunger is hunger of food; not of warm drink or of a particular
kind of food, with the single exception of course that the very fact of
our desiring anything implies that it is good. When relative terms have no
attributes, their correlatives have no attributes; when they have attributes,
their correlatives also have them. For example, the term 'greater' is simply
relative to 'less,' and knowledge refers to a subject of knowledge. But on the
other hand, a particular knowledge is of a particular subject. Again, every
science has a distinct character, which is defined by an object; medicine,
for example, is the science of health, although not to be confounded with
health. Having cleared our ideas thus far, let us return to the original
instance of thirst, which has a definite object—drink. Now the thirsty soul
may feel two distinct impulses; the animal one saying 'Drink;' the rational
one, which says 'Do not drink.' The two impulses are contradictory; and
therefore we may assume that they spring from distinct principles in the
soul. But is passion a third principle, or akin to desire? There is a story
of a certain Leontius which throws some light on this question. He was
coming up from the Piraeus outside the north wall, and he passed a spot
where there were dead bodies lying by the executioner. He felt a longing
desire to see them and also an abhorrence of them; at first he turned
away and shut his eyes, then, suddenly tearing them open, he said,—'Take
your fill, ye wretches, of the fair sight.' Now is there not here a third

principle which is often found to come to the assistance of reason against desire, but never of desire against reason? This is passion or spirit, of the separate existence of which we may further convince ourselves by putting the following case:—When a man suffers justly, if he be of a generous nature he is not indignant at the hardships which he undergoes: but when he suffers unjustly, his indignation is his great support; hunger and thirst cannot tame him; the spirit within him must do or die, until the voice of the shepherd, that is, of reason, bidding his dog bark no more, is heard within. This shows that passion is the ally of reason. Is passion then the same with reason? No, for the former exists in children and brutes; and Homer affords a proof of the distinction between them when he says, 'He smote his breast, and thus rebuked his soul.'

And now, at last, we have reached firm ground, and are able to infer that the virtues of the State and of the individual are the same. For wisdom and courage and justice in the State are severally the wisdom and courage and justice in the individuals who form the State. Each of the three classes will do the work of its own class in the State, and each part in the individual soul; reason, the superior, and passion, the inferior, will be harmonized by the influence of music and gymnastic. The counsellor and the warrior, the head and the arm, will act together in the town of Mansoul, and keep the desires in proper subjection. The courage of the warrior is that quality which preserves a right opinion about dangers in spite of pleasures and pains. The wisdom of the counsellor is that small part of the soul which has authority and reason. The virtue of temperance is the friendship of the ruling and the subject principles, both in the State and in the individual. Of justice we have already spoken; and the notion already given of it may be confirmed by common instances. Will the just state or the just individual steal, lie, commit adultery, or be guilty of impiety to gods and men? 'No.' And is not the reason of this that the several principles, whether in the state or in the individual, do their own business? And justice is the quality which makes just men and just states. Moreover, our old division of labour, which required that there should be one man for one use, was a dream or anticipation of what was to follow; and that dream has now been realized in justice, which begins by binding together the three chords of the soul, and then acts harmoniously in every relation of life. And injustice, which is the insubordination and disobedience of the inferior elements in the soul, is the opposite of justice, and is inharmonious and unnatural, being to the soul what disease is to the body; for in the soul as well as in the body, good or bad actions produce good or bad habits. And virtue is the health and beauty and well-being of the soul, and vice is the disease and weakness and deformity of the soul.

Again the old question returns upon us: Is justice or injustice the more profitable? The question has become ridiculous. For injustice, like mortal disease, makes life not worth having. Come up with me to the hill which overhangs the city and look down upon the single form of virtue, and the infinite forms of vice, among which are four special ones, characteristic both of states and of individuals. And the state which corresponds to the single form of virtue is that which we have been describing, wherein reason rules under one of two names—monarchy and aristocracy. Thus there are five forms in all, both of states and of souls...

In attempting to prove that the soul has three separate faculties, Plato takes occasion to discuss what makes difference of faculties. And the criterion which he proposes is difference in the working of the faculties. The same faculty cannot produce contradictory effects. But the path of early reasoners is beset by thorny entanglements, and he will not proceed a step without first clearing the ground. This leads him into a tiresome digression, which is intended to explain the nature of contradiction. First, the contradiction must be at the same time and in the same relation. Secondly, no extraneous word must be introduced into either of the terms in which the contradictory proposition is expressed: for example, thirst is of drink, not of warm drink. He implies, what he does not say, that if, by the advice of reason, or by the impulse of anger, a man is restrained from drinking, this proves that thirst, or desire under which thirst is included, is distinct from anger and reason. But suppose that we allow the term 'thirst' or 'desire' to be modified, and say an 'angry thirst,' or a 'revengeful desire,' then the two spheres of desire and anger overlap and become confused.

This case therefore has to be excluded. And still there remains an exception to the rule in the use of the term 'good,' which is always implied in the object of desire. These are the discussions of an age before logic; and any one who is wearied by them should remember that they are necessary to the clearing up of ideas in the first development of the human faculties.

The psychology of Plato extends no further than the division of the soul into the rational, irascible, and concupiscent elements, which, as far as we know, was first made by him, and has been retained by Aristotle and succeeding ethical writers. The chief difficulty in this early analysis of the mind is to define exactly the place of the irascible faculty (Greek), which may be variously described under the terms righteous indignation, spirit, passion. It is the foundation of courage, which includes in Plato moral courage, the courage of enduring pain, and of surmounting intellectual difficulties, as well as of meeting dangers in war. Though irrational, it inclines to side with the rational: it cannot be aroused by punishment when justly inflicted: it sometimes takes the form of an enthusiasm which sustains a man in the performance of great actions. It is the 'lion heart' with which the reason makes a treaty. On the other hand it is negative rather than positive; it is indignant at wrong or falsehood, but does not, like Love in the Symposium and Phaedrus, aspire to the vision of Truth or Good. It is the peremptory military spirit which prevails in the government of honour. It differs from anger (Greek), this latter term having no accessory notion of righteous indignation. Although Aristotle has retained the word, yet we may observe that 'passion' (Greek) has with him lost its affinity to the rational and has become indistinguishable from 'anger' (Greek). And to this vernacular use Plato himself in the Laws seems to revert, though not always. By modern philosophy too, as well as in our ordinary conversation, the words anger or passion are employed almost exclusively in a bad sense; there is no connotation of a just or reasonable cause by which they are aroused. The feeling of 'righteous indignation' is too partial and accidental to admit of our regarding it as a separate virtue or habit. We are tempted also to doubt whether Plato is right in supposing that an offender, however justly condemned, could be expected to acknowledge the justice of his sentence; this is the spirit of a philosopher or martyr rather than of a criminal.

We may observe how nearly Plato approaches Aristotle's famous thesis, that 'good actions produce good habits.' The words 'as healthy practices (Greek) produce health, so do just practices produce justice,' have a sound very like the Nicomachean Ethics. But we note also that an incidental remark in Plato has become a far-reaching principle in Aristotle, and an inseparable part of a great Ethical system.

There is a difficulty in understanding what Plato meant by 'the longer way': he seems to intimate some metaphysic of the future which will not be satisfied with arguing from the principle of contradiction. In the sixth and seventh books (compare Sophist and Parmenides) he has given us a sketch of such a metaphysic; but when Glaucon asks for the final revelation of the idea of good, he is put off with the declaration that he has not yet studied the preliminary sciences. How he would have filled up the sketch, or argued about such questions from a higher point of view, we can only conjecture. Perhaps he hoped to find some a priori method of developing the parts out of the whole; or he might have asked which of the ideas contains the other ideas, and possibly have stumbled on the Hegelian identity of the 'ego' and the 'universal.' Or he may have imagined that ideas might be constructed in some manner analogous to the construction of figures and numbers in the mathematical sciences. The most certain and necessary truth was to Plato the universal; and to this he was always seeking to refer all knowledge or opinion, just as in modern times we seek to rest them on the opposite pole of induction and experience. The aspirations of metaphysicians have always tended to pass beyond the limits of human thought and language: they seem to have reached a height at which they are 'moving about in worlds unrealized,' and their conceptions, although profoundly affecting their own minds, become invisible or unintelligible to others. We are not therefore surprised to find that Plato himself has nowhere clearly explained his doctrine of ideas; or that his school in a later generation, like his contemporaries Glaucon and Adeimantus, were unable to follow him in this region of speculation. In the Sophist, where he is refuting the scepticism which maintained either that there was no such thing as predication, or that all might be predicated of all, he arrives at the conclusion that some ideas combine with some, but not all with all. But he makes only one or two steps forward on this path; he nowhere attains to any connected system of ideas, or even to a knowledge of the most elementary relations of the sciences to one another.

Book V - Introduction & Analysis
Matrimony & Philosophy

I was going to enumerate the four forms of vice or decline in states, when Polemarchus—he was sitting a little farther from me than Adeimantus—taking him by the coat and leaning towards him, said something in an undertone, of which I only caught the words, 'Shall we let him off?' 'Certainly not,' said Adeimantus, raising his voice. Whom, I said, are you not going to let off? 'You,' he said. Why? 'Because we think that you are not dealing fairly with us in omitting women and children, of whom you have slily disposed under the general formula that friends have all things in common.' And was I not right? 'Yes,' he replied, 'but there are many sorts of communism or community, and we want to know which of them is right. The company, as you have just heard, are resolved to have a further explanation.' Thrasymachus said, 'Do you think that we have come hither to dig for gold, or to hear you discourse?' Yes, I said; but the discourse should be of a reasonable length. Glaucon added, 'Yes, Socrates, and there is reason in spending the whole of life in such discussions; but pray, without more ado, tell us how this community is to be carried out, and how the interval between birth and education is to be filled up.' Well, I said, the subject has several difficulties—What is possible? is the first question. What is desirable? is the second. 'Fear not,' he replied, 'for you are speaking among friends.' That, I replied, is a sorry consolation; I shall destroy my friends as well as myself. Not that I mind a little innocent laughter; but he who kills the truth is a murderer. 'Then,' said Glaucon, laughing, 'in case you should murder us we will acquit you beforehand, and you shall be held free from the guilt of deceiving us.'

Socrates proceeds:—The guardians of our state are to be watch-dogs, as we have already said. Now dogs are not divided into hes and shes—we do not take the masculine gender out to hunt and leave the females at home to look after their puppies. They have the same employments—the only difference between them is that the one sex is stronger and the other weaker. But if women are to have the same employments as men, they must have the same education—they must be taught music and gymnastics, and the art of war. I know that a great joke will be made of their riding on horseback and carrying weapons; the sight of the naked old wrinkled women showing their agility in the palaestra will certainly not be a vision of beauty, and may be expected to become a famous jest. But we must not mind the wits; there was a time when they might have laughed at our present gymnastics. All is habit: people have at last found out that the exposure is better than the concealment of the person, and now they laugh no more. Evil only should be the subject of ridicule.

The first question is, whether women are able either wholly or partially to share in the employments of men. And here we may be charged with inconsistency in making the proposal at all. For we started originally with the division of labour; and the diversity of employments was based on the difference of natures. But is there no difference between men and women? Nay, are they not wholly different? THERE was the difficulty, Glaucon, which made me unwilling to speak of family relations. However, when a man is out of his depth, whether in a pool or in an ocean, he can only swim for his life; and we must try to find a way of escape, if we can.

The argument is, that different natures have different uses, and the natures of men and women are said to differ. But this is only a verbal opposition. We do not consider that the difference may be purely nominal and accidental; for example, a bald man and a hairy man are opposed in a single point of view, but you cannot infer that because a bald man is a cobbler a hairy man ought not to be a cobbler. Now why is such an inference erroneous? Simply because the opposition between them is partial only, like the difference between a male physician and a female physician, not running through the whole nature, like the difference between a physician and a carpenter. And if the difference of the sexes is only that the one beget and the other bear children, this does not prove that they ought to have distinct educations. Admitting that women differ from men in capacity, do not men equally differ from one another? Has not nature scattered all the qualities which our citizens require indifferently up and down among the two sexes? and even in their peculiar pursuits, are not women often, though in some cases superior to men, ridiculously enough surpassed by them? Women are the same in kind as men, and have the same aptitude or want of aptitude for medicine or gymnastic or war, but in a less degree. One woman will be a good guardian, another not; and the good must be chosen to be the colleagues of our guardians. If however their natures are the same, the inference is that their education must also be the same; there is no longer anything unnatural or impossible in a woman learning music and gymnastic. And the education which we give them will be the very best, far superior to that of cobblers, and will train up the very best women, and nothing can be more advantageous to the State than this. Therefore let them strip, clothed in their chastity, and share in the toils of war and in the defence of their country; he who laughs at them is a fool for his pains.

The first wave is past, and the argument is compelled to admit that men and women have common duties and pursuits. A second and greater wave is rolling in—community of wives and children; is this either expedient or possible? The expediency I do not doubt; I am not so sure of the possibility. 'Nay, I think that a considerable doubt will be entertained on both points.' I meant to have escaped the trouble of proving the first, but as you have detected the little stratagem I must even submit. Only allow me to feed my fancy like the solitary in his walks, with a dream of what might be, and then I will return to the question of what can be.

In the first place our rulers will enforce the laws and make new ones where they are wanted, and their allies or ministers will obey. You, as legislator, have already selected the men; and now you shall select the women. After the selection has been made, they will dwell in common houses and have their meals in common, and will be brought together by a necessity more certain than that of mathematics. But they cannot be allowed to live in licentiousness; that is an unholy thing, which the rulers are determined to prevent. For the avoidance of this, holy marriage festivals will be instituted, and their holiness will be in proportion to their usefulness. And here, Glaucon, I should like to ask (as I know that you are a breeder of birds and animals), Do you not take the greatest care in the mating? 'Certainly.' And there is no reason to suppose that less care is required in the marriage of human beings. But then our rulers must be skilful physicians of the State, for they will often need a strong dose of falsehood in order to bring about desirable unions between their subjects. The good must be paired with the good, and the bad with the bad, and the offspring of the one must be reared, and of the other destroyed; in this way the flock will be preserved in prime condition. Hymeneal festivals will be celebrated at times fixed with an eye to population, and the brides and bridegrooms will meet at them; and by an ingenious system of lots the rulers will contrive that the brave and the fair come together, and that those of inferior breed are paired with inferiors—the latter will ascribe to chance what is really the invention of the rulers. And when children are born, the offspring of the brave and fair will be carried to an enclosure in a certain part of the city, and there attended by suitable nurses; the rest will be hurried away to places unknown. The mothers will be brought to the fold and will suckle the children; care however must be taken that none of them recognise their own offspring; and if necessary other nurses may also be hired. The trouble of watching and getting up at night will be transferred to attendants. 'Then the wives of our guardians will have a fine easy time when they are having children.' And quite right too, I said, that they should.

The parents ought to be in the prime of life, which for a man may be reckoned at thirty years—from twenty-five, when he has 'passed the point at which the speed of life is greatest,' to fifty-five; and at twenty years for a woman—from twenty to forty. Any one above or below those ages who partakes in the hymeneals shall be guilty of impiety; also every one who forms a marriage connexion at other times without the consent of the rulers. This latter regulation applies to those who are within the specified ages, after which they may range at will, provided they avoid the prohibited degrees of parents and children, or of brothers and sisters, which last, however, are not absolutely prohibited, if a dispensation be procured. 'But how shall we know the degrees of affinity, when all things are common?' The answer is, that brothers and sisters are all such as are born seven or nine months after the espousals, and their parents those who are then espoused, and every one will have many children and every child many parents.

Socrates proceeds: I have now to prove that this scheme is advantageous and also consistent with our entire polity. The greatest good of a State is unity; the greatest evil, discord and distraction. And there will be unity where there are no private pleasures or pains or interests—where if one member suffers all the members suffer, if one citizen is touched all are quickly sensitive; and the least hurt to the little finger of the State runs through the whole body and vibrates to the soul. For the true State, like an individual, is injured as a whole when any part is affected. Every State has subjects and rulers, who in a democracy are called rulers, and in other States masters: but in our State they are called saviours and allies; and the subjects who in other States are termed slaves, are by us termed nurturers and paymasters, and those who are termed comrades and colleagues in other places, are by us called fathers and brothers. And whereas in other States members of the same government regard one of their colleagues as a friend and another as an enemy, in our State no man is a stranger to another; for every citizen is connected with every other by ties of blood, and these names and this way of speaking will have a corresponding reality—brother, father, sister, mother, repeated from infancy in the ears of children, will not be mere words. Then again the citizens will have all things in common, in having common property they will have common pleasures and pains.

Can there be strife and contention among those who are of one mind; or lawsuits about property when men have nothing but their bodies which

they call their own; or suits about violence when every one is bound
to defend himself? The permission to strike when insulted will be an
'antidote' to the knife and will prevent disturbances in the State. But no
younger man will strike an elder; reverence will prevent him from laying
hands on his kindred, and he will fear that the rest of the family may
retaliate. Moreover, our citizens will be rid of the lesser evils of life; there
will be no flattery of the rich, no sordid household cares, no borrowing
and not paying. Compared with the citizens of other States, ours will
be Olympic victors, and crowned with blessings greater still—they and
their children having a better maintenance during life, and after death an
honourable burial. Nor has the happiness of the individual been sacrificed
to the happiness of the State; our Olympic victor has not been turned into
a cobbler, but he has a happiness beyond that of any cobbler. At the same
time, if any conceited youth begins to dream of appropriating the State to
himself, he must be reminded that 'half is better than the whole.' 'I should
certainly advise him to stay where he is when he has the promise of such a
brave life.'

But is such a community possible?—as among the animals, so also
among men; and if possible, in what way possible? About war there is
no difficulty; the principle of communism is adapted to military service.
Parents will take their children to look on at a battle, just as potters' boys
are trained to the business by looking on at the wheel. And to the parents
themselves, as to other animals, the sight of their young ones will prove a
great incentive to bravery. Young warriors must learn, but they must not
run into danger, although a certain degree of risk is worth incurring when
the benefit is great. The young creatures should be placed under the care
of experienced veterans, and they should have wings—that is to say, swift
and tractable steeds on which they may fly away and escape. One of the
first things to be done is to teach a youth to ride.

Cowards and deserters shall be degraded to the class of husbandmen;
gentlemen who allow themselves to be taken prisoners, may be presented
to the enemy. But what shall be done to the hero? First of all he shall
be crowned by all the youths in the army; secondly, he shall receive the

right hand of fellowship; and thirdly, do you think that there is any harm in his being kissed? We have already determined that he shall have more wives than others, in order that he may have as many children as possible. And at a feast he shall have more to eat; we have the authority of Homer for honouring brave men with 'long chines,' which is an appropriate compliment, because meat is a very strengthening thing. Fill the bowl then, and give the best seats and meats to the brave—may they do them good! And he who dies in battle will be at once declared to be of the golden race, and will, as we believe, become one of Hesiod's guardian angels. He shall be worshipped after death in the manner prescribed by the oracle; and not only he, but all other benefactors of the State who die in any other way, shall be admitted to the same honours.

The next question is, How shall we treat our enemies? Shall Hellenes be enslaved? No; for there is too great a risk of the whole race passing under the yoke of the barbarians. Or shall the dead be despoiled? Certainly not; for that sort of thing is an excuse for skulking, and has been the ruin of many an army. There is meanness and feminine malice in making an enemy of the dead body, when the soul which was the owner has fled—like a dog who cannot reach his assailants, and quarrels with the stones which are thrown at him instead. Again, the arms of Hellenes should not be offered up in the temples of the Gods; they are a pollution, for they are taken from brethren. And on similar grounds there should be a limit to the devastation of Hellenic territory—the houses should not be burnt, nor more than the annual produce carried off. For war is of two kinds, civil and foreign; the first of which is properly termed 'discord,' and only the second 'war;' and war between Hellenes is in reality civil war—a quarrel in a family, which is ever to be regarded as unpatriotic and unnatural, and ought to be prosecuted with a view to reconciliation in a true phil-Hellenic spirit, as of those who would chasten but not utterly enslave. The war is not against a whole nation who are a friendly multitude of men, women, and children, but only against a few guilty persons; when they are punished peace will be restored. That is the way in which Hellenes should war against one another—and against barbarians, as they war against one another now.

'But, my dear Socrates, you are forgetting the main question: Is such a State possible? I grant all and more than you say about the blessedness of being one family—fathers, brothers, mothers, daughters, going out to war together; but I want to ascertain the possibility of this ideal State.' You are too unmerciful. The first wave and the second wave I have hardly escaped, and now you will certainly drown me with the third. When you see the towering crest of the wave, I expect you to take pity. 'Not a whit.'

Well, then, we were led to form our ideal polity in the search after justice, and the just man answered to the just State. Is this ideal at all the worse for being impracticable? Would the picture of a perfectly beautiful man be any the worse because no such man ever lived? Can any reality come up to the idea? Nature will not allow words to be fully realized; but if I am to try and realize the ideal of the State in a measure, I think that an approach may be made to the perfection of which I dream by one or two, I do not say slight, but possible changes in the present constitution of States. I would reduce them to a single one—the great wave, as I call it. Until, then, kings are philosophers, or philosophers are kings, cities will never cease from ill: no, nor the human race; nor will our ideal polity ever come into being. I know that this is a hard saying, which few will be able to receive. 'Socrates, all the world will take off his coat and rush upon you with sticks and stones, and therefore I would advise you to prepare an answer.' You got me into the scrape, I said. 'And I was right,' he replied; 'however, I will stand by you as a sort of do-nothing, well-meaning ally.' Having the help of such a champion, I will do my best to maintain my position. And first, I must explain of whom I speak and what sort of natures these are who are to be philosophers and rulers. As you are a man of pleasure, you will not have forgotten how indiscriminate lovers are in their attachments; they love all, and turn blemishes into beauties. The snub-nosed youth is said to have a winning grace; the beak of another has a royal look; the featureless are faultless; the dark are manly, the fair angels; the sickly have a new term of endearment invented expressly for them, which is 'honey-pale.' Lovers of wine and lovers of ambition also desire the objects of their affection in every form. Now here comes the point:—The philosopher too is a lover of knowledge in every form; he has an insatiable curiosity. 'But will curiosity make a philosopher? Are the lovers of sights and sounds, who let out their ears to every chorus at the Dionysiac festivals, to be called philosophers?' They are not true philosophers, but only an imitation. 'Then how are we to describe the true?'

You would acknowledge the existence of abstract ideas, such as justice, beauty, good, evil, which are severally one, yet in their various combinations appear to be many. Those who recognize these realities are philosophers; whereas the other class hear sounds and see colours, and understand their use in the arts, but cannot attain to the true or waking vision of absolute justice or beauty or truth; they have not the light of knowledge, but of opinion, and what they see is a dream only. Perhaps he of whom we say the last will be angry with us; can we pacify him without revealing the disorder of his mind? Suppose we say that, if he has knowledge we rejoice to hear it, but knowledge must be of something which is, as ignorance is of something which is not; and there is a third thing, which both is and is not, and is matter of opinion only. Opinion and knowledge, then, having distinct objects, must also be distinct faculties. And by faculties I mean powers unseen and distinguishable only by the difference in their objects, as opinion and knowledge differ, since the one is liable to err, but the other is unerring and is the mightiest of all our faculties. If being is the object of knowledge, and not-being of ignorance, and these are the extremes, opinion must lie between them, and may be called darker than the one and brighter than the other. This intermediate or contingent matter is and is not at the same time, and partakes both of existence and of non-existence. Now I would ask my good friend, who denies abstract beauty and justice, and affirms a many beautiful and a many just, whether everything he sees is not in some point of view different—the beautiful ugly, the pious impious, the just unjust? Is not the double also the half, and are not heavy and light relative terms which pass into one another? Everything is and is not, as in the old riddle—'A man and not a man shot and did not shoot a bird and not a bird with a stone and not a stone.' The mind cannot be fixed on either alternative; and these ambiguous, intermediate, erring, half-lighted objects, which have a disorderly movement in the region between being and not-being, are the proper matter of opinion, as the immutable objects are the proper matter of knowledge. And he who grovels in the world of sense, and has only this uncertain perception of things, is not a philosopher, but a lover of opinion only...

The fifth book is the new beginning of the Republic, in which the community of property and of family are first maintained, and the transition is made to the kingdom of philosophers. For both of these Plato, after his manner, has been preparing in some chance words of Book IV, which fall unperceived on the reader's mind, as they are supposed at first to have fallen on the ear of Glaucon and Adeimantus. The 'paradoxes,' as Morgenstern terms them, of this book of the Republic will be reserved for another place; a few remarks on the style, and some explanations of difficulties, may be briefly added.

First, there is the image of the waves, which serves for a sort of scheme or plan of the book. The first wave, the second wave, the third and greatest wave come rolling in, and we hear the roar of them. All that can be said of the extravagance of Plato's proposals is anticipated by himself. Nothing is more admirable than the hesitation with which he proposes the solemn text, 'Until kings are philosophers,' etc.; or the reaction from the sublime to the ridiculous, when Glaucon describes the manner in which the new truth will be received by mankind.

Some defects and difficulties may be noted in the execution of the communistic plan. Nothing is told us of the application of communism to the lower classes; nor is the table of prohibited degrees capable of being made out. It is quite possible that a child born at one hymeneal festival may marry one of its own brothers or sisters, or even one of its parents, at another. Plato is afraid of incestuous unions, but at the same time he does not wish to bring before us the fact that the city would be divided into families of those born seven and nine months after each hymeneal festival. If it were worth while to argue seriously about such fancies, we might remark that while all the old affinities are abolished, the newly prohibited affinity rests not on any natural or rational principle, but only upon the accident of children having been born in the same month and year. Nor does he explain how the lots could be so manipulated by the legislature as to bring together the fairest and best. The singular expression which is employed to describe the age of five-and-twenty may perhaps be taken from some poet.

In the delineation of the philosopher, the illustrations of the nature of philosophy derived from love are more suited to the apprehension of Glaucon, the Athenian man of pleasure, than to modern tastes or feelings. They are partly facetious, but also contain a germ of truth. That science is a whole, remains a true principle of inductive as well as of metaphysical philosophy; and the love of universal knowledge is still the characteristic of the philosopher in modern as well as in ancient times.

At the end of the fifth book Plato introduces the figment of contingent matter, which has exercised so great an influence both on the Ethics and Theology of the modern world, and which occurs here for the first time in the history of philosophy. He did not remark that the degrees of knowledge in the subject have nothing corresponding to them in the object. With him a word must answer to an idea; and he could not conceive of an opinion which was an opinion about nothing. The influence of analogy led him to invent 'parallels and conjugates' and to overlook facts. To us some of his difficulties are puzzling only from their simplicity: we do not perceive that the answer to them 'is tumbling out at our feet.' To the mind of early thinkers, the conception of not-being was dark and mysterious; they did not see that this terrible apparition which threatened destruction to all knowledge was only a logical determination. The common term under which, through the accidental use of language, two entirely different ideas were included was another source of confusion. Thus through the ambiguity of (Greek) Plato, attempting to introduce order into the first chaos of human thought, seems to have confused perception and opinion, and to have failed to distinguish the contingent from the relative. In the Theaetetus the first of these difficulties begins to clear up; in the Sophist the second; and for this, as well as for other reasons, both these dialogues are probably to be regarded as later than the Republic.

Book VI - Introduction & Analysis
Philosophy of Government

Having determined that the many have no knowledge of true being, and have no clear patterns in their minds of justice, beauty, truth, and that philosophers have such patterns, we have now to ask whether they or the many shall be rulers in our State. But who can doubt that philosophers should be chosen, if they have the other qualities which are required in a ruler? For they are lovers of the knowledge of the eternal and of all truth; they are haters of falsehood; their meaner desires are absorbed in the interests of knowledge; they are spectators of all time and all existence; and in the magnificence of their contemplation the life of man is as nothing to them, nor is death fearful. Also they are of a social, gracious disposition, equally free from cowardice and arrogance. They learn and remember easily; they have harmonious, well-regulated minds; truth flows to them sweetly by nature. Can the god of Jealousy himself find any fault with such an assemblage of good qualities?

Here Adeimantus interposes:—'No man can answer you, Socrates; but every man feels that this is owing to his own deficiency in argument. He is driven from one position to another, until he has nothing more to say, just as an unskilful player at draughts is reduced to his last move by a more skilled opponent. And yet all the time he may be right. He may know, in this very instance, that those who make philosophy the business of their lives, generally turn out rogues if they are bad men, and fools if they are good. What do you say?' I should say that he is quite right. 'Then how is such an admission reconcileable with the doctrine that philosophers should be kings?'

I shall answer you in a parable which will also let you see how poor a hand I am at the invention of allegories. The relation of good men to their governments is so peculiar, that in order to defend them I must take an illustration from the world of fiction. Conceive the captain of a ship, taller by a head and shoulders than any of the crew, yet a little deaf, a little blind, and rather ignorant of the seaman's art. The sailors want to steer, although they know nothing of the art; and they have a theory that it cannot be learned. If the helm is refused them, they drug the captain's posset, bind him hand and foot, and take possession of the ship. He who joins in the mutiny is termed a good pilot and what not; they have no conception that the true pilot must observe the winds and the stars, and must be their master, whether they like it or not;—such an one would be called by them fool, prater, star-gazer. This is my parable; which I will beg you to interpret for me to those gentlemen who ask why the philosopher has such an evil name, and to explain to them that not he, but those who will not use him, are to blame for his uselessness. The philosopher should not beg of mankind to be put in authority over them. The wise man should not seek the rich, as the proverb bids, but every man, whether rich or poor, must knock at the door of the physician when he has need of him. Now the pilot is the philosopher—he whom in the parable they call star-gazer, and the mutinous sailors are the mob of politicians by whom he is rendered useless. Not that these are the worst enemies of philosophy, who is far more dishonoured by her own professing sons when they are corrupted by the world. Need I recall the original image of the philosopher? Did we not say of him just now, that he loved truth and hated falsehood, and that he could not rest in the multiplicity of phenomena, but was led by a sympathy in his own nature to the contemplation of the absolute? All the virtues as well as truth, who is the leader of them, took up their abode in his soul. But as you were observing, if we turn aside to view the reality, we see that the persons who were thus described, with the exception of a small and useless class, are utter rogues.

The point which has to be considered, is the origin of this corruption in nature. Every one will admit that the philosopher, in our description of him, is a rare being. But what numberless causes tend to destroy these rare beings! There is no good thing which may not be a cause of evil—health, wealth, strength, rank, and the virtues themselves, when placed under unfavourable circumstances. For as in the animal or vegetable world the strongest seeds most need the accompaniment of good air and soil, so the best of human characters turn out the worst when they fall upon an unsuitable soil; whereas weak natures hardly ever do any considerable good or harm; they are not the stuff out of which either great criminals or great heroes are made. The philosopher follows the same analogy: he is either the best or the worst of all men. Some persons say that the Sophists are the corrupters of youth; but is not public opinion the real Sophist who is everywhere present—in those very persons, in the assembly, in the courts, in the camp, in the applauses and hisses of the theatre re-echoed by the surrounding hills? Will not a young man's heart leap amid these discordant sounds? and will any education save him from being carried away by the torrent? Nor is this all. For if he will not yield to opinion, there follows the gentle compulsion of exile or death. What principle of rival Sophists or anybody else can overcome in such an unequal contest? Characters there may be more than human, who are exceptions—God may save a man, but not his own strength. Further, I would have you consider that the hireling Sophist only gives back to the world their own opinions; he is the keeper of the monster, who knows how to flatter or anger him, and observes the meaning of his inarticulate grunts. Good is what pleases him, evil what he dislikes; truth and beauty are determined only by the taste of the brute. Such is the Sophist's wisdom, and such is the condition of those who make public opinion the test of truth, whether in art or in morals. The curse is laid upon them of being and doing what it approves, and when they attempt first principles the failure is ludicrous. Think of all this and ask yourself whether the world is more likely to be a believer in the unity

of the idea, or in the multiplicity of phenomena. And the world if not
a believer in the idea cannot be a philosopher, and must therefore be a
persecutor of philosophers. There is another evil:—the world does not like
to lose the gifted nature, and so they flatter the young (Alcibiades) into
a magnificent opinion of his own capacity; the tall, proper youth begins
to expand, and is dreaming of kingdoms and empires. If at this instant a
friend whispers to him, 'Now the gods lighten thee; thou art a great fool'
and must be educated—do you think that he will listen? Or suppose a
better sort of man who is attracted towards philosophy, will they not make
Herculean efforts to spoil and corrupt him? Are we not right in saying
that the love of knowledge, no less than riches, may divert him? Men of
this class (Critias) often become politicians—they are the authors of great
mischief in states, and sometimes also of great good. And thus philosophy
is deserted by her natural protectors, and others enter in and dishonour
her. Vulgar little minds see the land open and rush from the prisons of the
arts into her temple. A clever mechanic having a soul coarse as his body,
thinks that he will gain caste by becoming her suitor. For philosophy, even
in her fallen estate, has a dignity of her own—and he, like a bald little
blacksmith's apprentice as he is, having made some money and got out
of durance, washes and dresses himself as a bridegroom and marries his
master's daughter. What will be the issue of such marriages? Will they
not be vile and bastard, devoid of truth and nature? 'They will.' Small,
then, is the remnant of genuine philosophers; there may be a few who are
citizens of small states, in which politics are not worth thinking of, or who
have been detained by Theages' bridle of ill health; for my own case of
the oracular sign is almost unique, and too rare to be worth mentioning.
And these few when they have tasted the pleasures of philosophy, and have
taken a look at that den of thieves and place of wild beasts, which is human
life, will stand aside from the storm under the shelter of a wall, and try to
preserve their own innocence and to depart in peace. 'A great work, too,
will have been accomplished by them.' Great, yes, but not the greatest; for
man is a social being, and can only attain his highest development in the
society which is best suited to him.

Enough, then, of the causes why philosophy has such an evil name. Another question is, Which of existing states is suited to her? Not one of them; at present she is like some exotic seed which degenerates in a strange soil; only in her proper state will she be shown to be of heavenly growth. 'And is her proper state ours or some other?' Ours in all points but one, which was left undetermined. You may remember our saying that some living mind or witness of the legislator was needed in states. But we were afraid to enter upon a subject of such difficulty, and now the question recurs and has not grown easier:—How may philosophy be safely studied? Let us bring her into the light of day, and make an end of the inquiry.

In the first place, I say boldly that nothing can be worse than the present mode of study. Persons usually pick up a little philosophy in early youth, and in the intervals of business, but they never master the real difficulty, which is dialectic. Later, perhaps, they occasionally go to a lecture on philosophy. Years advance, and the sun of philosophy, unlike that of Heracleitus, sets never to rise again. This order of education should be reversed; it should begin with gymnastics in youth, and as the man strengthens, he should increase the gymnastics of his soul. Then, when active life is over, let him finally return to philosophy. 'You are in earnest, Socrates, but the world will be equally earnest in withstanding you—no more than Thrasymachus.' Do not make a quarrel between Thrasymachus and me, who were never enemies and are now good friends enough. And I shall do my best to convince him and all mankind of the truth of my words, or at any rate to prepare for the future when, in another life, we may again take part in similar discussions. 'That will be a long time hence.' Not long in comparison with eternity. The many will probably remain incredulous, for they have never seen the natural unity of ideas, but only artificial juxtapositions; not free and generous thoughts, but tricks of controversy and quips of law;—a perfect man ruling in a perfect state, even a single one they have not known. And we foresaw that there was no chance of perfection either in states or individuals until a necessity was laid upon philosophers—not the rogues, but those whom we called the useless class—of holding office; or until the sons of kings were inspired with a true love of philosophy. Whether in the infinity of past time there has been, or is in some distant land, or ever will be hereafter, an ideal such as we have described, we stoutly maintain that there has been, is, and will be such a state whenever the Muse of philosophy rules. Will you say that the world is of another mind? O, my friend, do not revile the world! They will soon change their opinion if they are gently entreated, and are taught the true nature of the philosopher. Who can hate a man who loves him? Or be jealous of one who has no jealousy? Consider, again, that the many hate not the true but the false philosophers—the pretenders who force their way in without invitation, and are always speaking of persons and not of principles, which is unlike the spirit of philosophy. For the true philosopher despises earthly strife; his eye is fixed on the eternal order in accordance with which he moulds himself into the Divine image (and not himself only, but other men), and is the creator of the virtues private as well as public. When mankind see that the happiness of states is only to be found in that image, will they be angry with us for attempting to delineate it? 'Certainly not. But what will be the process of delineation?' The artist will do nothing until he has made a tabula rasa; on this he will inscribe the constitution of a state, glancing often at the divine truth of nature, and from that deriving the godlike among men, mingling the two elements, rubbing out and painting in, until there is a perfect harmony or fusion of the divine and human. But perhaps the world will doubt the existence of such an artist. What will they doubt? That the philosopher is a lover of truth, having a nature akin to the best?—and if they admit this will they still quarrel with us for making philosophers our kings? 'They will be less disposed to quarrel.' Let us assume then that they are pacified. Still, a person may hesitate about the probability of the son of a king being a philosopher. And we do not deny that they are very liable to be corrupted; but yet surely in the course of ages there might be one exception—and one is enough. If one son of a king were a philosopher, and had obedient citizens, he might bring the ideal polity into being. Hence we conclude that our laws are not only the best, but that they are also possible, though not free from difficulty.

I gained nothing by evading the troublesome questions which arose
concerning women and children. I will be wiser now and acknowledge that
we must go to the bottom of another question: What is to be the education
of our guardians? It was agreed that they were to be lovers of their country,
and were to be tested in the refiner's fire of pleasures and pains, and
those who came forth pure and remained fixed in their principles were
to have honours and rewards in life and after death. But at this point,
the argument put on her veil and turned into another path. I hesitated
to make the assertion which I now hazard,—that our guardians must be
philosophers. You remember all the contradictory elements, which met
in the philosopher—how difficult to find them all in a single person!
Intelligence and spirit are not often combined with steadiness; the stolid,
fearless, nature is averse to intellectual toil. And yet these opposite elements
are all necessary, and therefore, as we were saying before, the aspirant must
be tested in pleasures and dangers; and also, as we must now further add,
in the highest branches of knowledge. You will remember, that when we
spoke of the virtues mention was made of a longer road, which you were
satisfied to leave unexplored. 'Enough seemed to have been said.' Enough,
my friend; but what is enough while anything remains wanting? Of all
men the guardian must not faint in the search after truth; he must be
prepared to take the longer road, or he will never reach that higher region
which is above the four virtues; and of the virtues too he must not only
get an outline, but a clear and distinct vision. (Strange that we should be
so precise about trifles, so careless about the highest truths!) 'And what
are the highest?' You to pretend unconsciousness, when you have so often
heard me speak of the idea of good, about which we know so little, and
without which though a man gain the world he has no profit of it! Some
people imagine that the good is wisdom; but this involves a circle,—the
good, they say, is wisdom, wisdom has to do with the good. According
to others the good is pleasure; but then comes the absurdity that good
is bad, for there are bad pleasures as well as good. Again, the good must
have reality; a man may desire the appearance of virtue, but he will not
desire the appearance of good. Ought our guardians then to be ignorant

of this supreme principle, of which every man has a presentiment, and without which no man has any real knowledge of anything? 'But, Socrates, what is this supreme principle, knowledge or pleasure, or what? You may think me troublesome, but I say that you have no business to be always repeating the doctrines of others instead of giving us your own.' Can I say what I do not know? 'You may offer an opinion.' And will the blindness and crookedness of opinion content you when you might have the light and certainty of science? 'I will only ask you to give such an explanation of the good as you have given already of temperance and justice.' I wish that I could, but in my present mood I cannot reach to the height of the knowledge of the good. To the parent or principal I cannot introduce you, but to the child begotten in his image, which I may compare with the interest on the principal, I will. (Audit the account, and do not let me give you a false statement of the debt.) You remember our old distinction of the many beautiful and the one beautiful, the particular and the universal, the objects of sight and the objects of thought? Did you ever consider that the objects of sight imply a faculty of sight which is the most complex and costly of our senses, requiring not only objects of sense, but also a medium, which is light; without which the sight will not distinguish between colours and all will be a blank? For light is the noble bond between the perceiving faculty and the thing perceived, and the god who gives us light is the sun, who is the eye of the day, but is not to be confounded with the eye of man. This eye of the day or sun is what I call the child of the good, standing in the same relation to the visible world as the good to the intellectual. When the sun shines the eye sees, and in the intellectual world where truth is, there is sight and light. Now that which is the sun of intelligent natures, is the idea of good, the cause of knowledge and truth, yet other and fairer than they are, and standing in the same relation to them in which the sun stands to light. O inconceivable height of beauty, which is above knowledge and above truth! ('You cannot surely mean pleasure,' he said. Peace, I replied.) And this idea of good, like the sun, is also the cause of growth, and the author not of knowledge only, but of being, yet greater far than either in dignity and power. 'That is a reach of thought more than human; but, pray, go on with the image, for I suspect that there is more behind.' There is, I said; and bearing in mind our two suns or principles, imagine further their corresponding worlds—one of the visible, the other of the intelligible; you may assist your fancy by figuring the distinction under the image of a line divided into two unequal parts, and may again subdivide each part into two lesser segments representative of the stages of knowledge in either sphere. The lower portion of the lower or visible sphere will consist of shadows and reflections, and its upper and smaller portion will contain real objects in the world of nature or of art. The sphere of the intelligible will also have two divisions,—one of mathematics, in which there is no ascent but all is descent; no inquiring into premises, but only drawing of inferences. In this division the mind works with figures and numbers, the images of which are taken not from the shadows, but from the objects, although the truth of them is seen only with the mind's eye; and they are used as hypotheses without being analysed. Whereas in the other division reason uses the hypotheses as stages or steps in the ascent to the idea of good, to which she fastens them, and then again descends, walking firmly in the region of ideas, and of ideas only, in her ascent as well as descent, and finally resting in them. 'I partly understand,' he replied; 'you mean that the ideas of science are superior to the hypothetical, metaphorical conceptions of geometry and the other arts or sciences, whichever is to be the name of them; and the latter conceptions you refuse to make subjects of pure intellect, because they have no first principle, although when resting on a first principle, they pass into the higher sphere.' You understand me very well, I said. And now to those four divisions of knowledge you may assign four corresponding faculties—pure intelligence to the highest sphere; active intelligence to the second; to the third, faith; to the fourth, the perception of shadows—and the clearness of the several faculties will be in the same ratio as the truth of the objects to which they are related...

Like Socrates, we may recapitulate the virtues of the philosopher. In language which seems to reach beyond the horizon of that age and country, he is described as 'the spectator of all time and all existence.' He has the

noblest gifts of nature, and makes the highest use of them. All his desires
are absorbed in the love of wisdom, which is the love of truth. None of
the graces of a beautiful soul are wanting in him; neither can he fear death,
or think much of human life. The ideal of modern times hardly retains the
simplicity of the antique; there is not the same originality either in truth or
error which characterized the Greeks. The philosopher is no longer living
in the unseen, nor is he sent by an oracle to convince mankind of ignorance;
nor does he regard knowledge as a system of ideas leading upwards by
regular stages to the idea of good. The eagerness of the pursuit has abated;
there is more division of labour and less of comprehensive reflection upon
nature and human life as a whole; more of exact observation and less of
anticipation and inspiration. Still, in the altered conditions of knowledge,
the parallel is not wholly lost; and there may be a use in translating the
conception of Plato into the language of our own age. The philosopher
in modern times is one who fixes his mind on the laws of nature in
their sequence and connexion, not on fragments or pictures of nature;
on history, not on controversy; on the truths which are acknowledged by
the few, not on the opinions of the many. He is aware of the importance
of 'classifying according to nature,' and will try to 'separate the limbs
of science without breaking them' (Phaedr.). There is no part of truth,
whether great or small, which he will dishonour; and in the least things he
will discern the greatest (Parmen.). Like the ancient philosopher he sees the
world pervaded by analogies, but he can also tell 'why in some cases a single
instance is sufficient for an induction' (Mill's Logic), while in other cases
a thousand examples would prove nothing. He inquires into a portion of
knowledge only, because the whole has grown too vast to be embraced by
a single mind or life. He has a clearer conception of the divisions of science
and of their relation to the mind of man than was possible to the ancients.
Like Plato, he has a vision of the unity of knowledge, not as the beginning
of philosophy to be attained by a study of elementary mathematics, but
as the far-off result of the working of many minds in many ages. He is
aware that mathematical studies are preliminary to almost every other; at
the same time, he will not reduce all varieties of knowledge to the type

of mathematics. He too must have a nobility of character, without which genius loses the better half of greatness. Regarding the world as a point in immensity, and each individual as a link in a never-ending chain of existence, he will not think much of his own life, or be greatly afraid of death.

Adeimantus objects first of all to the form of the Socratic reasoning, thus showing that Plato is aware of the imperfection of his own method. He brings the accusation against himself which might be brought against him by a modern logician—that he extracts the answer because he knows how to put the question. In a long argument words are apt to change their meaning slightly, or premises may be assumed or conclusions inferred with rather too much certainty or universality; the variation at each step may be unobserved, and yet at last the divergence becomes considerable. Hence the failure of attempts to apply arithmetical or algebraic formulae to logic. The imperfection, or rather the higher and more elastic nature of language, does not allow words to have the precision of numbers or of symbols. And this quality in language impairs the force of an argument which has many steps.

The objection, though fairly met by Socrates in this particular instance, may be regarded as implying a reflection upon the Socratic mode of reasoning. And here, as elsewhere, Plato seems to intimate that the time had come when the negative and interrogative method of Socrates must be superseded by a positive and constructive one, of which examples are given in some of the later dialogues. Adeimantus further argues that the ideal is wholly at variance with facts; for experience proves philosophers to be either useless or rogues. Contrary to all expectation Socrates has no hesitation in admitting the truth of this, and explains the anomaly in an allegory, first characteristically depreciating his own inventive powers. In this allegory the people are distinguished from the professional politicians, and, as elsewhere, are spoken of in a tone of pity rather than of censure under the image of 'the noble captain who is not very quick in his perceptions.'

The uselessness of philosophers is explained by the circumstance that mankind will not use them. The world in all ages has been divided between contempt and fear of those who employ the power of ideas and know no other weapons. Concerning the false philosopher, Socrates argues that the best is most liable to corruption; and that the finer nature is more likely to suffer from alien conditions. We too observe that there are some kinds of excellence which spring from a peculiar delicacy of constitution; as is evidently true of the poetical and imaginative temperament, which often seems to depend on impressions, and hence can only breathe or live in a certain atmosphere. The man of genius has greater pains and greater pleasures, greater powers and greater weaknesses, and often a greater play of character than is to be found in ordinary men. He can assume the disguise of virtue or disinterestedness without having them, or veil personal enmity in the language of patriotism and philosophy,—he can say the word which all men are thinking, he has an insight which is terrible into the follies and weaknesses of his fellow-men. An Alcibiades, a Mirabeau, or a Napoleon the First, are born either to be the authors of great evils in states, or 'of great good, when they are drawn in that direction.'

Yet the thesis, 'corruptio optimi pessima,' cannot be maintained generally or without regard to the kind of excellence which is corrupted. The alien conditions which are corrupting to one nature, may be the elements of culture to another. In general a man can only receive his highest development in a congenial state or family, among friends or fellow-workers. But also he may sometimes be stirred by adverse circumstances to such a degree that he rises up against them and reforms them. And while weaker or coarser characters will extract good out of evil, say in a corrupt state of the church or of society, and live on happily, allowing the evil to remain, the finer or stronger natures may be crushed or spoiled by surrounding influences—may become misanthrope and philanthrope by turns; or in a few instances, like the founders of the monastic orders, or the Reformers, owing to some peculiarity in themselves or in their age, may break away entirely from the world and from the church, sometimes into great good, sometimes into great evil, sometimes into both. And the same holds in the lesser sphere of a convent, a school, a family.

Plato would have us consider how easily the best natures are overpowered by public opinion, and what efforts the rest of mankind will make to get possession of them. The world, the church, their own profession, any political or party organization, are always carrying them off their legs and teaching them to apply high and holy names to their own prejudices and interests. The 'monster' corporation to which they belong judges right and truth to be the pleasure of the community. The individual becomes one with his order; or, if he resists, the world is too much for him, and will sooner or later be revenged on him. This is, perhaps, a one-sided but not wholly untrue picture of the maxims and practice of mankind when they 'sit down together at an assembly,' either in ancient or modern times.

When the higher natures are corrupted by politics, the lower take possession of the vacant place of philosophy. This is described in one of those continuous images in which the argument, to use a Platonic expression, 'veils herself,' and which is dropped and reappears at intervals. The question is asked,—Why are the citizens of states so hostile to philosophy? The answer is, that they do not know her. And yet there is also a better mind of the many; they would believe if they were taught. But hitherto they have only known a conventional imitation of philosophy, words without thoughts, systems which have no life in them; a (divine) person uttering the words of beauty and freedom, the friend of man holding communion with the Eternal, and seeking to frame the state in that image, they have never known. The same double feeling respecting the mass of mankind has always existed among men. The first thought is that the people are the enemies of truth and right; the second, that this only arises out of an accidental error and confusion, and that they do not really hate those who love them, if they could be educated to know them.

In the latter part of the sixth book, three questions have to be considered: 1st, the nature of the longer and more circuitous way, which is contrasted with the shorter and more imperfect method of Book IV; 2nd, the heavenly pattern or idea of the state; 3rd, the relation of the divisions of knowledge to one another and to the corresponding faculties of the soul:

1. Of the higher method of knowledge in Plato we have only a glimpse. Neither here nor in the Phaedrus or Symposium, nor yet in the Philebus or Sophist, does he give any clear explanation of his meaning. He would probably have described his method as proceeding by regular steps to a system of universal knowledge, which inferred the parts from the whole rather than the whole from the parts. This ideal logic is not practised by him in the search after justice, or in the analysis of the parts of the soul; there, like Aristotle in the Nicomachean Ethics, he argues from experience and the common use of language. But at the end of the sixth book he conceives another and more perfect method, in which all ideas are only steps or grades or moments of thought, forming a connected whole which is self-supporting, and in which consistency is the test of truth. He does not explain to us in detail the nature of the process. Like many other thinkers both in ancient and modern times his mind seems to be filled with a vacant form which he is unable to realize. He supposes the sciences to have a natural order and connexion in an age when they can hardly be said to exist. He is hastening on to the 'end of the intellectual world' without even making a beginning of them.

In modern times we hardly need to be reminded that the process of acquiring knowledge is here confused with the contemplation of absolute knowledge. In all science a priori and a posteriori truths mingle in various proportions. The a priori part is that which is derived from the most universal experience of men, or is universally accepted by them; the a posteriori is that which grows up around the more general principles and becomes imperceptibly one with them. But Plato erroneously imagines that the synthesis is separable from the analysis, and that the method of science can anticipate science. In entertaining such a vision of a priori knowledge he is sufficiently justified, or at least his meaning may be sufficiently explained by the similar attempts of Descartes, Kant, Hegel, and even of Bacon himself, in modern philosophy. Anticipations or divinations, or prophetic glimpses of truths whether concerning man or nature, seem to stand in the same relation to ancient philosophy which hypotheses bear to modern inductive science. These 'guesses at truth' were not made at random; they arose from a superficial impression of uniformities and first principles in nature which the genius of the Greek, contemplating the expanse of heaven and earth, seemed to recognize in the distance. Nor can we deny that in ancient times knowledge must have stood still, and the human mind been deprived of the very instruments of thought, if philosophy had been strictly confined to the results of experience.

2. Plato supposes that when the tablet has been made blank the artist will fill in the lineaments of the ideal state. Is this a pattern laid up in heaven, or mere vacancy on which he is supposed to gaze with wondering eye? The answer is, that such ideals are framed partly by the omission of particulars, partly by imagination perfecting the form which experience supplies (Phaedo). Plato represents these ideals in a figure as belonging to another world; and in modern times the idea will sometimes seem to precede, at other times to co-operate with the hand of the artist. As in science, so also in creative art, there is a synthetical as well as an analytical method. One man will have the whole in his mind before he begins; to another the processes of mind and hand will be simultaneous.

3. There is no difficulty in seeing that Plato's divisions of knowledge are based, first, on the fundamental antithesis of sensible and intellectual which pervades the whole pre-Socratic philosophy; in which is implied also the opposition of the permanent and transient, of the universal and particular. But the age of philosophy in which he lived seemed to require a further distinction;—numbers and figures were beginning to separate from ideas. The world could no longer regard justice as a cube, and was learning to see, though imperfectly, that the abstractions of sense were distinct from the abstractions of mind. Between the Eleatic being or essence and the shadows of phenomena, the Pythagorean principle of number found a place, and was, as Aristotle remarks, a conducting medium from one to the other. Hence Plato is led to introduce a third term which had not hitherto entered into the scheme of his philosophy.

He had observed the use of mathematics in education; they were the best preparation for higher studies. The subjective relation between them further suggested an objective one; although the passage from one to the other is really imaginary (Metaph.). For metaphysical and moral philosophy has no connexion with mathematics; number and figure are the abstractions of time and space, not the expressions of purely intellectual conceptions. When divested of metaphor, a straight line or a square has no more to do with right and justice than a crooked line with vice. The figurative association was mistaken for a real one; and thus the three latter divisions of the Platonic proportion were constructed.

There is more difficulty in comprehending how he arrived at the first term of the series, which is nowhere else mentioned, and has no reference to any other part of his system. Nor indeed does the relation of shadows to objects correspond to the relation of numbers to ideas. Probably Plato has been led by the love of analogy (Timaeus) to make four terms instead of three, although the objects perceived in both divisions of the lower sphere are equally objects of sense. He is also preparing the way, as his manner is, for the shadows of images at the beginning of the seventh book, and the imitation of an imitation in the tenth. The line may be regarded as reaching from unity to infinity, and is divided into two unequal parts, and subdivided into two more; each lower sphere is the multiplication of the preceding. Of the four faculties, faith in the lower division has an intermediate position (cp. for the use of the word faith or belief, (Greek), Timaeus), contrasting equally with the vagueness of the perception of shadows (Greek) and the higher certainty of understanding (Greek) and reason (Greek).

The difference between understanding and mind or reason (Greek) is analogous to the difference between acquiring knowledge in the parts and the contemplation of the whole. True knowledge is a whole, and is at rest; consistency and universality are the tests of truth. To this self-evidencing knowledge of the whole the faculty of mind is supposed to correspond. But there is a knowledge of the understanding which is incomplete and in motion always, because unable to rest in the subordinate ideas. Those ideas are called both images and hypotheses—images because they are clothed in sense, hypotheses because they are assumptions only, until they are brought into connexion with the idea of good.

The general meaning of the passage, 'Noble, then, is the bond which links together sight...And of this kind I spoke as the intelligible...' so far as the thought contained in it admits of being translated into the terms of modern philosophy, may be described or explained as follows:—There is a truth, one and self-existent, to which by the help of a ladder let down from above, the human intelligence may ascend. This unity is like the sun in the heavens, the light by which all things are seen, the being by which they are created and sustained. It is the IDEA of good. And the steps of the ladder leading up to this highest or universal existence are the mathematical sciences, which also contain in themselves an element of the universal. These, too, we see in a new manner when we connect them with the idea of good. They then cease to be hypotheses or pictures, and become essential parts of a higher truth which is at once their first principle and their final cause.

We cannot give any more precise meaning to this remarkable passage, but we may trace in it several rudiments or vestiges of thought which are common to us and to Plato: such as (1) the unity and correlation of the sciences, or rather of science, for in Plato's time they were not yet parted off or distinguished; (2) the existence of a Divine Power, or life or idea or cause or reason, not yet conceived or no longer conceived as in the Timaeus and elsewhere under the form of a person; (3) the recognition of the hypothetical and conditional character of the mathematical sciences, and in a measure of every science when isolated from the rest; (4) the conviction of a truth which is invisible, and of a law, though hardly a law of nature, which permeates the intellectual rather than the visible world.

The method of Socrates is hesitating and tentative, awaiting the fuller explanation of the idea of good, and of the nature of dialectic in the seventh book. The imperfect intelligence of Glaucon, and the reluctance of Socrates to make a beginning, mark the difficulty of the subject. The allusion to Theages' bridle, and to the internal oracle, or demonic sign, of

Socrates, which here, as always in Plato, is only prohibitory; the remark that the salvation of any remnant of good in the present evil state of the world is due to God only; the reference to a future state of existence, which is unknown to Glaucon in the tenth book, and in which the discussions of Socrates and his disciples would be resumed; the surprise in the answers; the fanciful irony of Socrates, where he pretends that he can only describe the strange position of the philosopher in a figure of speech; the original observation that the Sophists, after all, are only the representatives and not the leaders of public opinion; the picture of the philosopher standing aside in the shower of sleet under a wall; the figure of 'the great beast' followed by the expression of good-will towards the common people who would not have rejected the philosopher if they had known him; the 'right noble thought' that the highest truths demand the greatest exactness; the hesitation of Socrates in returning once more to his well-worn theme of the idea of good; the ludicrous earnestness of Glaucon; the comparison of philosophy to a deserted maiden who marries beneath her—are some of the most interesting characteristics of the sixth book.

Yet a few more words may be added, on the old theme, which was so oft discussed in the Socratic circle, of which we, like Glaucon and Adeimantus, would fain, if possible, have a clearer notion. Like them, we are dissatisfied when we are told that the idea of good can only be revealed to a student of the mathematical sciences, and we are inclined to think that neither we nor they could have been led along that path to any satisfactory goal. For we have learned that differences of quantity cannot pass into differences of quality, and that the mathematical sciences can never rise above themselves into the sphere of our higher thoughts, although they may sometimes furnish symbols and expressions of them, and may train the mind in habits of abstraction and self-concentration. The illusion which was natural to an ancient philosopher has ceased to be an illusion to us. But if the process by which we are supposed to arrive at the idea of good be really imaginary, may not the idea itself be also a mere abstraction? We remark, first, that in all ages, and especially in primitive philosophy, words such as being, essence, unity, good, have exerted an extraordinary influence

over the minds of men. The meagreness or negativeness of their content
has been in an inverse ratio to their power. They have become the forms
under which all things were comprehended. There was a need or instinct
in the human soul which they satisfied; they were not ideas, but gods, and
to this new mythology the men of a later generation began to attach the
powers and associations of the elder deities.

The idea of good is one of those sacred words or forms of thought, which
were beginning to take the place of the old mythology. It meant unity, in
which all time and all existence were gathered up. It was the truth of all
things, and also the light in which they shone forth, and became evident to
intelligences human and divine. It was the cause of all things, the power by
which they were brought into being. It was the universal reason divested
of a human personality. It was the life as well as the light of the world,
all knowledge and all power were comprehended in it. The way to it was
through the mathematical sciences, and these too were dependent on it. To
ask whether God was the maker of it, or made by it, would be like asking
whether God could be conceived apart from goodness, or goodness apart
from God. The God of the Timaeus is not really at variance with the idea of
good; they are aspects of the same, differing only as the personal from the
impersonal, or the masculine from the neuter, the one being the expression
or language of mythology, the other of philosophy.

This, or something like this, is the meaning of the idea of good as
conceived by Plato. Ideas of number, order, harmony, development may
also be said to enter into it. The paraphrase which has just been given of it
goes beyond the actual words of Plato. We have perhaps arrived at the stage
of philosophy which enables us to understand what he is aiming at, better
than he did himself. We are beginning to realize what he saw darkly and at
a distance. But if he could have been told that this, or some conception of
the same kind, but higher than this, was the truth at which he was aiming,
and the need which he sought to supply, he would gladly have recognized
that more was contained in his own thoughts than he himself knew. As
his words are few and his manner reticent and tentative, so must the style
of his interpreter be. We should not approach his meaning more nearly

by attempting to define it further. In translating him into the language of modern thought, we might insensibly lose the spirit of ancient philosophy. It is remarkable that although Plato speaks of the idea of good as the first principle of truth and being, it is nowhere mentioned in his writings except in this passage. Nor did it retain any hold upon the minds of his disciples in a later generation; it was probably unintelligible to them. Nor does the mention of it in Aristotle appear to have any reference to this or any other passage in his extant writings.

Book VII - Introduction & Analysis
Shadows & Realities in Education

And now I will describe in a figure the enlightenment or unenlightenment of our nature:—Imagine human beings living in an underground den which is open towards the light; they have been there from childhood, having their necks and legs chained, and can only see into the den. At a distance there is a fire, and between the fire and the prisoners a raised way, and a low wall is built along the way, like the screen over which marionette players show their puppets. Behind the wall appear moving figures, who hold in their hands various works of art, and among them images of men and animals, wood and stone, and some of the passers-by are talking and others silent. 'A strange parable,' he said, 'and strange captives.' They are ourselves, I replied; and they see only the shadows of the images which the fire throws on the wall of the den; to these they give names, and if we add an echo which returns from the wall, the voices of the passengers will seem to proceed from the shadows. Suppose now that you suddenly turn them round and make them look with pain and grief to themselves at the real images; will they believe them to be real? Will not their eyes be dazzled, and will they not try to get away from the light to something which they are able to behold without blinking? And suppose further, that they are dragged up a steep and rugged ascent into the presence of the sun himself, will not their sight be darkened with the excess of light? Some time will pass before they get the habit of perceiving at all; and at first they will be able to perceive only shadows and reflections in the water; then they will recognize the moon and the stars, and will at length behold the sun in his own proper place as he is. Last of all they will conclude:—This is he who gives us the year and the seasons, and is the author of all that we see. How will they rejoice in passing from darkness to light! How worthless to them will seem the honours and glories of the den! But now imagine further, that they descend into their old habitations;—in that underground dwelling they will not see as well as their fellows, and will not be able to compete with them in the measurement of the shadows on the wall; there will be many jokes about the man who went on a visit to the sun and lost his eyes, and if they find anybody trying to set free and enlighten one of their number, they will put him to death, if they can catch him. Now the cave or den is the world of sight, the fire is the sun, the way upwards is the way to knowledge, and in the world of knowledge the idea of good is last seen and with difficulty, but when seen is inferred to be the author of good and right—parent of the lord of light in this world, and of truth and understanding in the other. He who attains to the beatific vision is always going upwards; he is unwilling to descend into political assemblies and courts of law; for his eyes are apt to blink at the images or shadows of images which they behold in them—he cannot enter into the ideas of those who have never in their lives understood the relation of the shadow to the substance. But blindness is of two kinds, and may be caused either by passing out of darkness into light or out of light into darkness, and a man of sense will distinguish between them, and will not laugh equally at both of them, but the blindness which arises from fulness of light he will deem blessed, and pity the other; or if he laugh at the puzzled soul looking at the sun, he will have more reason to laugh than the inhabitants of the den at those who descend from above. There is a further lesson taught by this parable of ours. Some persons fancy that instruction is like giving eyes to the blind, but we say that the faculty of sight was always there, and that the soul only requires to be turned round towards the light. And this is conversion; other virtues are almost like bodily habits, and may be acquired in the same manner, but intelligence has a diviner life, and is indestructible, turning either to good or evil according to the direction given. Did you never observe how the mind of a clever rogue peers out of his eyes, and the more clearly he sees, the more evil he does? Now if you take such an one, and cut away from him those leaden weights of pleasure and desire which bind his soul to earth, his intelligence will be turned round, and he will behold the truth as clearly as he now discerns his meaner ends. And have we not decided that our rulers must neither be so uneducated as to have no fixed rule of life, nor so over-educated as to be unwilling to leave their paradise for the business of the world? We must choose out therefore the natures who are most likely to ascend to the light and knowledge of the good; but we must not allow them to remain in the region of light; they must be forced down again among the captives in the den to partake of their labours and honours. 'Will they not think this a hardship?' You should remember that our purpose in framing the State was not that our citizens should do what they like, but that they should serve the State for the common good of all. May we not fairly say to our philosopher,—Friend, we do you no wrong; for in other States philosophy grows wild, and a wild plant owes nothing to the gardener, but you have been trained by us to be the rulers and kings of our hive, and therefore we must insist on your descending into the den. You must, each of you, take your turn, and become able to use your eyes in the dark, and with a little practice you will see far better than those who quarrel about the shadows, whose knowledge is a dream only, whilst yours is a waking reality. It may be that the saint or philosopher who is best fitted, may also be the least inclined to rule, but necessity is laid upon him, and he must no longer live in the heaven of ideas. And this will be the salvation of the State. For those who rule must not be those who are desirous to rule; and, if you can offer to our citizens a better life than that of rulers generally is, there will be a chance that the rich, not only in this world's goods, but in virtue and wisdom, may bear rule. And the only life which is better than the life of political ambition is that of philosophy, which is also the best preparation for the government of a State.

Then now comes the question,—How shall we create our rulers; what way is there from darkness to light? The change is effected by philosophy; it is not the turning over of an oyster-shell, but the conversion of a soul from night to day, from becoming to being. And what training will draw the soul upwards? Our former education had two branches, gymnastic, which was occupied with the body, and music, the sister art, which infused a natural harmony into mind and literature; but neither of these sciences gave any promise of doing what we want. Nothing remains to us but that universal or primary science of which all the arts and sciences are partakers, I mean number or calculation. 'Very true.' Including the art of war? 'Yes, certainly.' Then there is something ludicrous about Palamedes in the tragedy, coming in and saying that he had invented number, and had counted the ranks and set them in order. For if Agamemnon could not count his feet (and without number how could he?) he must have been a pretty sort of general indeed. No man should be a soldier who cannot count, and indeed he is hardly to be called a man. But I am not speaking of these practical applications of arithmetic, for number, in my view, is rather to be regarded as a conductor to thought and being. I will explain what I mean by the last expression:—Things sensible are of two kinds; the one class invite or stimulate the mind, while in the other the mind acquiesces. Now the stimulating class are the things which suggest contrast and relation. For example, suppose that I hold up to the eyes three fingers—a fore finger, a middle finger, a little finger—the sight equally recognizes all three fingers, but without number cannot further distinguish them. Or again, suppose two objects to be relatively great and small, these ideas of greatness and smallness are supplied not by the sense, but by the mind. And the perception of their contrast or relation quickens and sets in motion the mind, which is puzzled by the confused intimations of sense, and has recourse to number in order to find out whether the things indicated are one or more than one. Number replies that they are two and not one, and are to be distinguished from one another. Again, the sight beholds great and small, but only in a confused chaos, and not until they are distinguished does the question arise of their respective natures;

we are thus led on to the distinction between the visible and intelligible. That was what I meant when I spoke of stimulants to the intellect; I was thinking of the contradictions which arise in perception. The idea of unity, for example, like that of a finger, does not arouse thought unless involving some conception of plurality; but when the one is also the opposite of one, the contradiction gives rise to reflection; an example of this is afforded by any object of sight. All number has also an elevating effect; it raises the mind out of the foam and flux of generation to the contemplation of being, having lesser military and retail uses also. The retail use is not required by us; but as our guardian is to be a soldier as well as a philosopher, the military one may be retained. And to our higher purpose no science can be better adapted; but it must be pursued in the spirit of a philosopher, not of a shopkeeper. It is concerned, not with visible objects, but with abstract truth; for numbers are pure abstractions—the true arithmetician indignantly denies that his unit is capable of division. When you divide, he insists that you are only multiplying; his 'one' is not material or resolvable into fractions, but an unvarying and absolute equality; and this proves the purely intellectual character of his study. Note also the great power which arithmetic has of sharpening the wits; no other discipline is equally severe, or an equal test of general ability, or equally improving to a stupid person.

Let our second branch of education be geometry. 'I can easily see,' replied Glaucon, 'that the skill of the general will be doubled by his knowledge of geometry.' That is a small matter; the use of geometry, to which I refer, is the assistance given by it in the contemplation of the idea of good, and the compelling the mind to look at true being, and not at generation only. Yet the present mode of pursuing these studies, as any one who is the least of a mathematician is aware, is mean and ridiculous; they are made to look downwards to the arts, and not upwards to eternal existence. The geometer is always talking of squaring, subtending, apposing, as if he had in view action; whereas knowledge is the real object of the study. It should elevate the soul, and create the mind of philosophy; it should raise up what has fallen down, not to speak of lesser uses in war and military tactics, and in the improvement of the faculties.

Shall we propose, as a third branch of our education, astronomy? 'Very good,' replied Glaucon; 'the knowledge of the heavens is necessary at once for husbandry, navigation, military tactics.' I like your way of giving useful reasons for everything in order to make friends of the world. And there is a difficulty in proving to mankind that education is not only useful information but a purification of the eye of the soul, which is better than the bodily eye, for by this alone is truth seen. Now, will you appeal to mankind in general or to the philosopher? or would you prefer to look to yourself only? 'Every man is his own best friend.' Then take a step backward, for we are out of order, and insert the third dimension which is of solids, after the second which is of planes, and then you may proceed to solids in motion. But solid geometry is not popular and has not the patronage of the State, nor is the use of it fully recognized; the difficulty is great, and the votaries of the study are conceited and impatient. Still the charm of the pursuit wins upon men, and, if government would lend a little assistance, there might be great progress made. 'Very true,' replied Glaucon; 'but do I understand you now to begin with plane geometry, and to place next geometry of solids, and thirdly, astronomy, or the motion of solids?' Yes, I said; my hastiness has only hindered us.

'Very good, and now let us proceed to astronomy, about which I am willing to speak in your lofty strain. No one can fail to see that the contemplation of the heavens draws the soul upwards.' I am an exception, then; astronomy as studied at present appears to me to draw the soul not upwards, but downwards. Star-gazing is just looking up at the ceiling—no better; a man may lie on his back on land or on water—he may look up or look down, but there is no science in that. The vision of knowledge of which I speak is seen not with the eyes, but with the mind. All the magnificence of the heavens is but the embroidery of a copy which falls far short of the divine Original, and teaches nothing about the absolute harmonies or motions of things. Their beauty is like the beauty of figures drawn by the hand of Daedalus or any other great artist, which may be used for illustration, but no mathematician would seek to obtain from them true conceptions of equality or numerical relations. How ridiculous then to look for these in the map of the heavens, in which the imperfection of matter comes in everywhere as a disturbing element, marring the symmetry of day and night, of months and years, of the sun and stars in their courses. Only by problems can we place astronomy on a truly scientific basis. Let the heavens alone, and exert the intellect.

Still, mathematics admit of other applications, as the Pythagoreans say, and we agree. There is a sister science of harmonical motion, adapted to the ear as astronomy is to the eye, and there may be other applications also. Let us inquire of the Pythagoreans about them, not forgetting that we have an aim higher than theirs, which is the relation of these sciences to the idea of good. The error which pervades astronomy also pervades harmonics. The musicians put their ears in the place of their minds. 'Yes,' replied Glaucon, 'I like to see them laying their ears alongside of their neighbours' faces—some saying, "That's a new note," others declaring that the two notes are the same.' Yes, I said; but you mean the empirics who are always twisting and torturing the strings of the lyre, and quarrelling about the tempers of the strings; I am referring rather to the Pythagorean harmonists, who are almost equally in error. For they investigate only the numbers of the consonances which are heard, and ascend no higher,—of the true numerical harmony which is unheard, and is only to be found in problems, they have not even a conception. 'That last,' he said, 'must be a marvellous thing.' A thing, I replied, which is only useful if pursued with a view to the good.

All these sciences are the prelude of the strain, and are profitable if they are regarded in their natural relations to one another. 'I dare say, Socrates,' said Glaucon; 'but such a study will be an endless business.' What study do you mean—of the prelude, or what? For all these things are only the prelude, and you surely do not suppose that a mere mathematician is also a dialectician? 'Certainly not. I have hardly ever known a mathematician who could reason.' And yet, Glaucon, is not true reasoning that hymn of dialectic which is the music of the intellectual world, and which was by us compared to the effort of sight, when from beholding the shadows on the wall we arrived at last at the images which gave the shadows? Even so the

dialectical faculty withdrawing from sense arrives by the pure intellect at
the contemplation of the idea of good, and never rests but at the very end of
the intellectual world. And the royal road out of the cave into the light, and
the blinking of the eyes at the sun and turning to contemplate the shadows
of reality, not the shadows of an image only—this progress and gradual
acquisition of a new faculty of sight by the help of the mathematical
sciences, is the elevation of the soul to the contemplation of the highest
ideal of being.

'So far, I agree with you. But now, leaving the prelude, let us proceed
to the hymn. What, then, is the nature of dialectic, and what are the
paths which lead thither?' Dear Glaucon, you cannot follow me here.
There can be no revelation of the absolute truth to one who has not
been disciplined in the previous sciences. But that there is a science
of absolute truth, which is attained in some way very different from
those now practised, I am confident. For all other arts or sciences are
relative to human needs and opinions; and the mathematical sciences are
but a dream or hypothesis of true being, and never analyse their own
principles. Dialectic alone rises to the principle which is above hypotheses,
converting and gently leading the eye of the soul out of the barbarous
slough of ignorance into the light of the upper world, with the help
of the sciences which we have been describing—sciences, as they are
often termed, although they require some other name, implying greater
clearness than opinion and less clearness than science, and this in our
previous sketch was understanding. And so we get four names—two
for intellect, and two for opinion,—reason or mind, understanding,
faith, perception of shadows—which make a proportion—
being:becoming::intellect:opinion—and science:belief::understanding:
perception of shadows. Dialectic may be further described as that science
which defines and explains the essence or being of each nature, which
distinguishes and abstracts the good, and is ready to do battle against all
opponents in the cause of good. To him who is not a dialectician life is but
a sleepy dream; and many a man is in his grave before his is well waked up.
And would you have the future rulers of your ideal State intelligent beings,

or stupid as posts? 'Certainly not the latter.' Then you must train them in dialectic, which will teach them to ask and answer questions, and is the coping-stone of the sciences.

I dare say that you have not forgotten how our rulers were chosen; and the process of selection may be carried a step further:—As before, they must be constant and valiant, good-looking, and of noble manners, but now they must also have natural ability which education will improve; that is to say, they must be quick at learning, capable of mental toil, retentive, solid, diligent natures, who combine intellectual with moral virtues; not lame and one-sided, diligent in bodily exercise and indolent in mind, or conversely; not a maimed soul, which hates falsehood and yet unintentionally is always wallowing in the mire of ignorance; not a bastard or feeble person, but sound in wind and limb, and in perfect condition for the great gymnastic trial of the mind. Justice herself can find no fault with natures such as these; and they will be the saviours of our State; disciples of another sort would only make philosophy more ridiculous than she is at present. Forgive my enthusiasm; I am becoming excited; but when I see her trampled underfoot, I am angry at the authors of her disgrace. 'I did not notice that you were more excited than you ought to have been.' But I felt that I was. Now do not let us forget another point in the selection of our disciples—that they must be young and not old. For Solon is mistaken in saying that an old man can be always learning; youth is the time of study, and here we must remember that the mind is free and dainty, and, unlike the body, must not be made to work against the grain. Learning should be at first a sort of play, in which the natural bent is detected. As in training them for war, the young dogs should at first only taste blood; but when the necessary gymnastics are over which during two or three years divide life between sleep and bodily exercise, then the education of the soul will become a more serious matter. At twenty years of age, a selection must be made of the more promising disciples, with whom a new epoch of education will begin. The sciences which they have hitherto learned in fragments will now be brought into relation with each other and with true being; for the power of combining them is the test of speculative and dialectical ability. And afterwards at thirty a further selection shall be made of those who are able to withdraw from the world of sense into the abstraction of ideas. But at this point, judging from present experience, there is a danger that dialectic may be the source of many evils. The danger may be illustrated by a parallel case:—Imagine a person who has been brought up in wealth and luxury amid a crowd of flatterers, and who is suddenly informed that he is a supposititious son. He has hitherto honoured his reputed parents and disregarded the flatterers, and now he does the reverse. This is just what happens with a man's principles. There are certain doctrines which he learnt at home and which exercised a parental authority over him. Presently he finds that imputations are cast upon them; a troublesome querist comes and asks, 'What is the just and good?' or proves that virtue is vice and vice virtue, and his mind becomes unsettled, and he ceases to love, honour, and obey them as he has hitherto done. He is seduced into the life of pleasure, and becomes a lawless person and a rogue. The case of such speculators is very pitiable, and, in order that our thirty years' old pupils may not require this pity, let us take every possible care that young persons do not study philosophy too early. For a young man is a sort of puppy who only plays with an argument; and is reasoned into and out of his opinions every day; he soon begins to believe nothing, and brings himself and philosophy into discredit. A man of thirty does not run on in this way; he will argue and not merely contradict, and adds new honour to philosophy by the sobriety of his conduct. What time shall we allow for this second gymnastic training of the soul?—say, twice the time required for the gymnastics of the body; six, or perhaps five years, to commence at thirty, and then for fifteen years let the student go down into the den, and command armies, and gain experience of life. At fifty let him return to the end of all things, and have his eyes uplifted to the idea of good, and order his life after that pattern; if necessary, taking his turn at the helm of State, and training up others to be his successors. When his time comes he shall depart in peace to the islands of the blest. He shall be honoured with sacrifices, and receive such worship as the Pythian oracle approves.

'You are a statuary, Socrates, and have made a perfect image of our governors.' Yes, and of our governesses, for the women will share in all things with the men. And you will admit that our State is not a mere aspiration, but may really come into being when there shall arise philosopher-kings, one or more, who will despise earthly vanities, and will be the servants of justice only. 'And how will they begin their work?' Their first act will be to send away into the country all those who are more than ten years of age, and to proceed with those who are left...

At the commencement of the sixth book, Plato anticipated his explanation of the relation of the philosopher to the world in an allegory, in this, as in other passages, following the order which he prescribes in education, and proceeding from the concrete to the abstract. At the commencement of Book VII, under the figure of a cave having an opening towards a fire and a way upwards to the true light, he returns to view the divisions of knowledge, exhibiting familiarly, as in a picture, the result which had been hardly won by a great effort of thought in the previous discussion; at the same time casting a glance onward at the dialectical process, which is represented by the way leading from darkness to light. The shadows, the images, the reflection of the sun and stars in the water, the stars and sun themselves, severally correspond,—the first, to the realm of fancy and poetry,—the second, to the world of sense,—the third, to the abstractions or universals of sense, of which the mathematical sciences furnish the type,—the fourth and last to the same abstractions, when seen in the unity of the idea, from which they derive a new meaning and power. The true dialectical process begins with the contemplation of the real stars, and not mere reflections of them, and ends with the recognition of the sun, or idea of good, as the parent not only of light but of warmth and growth. To the divisions of knowledge the stages of education partly answer:—first, there is the early education of childhood and youth in the fancies of the poets, and in the laws and customs of the State;—then there is the training of the body to be a warrior athlete, and a good servant of the mind;—and thirdly, after an interval follows the education of later life, which begins with mathematics and proceeds to philosophy in general.

There seem to be two great aims in the philosophy of Plato,—first, to realize abstractions; secondly, to connect them. According to him, the true education is that which draws men from becoming to being, and to a comprehensive survey of all being. He desires to develop in the human mind the faculty of seeing the universal in all things; until at last the particulars of sense drop away and the universal alone remains. He then seeks to combine the universals which he has disengaged from sense, not perceiving that the correlation of them has no other basis but the common use of language. He never understands that abstractions, as Hegel says, are 'mere abstractions'—of use when employed in the arrangement of facts, but adding nothing to the sum of knowledge when pursued apart from them, or with reference to an imaginary idea of good. Still the exercise of the faculty of abstraction apart from facts has enlarged the mind, and played a great part in the education of the human race. Plato appreciated the value of this faculty, and saw that it might be quickened by the study of number and relation. All things in which there is opposition or proportion are suggestive of reflection. The mere impression of sense evokes no power of thought or of mind, but when sensible objects ask to be compared and distinguished, then philosophy begins. The science of arithmetic first suggests such distinctions. The follow in order the other sciences of plain and solid geometry, and of solids in motion, one branch of which is astronomy or the harmony of the spheres,—to this is appended the sister science of the harmony of sounds. Plato seems also to hint at the possibility of other applications of arithmetical or mathematical proportions, such as we employ in chemistry and natural philosophy, such as the Pythagoreans and even Aristotle make use of in Ethics and Politics, e.g. his distinction between arithmetical and geometrical proportion in the Ethics (Book V), or between numerical and proportional equality in the Politics.

The modern mathematician will readily sympathise with Plato's delight in the properties of pure mathematics. He will not be disinclined to say with him:—Let alone the heavens, and study the beauties of number and figure in themselves. He too will be apt to depreciate their application to the arts. He will observe that Plato has a conception of geometry, in which

figures are to be dispensed with; thus in a distant and shadowy way seeming
to anticipate the possibility of working geometrical problems by a more
general mode of analysis. He will remark with interest on the backward
state of solid geometry, which, alas! was not encouraged by the aid of the
State in the age of Plato; and he will recognize the grasp of Plato's mind in
his ability to conceive of one science of solids in motion including the earth
as well as the heavens,—not forgetting to notice the intimation to which
allusion has been already made, that besides astronomy and harmonics the
science of solids in motion may have other applications. Still more will he
be struck with the comprehensiveness of view which led Plato, at a time
when these sciences hardly existed, to say that they must be studied in
relation to one another, and to the idea of good, or common principle
of truth and being. But he will also see (and perhaps without surprise)
that in that stage of physical and mathematical knowledge, Plato has fallen
into the error of supposing that he can construct the heavens a priori
by mathematical problems, and determine the principles of harmony
irrespective of the adaptation of sounds to the human ear. The illusion
was a natural one in that age and country. The simplicity and certainty
of astronomy and harmonics seemed to contrast with the variation and
complexity of the world of sense; hence the circumstance that there was
some elementary basis of fact, some measurement of distance or time or
vibrations on which they must ultimately rest, was overlooked by him. The
modern predecessors of Newton fell into errors equally great; and Plato
can hardly be said to have been very far wrong, or may even claim a sort of
prophetic insight into the subject, when we consider that the greater part
of astronomy at the present day consists of abstract dynamics, by the help
of which most astronomical discoveries have been made.

The metaphysical philosopher from his point of view recognizes
mathematics as an instrument of education,—which strengthens the
power of attention, develops the sense of order and the faculty of
construction, and enables the mind to grasp under simple formulae the
quantitative differences of physical phenomena. But while acknowledging
their value in education, he sees also that they have no connexion with

our higher moral and intellectual ideas. In the attempt which Plato makes to connect them, we easily trace the influences of ancient Pythagorean notions. There is no reason to suppose that he is speaking of the ideal numbers; but he is describing numbers which are pure abstractions, to which he assigns a real and separate existence, which, as 'the teachers of the art' (meaning probably the Pythagoreans) would have affirmed, repel all attempts at subdivision, and in which unity and every other number are conceived of as absolute. The truth and certainty of numbers, when thus disengaged from phenomena, gave them a kind of sacredness in the eyes of an ancient philosopher. Nor is it easy to say how far ideas of order and fixedness may have had a moral and elevating influence on the minds of men, 'who,' in the words of the Timaeus, 'might learn to regulate their erring lives according to them.' It is worthy of remark that the old Pythagorean ethical symbols still exist as figures of speech among ourselves. And those who in modern times see the world pervaded by universal law, may also see an anticipation of this last word of modern philosophy in the Platonic idea of good, which is the source and measure of all things, and yet only an abstraction (Philebus).

Two passages seem to require more particular explanations. First, that which relates to the analysis of vision. The difficulty in this passage may be explained, like many others, from differences in the modes of conception prevailing among ancient and modern thinkers. To us, the perceptions of sense are inseparable from the act of the mind which accompanies them. The consciousness of form, colour, distance, is indistinguishable from the simple sensation, which is the medium of them. Whereas to Plato sense is the Heraclitean flux of sense, not the vision of objects in the order in which they actually present themselves to the experienced sight, but as they may be imagined to appear confused and blurred to the half-awakened eye of the infant. The first action of the mind is aroused by the attempt to set in order this chaos, and the reason is required to frame distinct conceptions under which the confused impressions of sense may be arranged. Hence arises the question, 'What is great, what is small?' and thus begins the distinction of the visible and the intelligible.

The second difficulty relates to Plato's conception of harmonics. Three classes of harmonists are distinguished by him:—first, the Pythagoreans, whom he proposes to consult as in the previous discussion on music he was to consult Damon—they are acknowledged to be masters in the art, but are altogether deficient in the knowledge of its higher import and relation to the good; secondly, the mere empirics, whom Glaucon appears to confuse with them, and whom both he and Socrates ludicrously describe as experimenting by mere auscultation on the intervals of sounds. Both of these fall short in different degrees of the Platonic idea of harmony, which must be studied in a purely abstract way, first by the method of problems, and secondly as a part of universal knowledge in relation to the idea of good.

The allegory has a political as well as a philosophical meaning. The den or cave represents the narrow sphere of politics or law (compare the description of the philosopher and lawyer in the Theaetetus), and the light of the eternal ideas is supposed to exercise a disturbing influence on the minds of those who return to this lower world. In other words, their principles are too wide for practical application; they are looking far away into the past and future, when their business is with the present. The ideal is not easily reduced to the conditions of actual life, and may often be at variance with them. And at first, those who return are unable to compete with the inhabitants of the den in the measurement of the shadows, and are derided and persecuted by them; but after a while they see the things below in far truer proportions than those who have never ascended into the upper world. The difference between the politician turned into a philosopher and the philosopher turned into a politician, is symbolized by the two kinds of disordered eyesight, the one which is experienced by the captive who is transferred from darkness to day, the other, of the heavenly messenger who voluntarily for the good of his fellow-men descends into the den. In what way the brighter light is to dawn on the inhabitants of the lower world, or how the idea of good is to become the guiding principle of politics, is left unexplained by Plato. Like the nature and divisions of dialectic, of which Glaucon impatiently demands to be informed, perhaps he would have said that the explanation could not be given except to a disciple of the previous sciences. (Symposium.)

Many illustrations of this part of the Republic may be found in modern Politics and in daily life. For among ourselves, too, there have been two sorts of Politicians or Statesmen, whose eyesight has become disordered in two different ways. First, there have been great men who, in the language of Burke, 'have been too much given to general maxims,' who, like J.S. Mill or Burke himself, have been theorists or philosophers before they were politicians, or who, having been students of history, have allowed some great historical parallel, such as the English Revolution of 1688, or possibly Athenian democracy or Roman Imperialism, to be the medium through which they viewed contemporary events. Or perhaps the long projecting shadow of some existing institution may have darkened their vision. The Church of the future, the Commonwealth of the future, the Society of the future, have so absorbed their minds, that they are unable to see in their true proportions the Politics of to-day. They have been intoxicated with great ideas, such as liberty, or equality, or the greatest happiness of the greatest number, or the brotherhood of humanity, and they no longer care to consider how these ideas must be limited in practice or harmonized with the conditions of human life. They are full of light, but the light to them has become only a sort of luminous mist or blindness. Almost every one has known some enthusiastic half-educated person, who sees everything at false distances, and in erroneous proportions.

With this disorder of eyesight may be contrasted another—of those who see not far into the distance, but what is near only; who have been engaged all their lives in a trade or a profession; who are limited to a set or sect of their own. Men of this kind have no universal except their own interests or the interests of their class, no principle but the opinion of persons like themselves, no knowledge of affairs beyond what they pick up in the streets or at their club. Suppose them to be sent into a larger world, to undertake some higher calling, from being tradesmen to turn generals or politicians, from being schoolmasters to become philosophers:—or imagine them on a sudden to receive an inward light which reveals to them for the first time in their lives a higher idea of God and the existence of a spiritual world, by this sudden conversion or change is not their daily life likely to be upset; and on the other hand will not many of their old prejudices and narrownesses still adhere to them long after they have begun to take a more comprehensive view of human things? From familiar examples like these we may learn what Plato meant by the eyesight which is liable to two kinds of disorders.

Nor have we any difficulty in drawing a parallel between the young Athenian in the fifth century before Christ who became unsettled by new ideas, and the student of a modern University who has been the subject of a similar 'aufklärung.' We too observe that when young men begin to criticise customary beliefs, or to analyse the constitution of human nature, they are apt to lose hold of solid principle (ἄπαν τὸ βέβαιον αὐτῶν ἐξοίχεται). They are like trees which have been frequently transplanted. The earth about them is loose, and they have no roots reaching far into the soil. They 'light upon every flower,' following their own wayward wills, or because the wind blows them. They catch opinions, as diseases are caught—when they are in the air. Borne hither and thither, 'they speedily fall into beliefs' the opposite of those in which they were brought up. They hardly retain the distinction of right and wrong; they seem to think one thing as good as another. They suppose themselves to be searching after truth when they are playing the game of 'follow my leader.' They fall in love 'at first sight' with paradoxes respecting morality, some fancy about art, some novelty or eccentricity in religion, and like lovers they are so absorbed for a time in their new notion that they can think of nothing else. The resolution of some philosophical or theological question seems to them more interesting and important than any substantial knowledge of literature or science or even than a good life. Like the youth in the Philebus, they are ready to discourse to any one about a new philosophy. They are generally the disciples of some eminent professor or sophist, whom they rather imitate than understand. They may be counted happy if in later years they retain some of the simple truths which they acquired in early education, and which they may, perhaps, find to be worth all the rest. Such is the picture which Plato draws and which we only reproduce, partly in his own words, of the dangers which beset youth in times of transition, when old opinions are fading away and the new are not yet firmly established. Their condition is ingeniously compared by him to that of a supposititious son, who has made the discovery that his reputed parents are not his real ones, and, in consequence, they have lost their authority over him.

The distinction between the mathematician and the dialectician is also noticeable. Plato is very well aware that the faculty of the mathematician is quite distinct from the higher philosophical sense which recognizes and combines first principles. The contempt which he expresses for distinctions of words, the danger of involuntary falsehood, the apology which Socrates makes for his earnestness of speech, are highly characteristic of the Platonic style and mode of thought. The quaint notion that if Palamedes was the inventor of number Agamemnon could not have counted his feet; the art by which we are made to believe that this State of ours is not a dream only; the gravity with which the first step is taken in the actual creation of the State, namely, the sending out of the city all who had arrived at ten years of age, in order to expedite the business of education by a generation, are also truly Platonic. (For the last, compare the passage at the end of the third book, in which he expects the lie about the earthborn men to be believed in the second generation.)

Book VIII - Introduction & Analysis
Four Forms of Government

And so we have arrived at the conclusion, that in the perfect State wives and children are to be in common; and the education and pursuits of men and women, both in war and peace, are to be common, and kings are to be philosophers and warriors, and the soldiers of the State are to live together, having all things in common; and they are to be warrior athletes, receiving no pay but only their food, from the other citizens. Now let us return to the point at which we digressed. 'That is easily done,' he replied: 'You were speaking of the State which you had constructed, and of the individual who answered to this, both of whom you affirmed to be good; and you said that of inferior States there were four forms and four individuals corresponding to them, which although deficient in various degrees, were all of them worth inspecting with a view to determining the relative happiness or misery of the best or worst man. Then Polemarchus and Adeimantus interrupted you, and this led to another argument,—and so here we are.' Suppose that we put ourselves again in the same position, and do you repeat your question. 'I should like to know of what constitutions you were speaking?' Besides the perfect State there are only four of any note in Hellas:—first, the famous Lacedaemonian or Cretan commonwealth; secondly, oligarchy, a State full of evils; thirdly, democracy, which follows next in order; fourthly, tyranny, which is the disease or death of all government. Now, States are not made of 'oak and rock,' but of flesh and blood; and therefore as there are five States there must be five human natures in individuals, which correspond to them. And first, there is the ambitious nature, which answers to the Lacedaemonian State; secondly, the oligarchical nature; thirdly, the democratical; and fourthly, the tyrannical. This last will have to be compared with the perfectly just, which is the fifth, that we may know which is the happier, and then we shall be able to determine whether the argument of Thrasymachus or our own is the more convincing. And as before we began with the State and went on to the individual, so now, beginning with timocracy, let us go on to the timocratical man, and then proceed to the other forms of government, and the individuals who answer to them.

But how did timocracy arise out of the perfect State? Plainly, like all changes of government, from division in the rulers. But whence came division? 'Sing, heavenly Muses,' as Homer says;—let them condescend to answer us, as if we were children, to whom they put on a solemn face in jest. 'And what will they say?' They will say that human things are fated to decay, and even the perfect State will not escape from this law of destiny, when 'the wheel comes full circle' in a period short or long. Plants or animals have times of fertility and sterility, which the intelligence of rulers because alloyed by sense will not enable them to ascertain, and children will be born out of season. For whereas divine creations are in a perfect cycle or number, the human creation is in a number which declines from perfection, and has four terms and three intervals of numbers, increasing, waning, assimilating, dissimilating, and yet perfectly commensurate with each other. The base of the number with a fourth added (or which is 3:4), multiplied by five and cubed, gives two harmonies:—the first a square number, which is a hundred times the base (or a hundred times a hundred); the second, an oblong, being a hundred squares of the rational diameter of a figure the side of which is five, subtracting one from each square or two perfect squares from all, and adding a hundred cubes of three. This entire number is geometrical and contains the rule or law of generation. When this law is neglected marriages will be unpropitious; the inferior

offspring who are then born will in time become the rulers; the State
will decline, and education fall into decay; gymnastic will be preferred
to music, and the gold and silver and brass and iron will form a chaotic
mass—thus division will arise. Such is the Muses' answer to our question.
'And a true answer, of course:—but what more have they to say?' They say
that the two races, the iron and brass, and the silver and gold, will draw
the State different ways;—the one will take to trade and moneymaking,
and the others, having the true riches and not caring for money, will resist
them: the contest will end in a compromise; they will agree to have private
property, and will enslave their fellow-citizens who were once their friends
and nurturers. But they will retain their warlike character, and will be
chiefly occupied in fighting and exercising rule. Thus arises timocracy,
which is intermediate between aristocracy and oligarchy.

The new form of government resembles the ideal in obedience to rulers
and contempt for trade, and having common meals, and in devotion to
warlike and gymnastic exercises. But corruption has crept into philosophy,
and simplicity of character, which was once her note, is now looked for
only in the military class. Arts of war begin to prevail over arts of peace; the
ruler is no longer a philosopher; as in oligarchies, there springs up among
them an extravagant love of gain—get another man's and save your own,
is their principle; and they have dark places in which they hoard their gold
and silver, for the use of their women and others; they take their pleasures
by stealth, like boys who are running away from their father—the law; and
their education is not inspired by the Muse, but imposed by the strong
arm of power. The leading characteristic of this State is party spirit and
ambition.

And what manner of man answers to such a State? 'In love of
contention,' replied Adeimantus, 'he will be like our friend Glaucon.'
In that respect, perhaps, but not in others. He is self-asserting and
ill-educated, yet fond of literature, although not himself a speaker,—fierce
with slaves, but obedient to rulers, a lover of power and honour, which
he hopes to gain by deeds of arms,—fond, too, of gymnastics and of
hunting. As he advances in years he grows avaricious, for he has lost

philosophy, which is the only saviour and guardian of men. His origin is
as follows:—His father is a good man dwelling in an ill-ordered State, who
has retired from politics in order that he may lead a quiet life. His mother is
angry at her loss of precedence among other women; she is disgusted at her
husband's selfishness, and she expatiates to her son on the unmanliness and
indolence of his father. The old family servant takes up the tale, and says
to the youth:—'When you grow up you must be more of a man than your
father.' All the world are agreed that he who minds his own business is an
idiot, while a busybody is highly honoured and esteemed. The young man
compares this spirit with his father's words and ways, and as he is naturally
well disposed, although he has suffered from evil influences, he rests at a
middle point and becomes ambitious and a lover of honour.

And now let us set another city over against another man. The next
form of government is oligarchy, in which the rule is of the rich only; nor
is it difficult to see how such a State arises. The decline begins with the
possession of gold and silver; illegal modes of expenditure are invented; one
draws another on, and the multitude are infected; riches outweigh virtue;
lovers of money take the place of lovers of honour; misers of politicians;
and, in time, political privileges are confined by law to the rich, who do
not shrink from violence in order to effect their purposes.

Thus much of the origin,—let us next consider the evils of oligarchy.
Would a man who wanted to be safe on a voyage take a bad pilot because
he was rich, or refuse a good one because he was poor? And does not the
analogy apply still more to the State? And there are yet greater evils: two
nations are struggling together in one—the rich and the poor; and the rich
dare not put arms into the hands of the poor, and are unwilling to pay for
defenders out of their own money. And have we not already condemned
that State in which the same persons are warriors as well as shopkeepers?
The greatest evil of all is that a man may sell his property and have no
place in the State; while there is one class which has enormous wealth, the
other is entirely destitute. But observe that these destitutes had not really
any more of the governing nature in them when they were rich than now
that they are poor; they were miserable spendthrifts always. They are the

drones of the hive; only whereas the actual drone is unprovided by nature with a sting, the two-legged things whom we call drones are some of them without stings and some of them have dreadful stings; in other words, there are paupers and there are rogues. These are never far apart; and in oligarchical cities, where nearly everybody is a pauper who is not a ruler, you will find abundance of both. And this evil state of society originates in bad education and bad government.

Like State, like man,—the change in the latter begins with the representative of timocracy; he walks at first in the ways of his father, who may have been a statesman, or general, perhaps; and presently he sees him 'fallen from his high estate,' the victim of informers, dying in prison or exile, or by the hand of the executioner. The lesson which he thus receives, makes him cautious; he leaves politics, represses his pride, and saves pence. Avarice is enthroned as his bosom's lord, and assumes the style of the Great King; the rational and spirited elements sit humbly on the ground at either side, the one immersed in calculation, the other absorbed in the admiration of wealth. The love of honour turns to love of money; the conversion is instantaneous. The man is mean, saving, toiling, the slave of one passion which is the master of the rest: Is he not the very image of the State? He has had no education, or he would never have allowed the blind god of riches to lead the dance within him. And being uneducated he will have many slavish desires, some beggarly, some knavish, breeding in his soul. If he is the trustee of an orphan, and has the power to defraud, he will soon prove that he is not without the will, and that his passions are only restrained by fear and not by reason. Hence he leads a divided existence; in which the better desires mostly prevail. But when he is contending for prizes and other distinctions, he is afraid to incur a loss which is to be repaid only by barren honour; in time of war he fights with a small part of his resources, and usually keeps his money and loses the victory.

Next comes democracy and the democratic man, out of oligarchy and the oligarchical man. Insatiable avarice is the ruling passion of an oligarchy; and they encourage expensive habits in order that they may gain by the ruin of extravagant youth. Thus men of family often lose their property or rights of citizenship; but they remain in the city, full of hatred against the new owners of their estates and ripe for revolution. The usurer with stooping walk pretends not to see them; he passes by, and leaves his sting—that is, his money—in some other victim; and many a man has to pay the parent or principal sum multiplied into a family of children, and is reduced into a state of dronage by him. The only way of diminishing the evil is either to limit a man in his use of his property, or to insist that he shall lend at his own risk. But the ruling class do not want remedies; they care only for money, and are as careless of virtue as the poorest of the citizens. Now there are occasions on which the governors and the governed meet together,—at festivals, on a journey, voyaging or fighting. The sturdy pauper finds that in the hour of danger he is not despised; he sees the rich man puffing and panting, and draws the conclusion which he privately imparts to his companions,—'that our people are not good for much;' and as a sickly frame is made ill by a mere touch from without, or sometimes without external impulse is ready to fall to pieces of itself, so from the least cause, or with none at all, the city falls ill and fights a battle for life or death. And democracy comes into power when the poor are the victors, killing some and exiling some, and giving equal shares in the government to all the rest.

The manner of life in such a State is that of democrats; there is freedom and plainness of speech, and every man does what is right in his own eyes, and has his own way of life. Hence arise the most various developments of character; the State is like a piece of embroidery of which the colours and figures are the manners of men, and there are many who, like women and children, prefer this variety to real beauty and excellence. The State is not one but many, like a bazaar at which you can buy anything. The great charm is, that you may do as you like; you may govern if you like, let it alone if you like; go to war and make peace if you feel disposed, and all quite irrespective of anybody else. When you condemn men to death they remain alive all the same; a gentleman is desired to go into exile, and he stalks about the streets like a hero; and nobody sees him or cares for him. Observe, too, how grandly Democracy sets her foot upon all our fine theories of education,—how little she cares for the training of her statesmen! The only qualification which she demands is the profession of patriotism. Such is democracy;—a pleasing, lawless, various sort of government, distributing equality to equals and unequals alike.

Let us now inspect the individual democrat; and first, as in the case of the State, we will trace his antecedents. He is the son of a miserly oligarch, and has been taught by him to restrain the love of unnecessary pleasures. Perhaps I ought to explain this latter term:—Necessary pleasures are those which are good, and which we cannot do without; unnecessary pleasures are those which do no good, and of which the desire might be eradicated by early training. For example, the pleasures of eating and drinking are necessary and healthy, up to a certain point; beyond that point they are alike hurtful to body and mind, and the excess may be avoided. When in excess, they may be rightly called expensive pleasures, in opposition to the useful ones. And the drone, as we called him, is the slave of these unnecessary pleasures and desires, whereas the miserly oligarch is subject only to the necessary.

The oligarch changes into the democrat in the following manner:—The youth who has had a miserly bringing up, gets a taste of the drone's honey; he meets with wild companions, who introduce him to every new pleasure. As in the State, so in the individual, there are allies on both sides, temptations from without and passions from within; there is reason also and external influences of parents and friends in alliance with the oligarchical principle; and the two factions are in violent conflict with one another. Sometimes the party of order prevails, but then again new desires and new disorders arise, and the whole mob of passions gets possession of the Acropolis, that is to say, the soul, which they find void and unguarded by true words and works. Falsehoods and illusions ascend to take their place; the prodigal goes back into the country of the Lotophagi or drones, and openly dwells there. And if any offer of alliance or parley of individual elders comes from home, the false spirits shut the gates of the castle and permit no one to enter,—there is a battle, and they gain the victory; and straightway making alliance with the desires, they banish modesty, which they call folly, and send temperance over the border. When the house has been swept and garnished, they dress up the exiled vices, and, crowning them with garlands, bring them back under new names. Insolence they call good breeding, anarchy freedom, waste magnificence, impudence courage. Such is the process by which the youth passes from the necessary pleasures to the unnecessary. After a while he divides his time impartially between them; and perhaps, when he gets older and the violence of passion has abated, he restores some of the exiles and lives in a sort of equilibrium, indulging first one pleasure and then another; and if reason comes and tells him that some pleasures are good and honourable, and others bad and vile, he shakes his head and says that he can make no distinction between them. Thus he lives in the fancy of the hour; sometimes he takes to drink, and then he turns abstainer; he practises in the gymnasium or he does nothing at all; then again he would be a philosopher or a politician; or again, he would be a warrior or a man of business; he is

'Every thing by starts and nothing long.'

There remains still the finest and fairest of all men and all States—tyranny and the tyrant. Tyranny springs from democracy much as democracy springs from oligarchy. Both arise from excess; the one from excess of wealth, the other from excess of freedom. 'The great natural good of life,' says the democrat, 'is freedom.' And this exclusive love of freedom and regardlessness of everything else, is the cause of the change from democracy to tyranny. The State demands the strong wine of freedom, and unless her rulers give her a plentiful draught, punishes and insults them; equality and fraternity of governors and governed is the approved principle. Anarchy is the law, not of the State only, but of private houses, and extends even to the animals. Father and son, citizen and foreigner, teacher and pupil, old and young, are all on a level; fathers and teachers fear their sons and pupils, and the wisdom of the young man is a match for the elder, and the old imitate the jaunty manners of the young because they are afraid of being thought morose. Slaves are on a level with their masters and mistresses, and there is no difference between men and women. Nay, the very animals in a democratic State have a freedom which is unknown

in other places. The she-dogs are as good as their she-mistresses, and horses
and asses march along with dignity and run their noses against anybody
who comes in their way. 'That has often been my experience.' At last the
citizens become so sensitive that they cannot endure the yoke of laws,
written or unwritten; they would have no man call himself their master.
Such is the glorious beginning of things out of which tyranny springs.
'Glorious, indeed; but what is to follow?' The ruin of oligarchy is the ruin
of democracy; for there is a law of contraries; the excess of freedom passes
into the excess of slavery, and the greater the freedom the greater the slavery.
You will remember that in the oligarchy were found two classes—rogues
and paupers, whom we compared to drones with and without stings.
These two classes are to the State what phlegm and bile are to the human
body; and the State-physician, or legislator, must get rid of them, just as
the bee-master keeps the drones out of the hive. Now in a democracy, too,
there are drones, but they are more numerous and more dangerous than
in the oligarchy; there they are inert and unpractised, here they are full of
life and animation; and the keener sort speak and act, while the others buzz
about the bema and prevent their opponents from being heard. And there
is another class in democratic States, of respectable, thriving individuals,
who can be squeezed when the drones have need of their possessions;
there is moreover a third class, who are the labourers and the artisans, and
they make up the mass of the people. When the people meet, they are
omnipotent, but they cannot be brought together unless they are attracted
by a little honey; and the rich are made to supply the honey, of which the
demagogues keep the greater part themselves, giving a taste only to the
mob. Their victims attempt to resist; they are driven mad by the stings
of the drones, and so become downright oligarchs in self-defence. Then
follow informations and convictions for treason. The people have some
protector whom they nurse into greatness, and from this root the tree of
tyranny springs. The nature of the change is indicated in the old fable of
the temple of Zeus Lycaeus, which tells how he who tastes human flesh
mixed up with the flesh of other victims will turn into a wolf. Even so the
protector, who tastes human blood, and slays some and exiles others with

or without law, who hints at abolition of debts and division of lands, must either perish or become a wolf—that is, a tyrant. Perhaps he is driven out, but he soon comes back from exile; and then if his enemies cannot get rid of him by lawful means, they plot his assassination. Thereupon the friend of the people makes his well-known request to them for a body-guard, which they readily grant, thinking only of his danger and not of their own. Now let the rich man make to himself wings, for he will never run away again if he does not do so then. And the Great Protector, having crushed all his rivals, stands proudly erect in the chariot of State, a full-blown tyrant: Let us enquire into the nature of his happiness.

In the early days of his tyranny he smiles and beams upon everybody; he is not a 'dominus,' no, not he: he has only come to put an end to debt and the monopoly of land. Having got rid of foreign enemies, he makes himself necessary to the State by always going to war. He is thus enabled to depress the poor by heavy taxes, and so keep them at work; and he can get rid of bolder spirits by handing them over to the enemy. Then comes unpopularity; some of his old associates have the courage to oppose him. The consequence is, that he has to make a purgation of the State; but, unlike the physician who purges away the bad, he must get rid of the high-spirited, the wise and the wealthy; for he has no choice between death and a life of shame and dishonour. And the more hated he is, the more he will require trusty guards; but how will he obtain them? 'They will come flocking like birds—for pay.' Will he not rather obtain them on the spot? He will take the slaves from their owners and make them his body-guard; these are his trusted friends, who admire and look up to him. Are not the tragic poets wise who magnify and exalt the tyrant, and say that he is wise by association with the wise? And are not their praises of tyranny alone a sufficient reason why we should exclude them from our State? They may go to other cities, and gather the mob about them with fine words, and change commonwealths into tyrannies and democracies, receiving honours and rewards for their services; but the higher they and their friends ascend constitution hill, the more their honour will fail and become 'too asthmatic to mount.' To return to the tyrant—How will he support that rare army of his? First, by robbing the temples of their treasures, which will enable him to lighten the taxes; then he will take all his father's property, and spend it on his companions, male or female. Now his father is the demus, and if the demus gets angry, and says that a great hulking son ought not to be a burden on his parents, and bids him and his riotous crew begone, then will the parent know what a monster he has been nurturing, and that the son whom he would fain expel is too strong for him. 'You do not mean to say that he will beat his father?' Yes, he will, after having taken away his arms. 'Then he is a parricide and a cruel, unnatural son.' And the people have jumped from the fear of slavery into slavery, out of the smoke into the fire. Thus liberty, when out of all order and reason, passes into the worst form of servitude...

In the previous books Plato has described the ideal State; now he returns to the perverted or declining forms, on which he had lightly touched at the end of Book IV. These he describes in a succession of parallels between the individuals and the States, tracing the origin of either in the State or individual which has preceded them. He begins by asking the point at which he digressed; and is thus led shortly to recapitulate the substance of the three former books, which also contain a parallel of the philosopher and the State.

Of the first decline he gives no intelligible account; he would not have liked to admit the most probable causes of the fall of his ideal State, which to us would appear to be the impracticability of communism or the natural antagonism of the ruling and subject classes. He throws a veil of mystery over the origin of the decline, which he attributes to ignorance of the law of population. Of this law the famous geometrical figure or number is the expression. Like the ancients in general, he had no idea of the gradual perfectibility of man or of the education of the human race. His ideal was not to be attained in the course of ages, but was to spring in full armour from the head of the legislator. When good laws had been given, he thought only of the manner in which they were likely to be corrupted, or of how they might be filled up in detail or restored in accordance with their original spirit. He appears not to have reflected upon the full meaning of his own words, 'In the brief space of human life, nothing great can be accomplished'; or again, as he afterwards says in the Laws, 'Infinite time is the maker of cities.' The order of constitutions which is adopted by him represents an order of thought rather than a succession of time, and may be considered as the first attempt to frame a philosophy of history.

The first of these declining States is timocracy, or the government of soldiers and lovers of honour, which answers to the Spartan State; this is a government of force, in which education is not inspired by the Muses, but imposed by the law, and in which all the finer elements of organization have disappeared. The philosopher himself has lost the love of truth, and the soldier, who is of a simpler and honester nature, rules in his stead. The individual who answers to timocracy has some noticeable qualities. He is described as ill educated, but, like the Spartan, a lover of literature; and although he is a harsh master to his servants he has no natural superiority over them. His character is based upon a reaction against the circumstances of his father, who in a troubled city has retired from politics; and his mother, who is dissatisfied at her own position, is always urging him towards the life of political ambition. Such a character may have had this origin, and indeed Livy attributes the Licinian laws to a feminine jealousy of a similar kind. But there is obviously no connection between the manner in which the timocratic State springs out of the ideal, and the mere accident by which the timocratic man is the son of a retired statesman.

The two next stages in the decline of constitutions have even less historical foundation. For there is no trace in Greek history of a polity like the Spartan or Cretan passing into an oligarchy of wealth, or of the oligarchy of wealth passing into a democracy. The order of history appears to be different; first, in the Homeric times there is the royal or patriarchal form of government, which a century or two later was succeeded by an oligarchy of birth rather than of wealth, and in which wealth was only the accident of the hereditary possession of land and power. Sometimes this oligarchical government gave way to a government based upon a qualification of property, which, according to Aristotle's mode of using words, would have been called a timocracy; and this in some cities, as at

Athens, became the conducting medium to democracy. But such was not the necessary order of succession in States; nor, indeed, can any order be discerned in the endless fluctuation of Greek history (like the tides in the Euripus), except, perhaps, in the almost uniform tendency from monarchy to aristocracy in the earliest times. At first sight there appears to be a similar inversion in the last step of the Platonic succession; for tyranny, instead of being the natural end of democracy, in early Greek history appears rather as a stage leading to democracy; the reign of Peisistratus and his sons is an episode which comes between the legislation of Solon and the constitution of Cleisthenes; and some secret cause common to them all seems to have led the greater part of Hellas at her first appearance in the dawn of history, e.g. Athens, Argos, Corinth, Sicyon, and nearly every State with the exception of Sparta, through a similar stage of tyranny which ended either in oligarchy or democracy. But then we must remember that Plato is describing rather the contemporary governments of the Sicilian States, which alternated between democracy and tyranny, than the ancient history of Athens or Corinth.

The portrait of the tyrant himself is just such as the later Greek delighted to draw of Phalaris and Dionysius, in which, as in the lives of mediaeval saints or mythic heroes, the conduct and actions of one were attributed to another in order to fill up the outline. There was no enormity which the Greek was not today to believe of them; the tyrant was the negation of government and law; his assassination was glorious; there was no crime, however unnatural, which might not with probability be attributed to him. In this, Plato was only following the common thought of his countrymen, which he embellished and exaggerated with all the power of his genius. There is no need to suppose that he drew from life; or that his knowledge of tyrants is derived from a personal acquaintance with Dionysius. The manner in which he speaks of them would rather tend to render doubtful his ever having 'consorted' with them, or entertained the schemes, which are attributed to him in the Epistles, of regenerating Sicily by their help.

Plato in a hyperbolical and serio-comic vein exaggerates the follies of democracy which he also sees reflected in social life. To him democracy is a state of individualism or dissolution; in which every one is doing what is right in his own eyes. Of a people animated by a common spirit of liberty, rising as one man to repel the Persian host, which is the leading idea of democracy in Herodotus and Thucydides, he never seems to think. But if he is not a believer in liberty, still less is he a lover of tyranny. His deeper and more serious condemnation is reserved for the tyrant, who is the ideal of wickedness and also of weakness, and who in his utter helplessness and suspiciousness is leading an almost impossible existence, without that remnant of good which, in Plato's opinion, was required to give power to evil (Book I). This ideal of wickedness living in helpless misery, is the reverse of that other portrait of perfect injustice ruling in happiness and splendour, which first of all Thrasymachus, and afterwards the sons of Ariston had drawn, and is also the reverse of the king whose rule of life is the good of his subjects.

Each of these governments and individuals has a corresponding ethical gradation: the ideal State is under the rule of reason, not extinguishing but harmonizing the passions, and training them in virtue; in the timocracy and the timocratic man the constitution, whether of the State or of the individual, is based, first, upon courage, and secondly, upon the love of honour; this latter virtue, which is hardly to be esteemed a virtue, has superseded all the rest. In the second stage of decline the virtues have altogether disappeared, and the love of gain has succeeded to them; in the third stage, or democracy, the various passions are allowed to have free play, and the virtues and vices are impartially cultivated. But this freedom, which leads to many curious extravagances of character, is in reality only a state of weakness and dissipation. At last, one monster passion takes possession of the whole nature of man—this is tyranny. In all of them excess—the excess first of wealth and then of freedom, is the element of decay.

The eighth book of the Republic abounds in pictures of life and fanciful allusions; the use of metaphorical language is carried to a greater extent than anywhere else in Plato. We may remark,

(1), the description of the two nations in one, which become more and more divided in the Greek Republics, as in feudal times, and perhaps also in our own;

(2), the notion of democracy expressed in a sort of Pythagorean formula as equality among unequals;

(3), the free and easy ways of men and animals, which are characteristic of liberty, as foreign mercenaries and universal mistrust are of the tyrant;

(4), the proposal that mere debts should not be recoverable by law is a speculation which has often been entertained by reformers of the law in modern times, and is in harmony with the tendencies of modern legislation. Debt and land were the two great difficulties of the ancient lawgiver: in modern times we may be said to have almost, if not quite, solved the first of these difficulties, but hardly the second.

Still more remarkable are the corresponding portraits of individuals: there is the family picture of the father and mother and the old servant of the timocratical man, and the outward respectability and inherent meanness of the oligarchical; the uncontrolled licence and freedom of the democrat, in which the young Alcibiades seems to be depicted, doing right or wrong as he pleases, and who at last, like the prodigal, goes into a far country (note here the play of language by which the democratic man is himself represented under the image of a State having a citadel and receiving embassies); and there is the wild-beast nature, which breaks loose in his successor. The hit about the tyrant being a parricide; the representation of the tyrant's life as an obscene dream; the rhetorical surprise of a more miserable than the most miserable of men in Book IX; the hint to the poets that if they are the friends of tyrants there is no place for them in a constitutional State, and that they are too clever not to see the propriety of their own expulsion; the continuous image of the drones who are of two kinds, swelling at last into the monster drone having wings (Book IX),—are among Plato's happiest touches.

There remains to be considered the great difficulty of this book of the
Republic, the so-called number of the State. This is a puzzle almost as
great as the Number of the Beast in the Book of Revelation, and though
apparently known to Aristotle, is referred to by Cicero as a proverb of
obscurity (Ep. ad Att.). And some have imagined that there is no answer to
the puzzle, and that Plato has been practising upon his readers. But such a
deception as this is inconsistent with the manner in which Aristotle speaks
of the number (Pol.), and would have been ridiculous to any reader of the
Republic who was acquainted with Greek mathematics. As little reason
is there for supposing that Plato intentionally used obscure expressions;
the obscurity arises from our want of familiarity with the subject. On the
other hand, Plato himself indicates that he is not altogether serious, and
in describing his number as a solemn jest of the Muses, he appears to
imply some degree of satire on the symbolical use of number. (Compare
Cratylus; Protag.)

Our hope of understanding the passage depends principally on an
accurate study of the words themselves; on which a faint light is thrown
by the parallel passage in the ninth book. Another help is the allusion
in Aristotle, who makes the important remark that the latter part of the
passage (Greek) describes a solid figure. (Pol.—'He only says that nothing
is abiding, but that all things change in a certain cycle; and that the origin of
the change is a base of numbers which are in the ratio of 4:3; and this when
combined with a figure of five gives two harmonies; he means when the
number of this figure becomes solid.') Some further clue may be gathered
from the appearance of the Pythagorean triangle, which is denoted by the
numbers 3, 4, 5, and in which, as in every right-angled triangle, the squares
of the two lesser sides equal the square of the hypotenuse (9 + 16 = 25).

Plato begins by speaking of a perfect or cyclical number (Tim.), i.e. a
number in which the sum of the divisors equals the whole; this is the divine
or perfect number in which all lesser cycles or revolutions are complete.
He also speaks of a human or imperfect number, having four terms and
three intervals of numbers which are related to one another in certain
proportions; these he converts into figures, and finds in them when they

have been raised to the third power certain elements of number, which give two 'harmonies,' the one square, the other oblong; but he does not say that the square number answers to the divine, or the oblong number to the human cycle; nor is any intimation given that the first or divine number represents the period of the world, the second the period of the state, or of the human race as Zeller supposes; nor is the divine number afterwards mentioned (Arist.). The second is the number of generations or births, and presides over them in the same mysterious manner in which the stars preside over them, or in which, according to the Pythagoreans, opportunity, justice, marriage, are represented by some number or figure. This is probably the number 216.

The explanation given in the text supposes the two harmonies to make up the number 8000. This explanation derives a certain plausibility from the circumstance that 8000 is the ancient number of the Spartan citizens (Herod.), and would be what Plato might have called 'a number which nearly concerns the population of a city'; the mysterious disappearance of the Spartan population may possibly have suggested to him the first cause of his decline of States. The lesser or square 'harmony,' of 400, might be a symbol of the guardians,—the larger or oblong 'harmony,' of the people, and the numbers 3, 4, 5 might refer respectively to the three orders in the State or parts of the soul, the four virtues, the five forms of government. The harmony of the musical scale, which is elsewhere used as a symbol of the harmony of the state, is also indicated. For the numbers 3, 4, 5, which represent the sides of the Pythagorean triangle, also denote the intervals of the scale.

The terms used in the statement of the problem may be explained as follows. A perfect number (Greek), as already stated, is one which is equal to the sum of its divisors. Thus 6, which is the first perfect or cyclical number, = 1 + 2 + 3. The words (Greek), 'terms' or 'notes,' and (Greek), 'intervals,' are applicable to music as well as to number and figure. (Greek) is the 'base' on which the whole calculation depends, or the 'lowest term' from which it can be worked out. The words (Greek) have been variously translated—'squared and cubed' (Donaldson), 'equalling and equalled in power' (Weber), 'by involution and evolution,' i.e. by raising the power and extracting the root (as in the translation). Numbers are called 'like and unlike' (Greek) when the factors or the sides of the planes and cubes which they represent are or are not in the same ratio: e.g. 8 and 27 = 2 cubed and 3 cubed; and conversely. 'Waxing' (Greek) numbers, called also 'increasing' (Greek), are those which are exceeded by the sum of their divisors: e.g. 12 and 18 are less than 16 and 21. 'Waning' (Greek) numbers, called also 'decreasing' (Greek) are those which succeed the sum of their divisors: e.g. 8 and 27 exceed 7 and 13. The words translated 'commensurable and agreeable to one another' (Greek) seem to be different ways of describing the same relation, with more or less precision. They are equivalent to 'expressible in terms having the same relation to one another,' like the series 8, 12, 18, 27, each of which numbers is in the relation of (1 and 1/2) to the preceding. The 'base,' or 'fundamental number, which has 1/3 added to it' (1 and 1/3) = 4/3 or a musical fourth. (Greek) is a 'proportion' of numbers as of musical notes, applied either to the parts or factors of a single number or to the relation of one number to another. The first harmony is a 'square' number (Greek); the second harmony is an 'oblong' number (Greek), i.e. a number representing a figure of which the opposite sides only are equal. (Greek) = 'numbers squared from' or 'upon diameters'; (Greek) = 'rational,' i.e. omitting fractions, (Greek), 'irrational,' i.e. including fractions; e.g. 49 is a square of the rational diameter of a figure the side of which = 5: 50, of an irrational diameter of the same. For several of the explanations here given and for a good deal besides I am indebted to an excellent article on the Platonic Number by Dr. Donaldson (Proc. of the Philol. Society).

The conclusions which he draws from these data are summed up by him as follows. Having assumed that the number of the perfect or divine cycle is the number of the world, and the number of the imperfect cycle the number of the state, he proceeds: 'The period of the world is defined by the perfect number 6, that of the state by the cube of that number or 216, which is the product of the last pair of terms in the Platonic Tetractys (a series of seven terms, 1, 2, 3, 4, 9, 8, 27); and if we take this as the basis of our computation, we shall have two cube numbers (Greek), viz. 8 and 27; and the mean proportionals between these, viz. 12 and 18, will furnish three intervals and four terms, and these terms and intervals stand related to one another in the sesqui-altera ratio, i.e. each term is to the preceding as 3/2. Now if we remember that the number 216 = 8 x 27 = 3 cubed + 4 cubed + 5 cubed, and 3 squared + 4 squared = 5 squared, we must admit that this number implies the numbers 3, 4, 5, to which musicians attach so much importance. And if we combine the ratio 4/3 with the number 5, or multiply the ratios of the sides by the hypotenuse, we shall by first squaring and then cubing obtain two expressions, which denote the ratio of the two last pairs of terms in the Platonic Tetractys, the former multiplied by the square, the latter by the cube of the number 10, the sum of the first four digits which constitute the Platonic Tetractys.' The two (Greek) he elsewhere explains as follows: 'The first (Greek) is (Greek), in other words (4/3 x 5) all squared = 100 x 2 squared over 3 squared. The second (Greek), a cube of the same root, is described as 100 multiplied (alpha) by the rational diameter of 5 diminished by unity, i.e., as shown above, 48: (beta) by two incommensurable diameters, i.e. the two first irrationals, or 2 and 3: and (gamma) by the cube of 3, or 27. Thus we have (48 + 5 + 27) 100 = 1000 x 2 cubed. This second harmony is to be the cube of the number of which the former harmony is the square, and therefore must be divided by the cube of 3. In other words, the whole expression will be: (1), for the first harmony, 400/9: (2), for the second harmony, 8000/27.'

The reasons which have inclined me to agree with Dr. Donaldson and also with Schleiermacher in supposing that 216 is the Platonic number of births are: (1) that it coincides with the description of the number given in the first part of the passage (Greek...): (2) that the number 216 with its permutations would have been familiar to a Greek mathematician, though unfamiliar to us: (3) that 216 is the cube of 6, and also the sum of 3 cubed, 4 cubed, 5 cubed, the numbers 3, 4, 5 representing the Pythagorean triangle, of which the sides when squared equal the square of the hypotenuse (9 + 16 = 25): (4) that it is also the period of the Pythagorean Metempsychosis: (5) the three ultimate terms or bases (3, 4, 5) of which 216 is composed answer to the third, fourth, fifth in the musical scale: (6) that the number 216 is the product of the cubes of 2 and 3, which are the two last terms in the Platonic Tetractys: (7) that the Pythagorean triangle is said by Plutarch (de Is. et Osir.), Proclus (super prima Eucl.), and Quintilian (de Musica) to be contained in this passage, so that the tradition of the school seems to point in the same direction: (8) that the Pythagorean triangle is called also the figure of marriage (Greek).

But though agreeing with Dr. Donaldson thus far, I see no reason for supposing, as he does, that the first or perfect number is the world, the human or imperfect number the state; nor has he given any proof that the second harmony is a cube. Nor do I think that (Greek) can mean 'two incommensurables,' which he arbitrarily assumes to be 2 and 3, but rather, as the preceding clause implies, (Greek), i.e. two square numbers based upon irrational diameters of a figure the side of which is 5 = 50 x 2.

The greatest objection to the translation is the sense given to the words (Greek), 'a base of three with a third added to it, multiplied by 5.' In this somewhat forced manner Plato introduces once more the numbers of the Pythagorean triangle. But the coincidences in the numbers which follow are in favour of the explanation. The first harmony of 400, as has been already remarked, probably represents the rulers; the second and oblong harmony of 7600, the people.

And here we take leave of the difficulty. The discovery of the riddle would be useless, and would throw no light on ancient mathematics. The point of interest is that Plato should have used such a symbol, and that so much of the Pythagorean spirit should have prevailed in him. His general meaning is that divine creation is perfect, and is represented or presided over by a perfect or cyclical number; human generation is imperfect, and represented or presided over by an imperfect number or series of numbers. The number 5040, which is the number of the citizens in the Laws, is expressly based by him on utilitarian grounds, namely, the convenience of the number for division; it is also made up of the first seven digits multiplied by one another. The contrast of the perfect and imperfect number may have been easily suggested by the corrections of the cycle,

which were made first by Meton and secondly by Callippus; (the latter
is said to have been a pupil of Plato). Of the degree of importance or
of exactness to be attributed to the problem, the number of the tyrant
in Book IX ($729 = 365 \times 2$), and the slight correction of the error in
the number 5040/12 (Laws), may furnish a criterion. There is nothing
surprising in the circumstance that those who were seeking for order in
nature and had found order in number, should have imagined one to give
law to the other. Plato believes in a power of number far beyond what
he could see realized in the world around him, and he knows the great
influence which 'the little matter of 1, 2, 3' exercises upon education. He
may even be thought to have a prophetic anticipation of the discoveries
of Quetelet and others, that numbers depend upon numbers; e.g.—in
population, the numbers of births and the respective numbers of children
born of either sex, on the respective ages of parents, i.e. on other numbers.

Book IX - Introduction & Analysis
Wrong or Right Government & Pleasures of Each

Last of all comes the tyrannical man, about whom we have to enquire, Whence is he, and how does he live—in happiness or in misery? There is, however, a previous question of the nature and number of the appetites, which I should like to consider first. Some of them are unlawful, and yet admit of being chastened and weakened in various degrees by the power of reason and law. 'What appetites do you mean?' I mean those which are awake when the reasoning powers are asleep, which get up and walk about naked without any self-respect or shame; and there is no conceivable folly or crime, however cruel or unnatural, of which, in imagination, they may not be guilty. 'True,' he said; 'very true.' But when a man's pulse beats temperately; and he has supped on a feast of reason and come to a knowledge of himself before going to rest, and has satisfied his desires just enough to prevent their perturbing his reason, which remains clear and luminous, and when he is free from quarrel and heat,—the visions which he has on his bed are least irregular and abnormal. Even in good men there is such an irregular wild-beast nature, which peers out in sleep.

To return:—You remember what was said of the democrat; that he was the son of a miserly father, who encouraged the saving desires and repressed the ornamental and expensive ones; presently the youth got into fine company, and began to entertain a dislike to his father's narrow ways; and being a better man than the corrupters of his youth, he came to a mean, and led a life, not of lawless or slavish passion, but of regular and successive indulgence. Now imagine that the youth has become a father, and has a son who is exposed to the same temptations, and has companions who lead him into every sort of iniquity, and parents and friends who try to keep him right. The counsellors of evil find that their only chance of retaining him is to implant in his soul a monster drone, or love; while other desires buzz around him and mystify him with sweet sounds and scents, this monster love takes possession of him, and puts an end to every true or modest thought or wish. Love, like drunkenness and madness, is a tyranny; and the tyrannical man, whether made by nature or habit, is just a drinking, lusting, furious sort of animal.

And how does such an one live? 'Nay, that you must tell me.' Well then, I fancy that he will live amid revelries and harlotries, and love will be the lord and master of the house. Many desires require much money, and so he spends all that he has and borrows more; and when he has nothing the young ravens are still in the nest in which they were hatched, crying for food. Love urges them on; and they must be gratified by force or fraud, or if not, they become painful and troublesome; and as the new pleasures succeed the old ones, so will the son take possession of the goods of his parents; if they show signs of refusing, he will defraud and deceive them; and if they openly resist, what then? 'I can only say, that I should not much like to be in their place.' But, O heavens, Adeimantus, to think that for some new-fangled and unnecessary love he will give up his old father and mother, best and dearest of friends, or enslave them to the fancies of the hour! Truly a tyrannical son is a blessing to his father and mother! When there is no more to be got out of them, he turns burglar or pickpocket, or robs a temple. Love overmasters the thoughts of his youth, and he becomes in sober reality the monster that he was sometimes in sleep. He waxes strong in all violence and lawlessness; and is ready for any deed of daring that will supply the wants of his rabble-rout. In a well-ordered State there are only a few such, and these in time of war go out and become the mercenaries of a tyrant. But in time of peace they stay at home and do mischief; they are the thieves, footpads, cut-purses, man-stealers of the community; or if they are able to speak, they turn false-witnesses and informers. 'No small catalogue of crimes truly, even if the perpetrators are few.' Yes, I said; but small and great are relative terms, and no crimes which are committed by them approach those of the tyrant, whom this class, growing strong and numerous, create out of themselves. If the people yield, well and good, but, if they resist, then, as before he beat his father and mother, so now he beats his fatherland and motherland, and places his mercenaries over them. Such men in their early days live with flatterers, and they themselves flatter others, in order to gain their ends; but they soon discard their followers when they have no longer any need of them; they are always either masters or servants,—the joys of friendship are unknown to them. And they are utterly treacherous and unjust, if the nature of justice be at all understood by us. They realize our dream; and he who is the most of a tyrant by nature, and leads the life of a tyrant for the longest time, will be the worst of them, and being the worst of them, will also be the most miserable.

Like man, like State,—the tyrannical man will answer to tyranny, which is the extreme opposite of the royal State; for one is the best and the other the worst. But which is the happier? Great and terrible as the tyrant may appear enthroned amid his satellites, let us not be afraid to go in and ask; and the answer is, that the monarchical is the happiest, and the tyrannical the most miserable of States. And may we not ask the same question about the men themselves, requesting some one to look into them who is able to penetrate the inner nature of man, and will not be panic-struck by the vain pomp of tyranny? I will suppose that he is one who has lived with him, and has seen him in family life, or perhaps in the hour of trouble and danger.

Assuming that we ourselves are the impartial judge for whom we seek, let us begin by comparing the individual and State, and ask first of all, whether the State is likely to be free or enslaved—Will there not be a little freedom and a great deal of slavery? And the freedom is of the bad, and the slavery of the good; and this applies to the man as well as to the State; for his soul is full of meanness and slavery, and the better part is enslaved to the worse. He cannot do what he would, and his mind is full of confusion; he is the very

reverse of a freeman. The State will be poor and full of misery and
sorrow; and the man's soul will also be poor and full of sorrows, and
he will be the most miserable of men. No, not the most miserable, for
there is yet a more miserable. 'Who is that?' The tyrannical man who
has the misfortune also to become a public tyrant. 'There I suspect that
you are right.' Say rather, 'I am sure;' conjecture is out of place in an
enquiry of this nature. He is like a wealthy owner of slaves, only he has
more of them than any private individual. You will say, 'The owners
of slaves are not generally in any fear of them.' But why? Because
the whole city is in a league which protects the individual. Suppose
however that one of these owners and his household is carried off by
a god into a wilderness, where there are no freemen to help him—will
he not be in an agony of terror?—will he not be compelled to flatter
his slaves and to promise them many things sore against his will? And
suppose the same god who carried him off were to surround him with
neighbours who declare that no man ought to have slaves, and that the
owners of them should be punished with death. 'Still worse and worse!
He will be in the midst of his enemies.' And is not our tyrant such a
captive soul, who is tormented by a swarm of passions which he cannot
indulge; living indoors always like a woman, and jealous of those who
can go out and see the world?

Having so many evils, will not the most miserable of men be still more
miserable in a public station? Master of others when he is not master of
himself; like a sick man who is compelled to be an athlete; the meanest of
slaves and the most abject of flatterers; wanting all things, and never able
to satisfy his desires; always in fear and distraction, like the State of which
he is the representative. His jealous, hateful, faithless temper grows worse
with command; he is more and more faithless, envious, unrighteous,—the
most wretched of men, a misery to himself and to others. And so let us have
a final trial and proclamation; need we hire a herald, or shall I proclaim the
result? 'Made the proclamation yourself.' The son of Ariston (the best)
is of opinion that the best and justest of men is also the happiest, and
that this is he who is the most royal master of himself; and that the unjust

man is he who is the greatest tyrant of himself and of his State. And I add further—'seen or unseen by gods or men.'

This is our first proof. The second is derived from the three kinds of pleasure, which answer to the three elements of the soul—reason, passion, desire; under which last is comprehended avarice as well as sensual appetite, while passion includes ambition, party-feeling, love of reputation. Reason, again, is solely directed to the attainment of truth, and careless of money and reputation. In accordance with the difference of men's natures, one of these three principles is in the ascendant, and they have their several pleasures corresponding to them. Interrogate now the three natures, and each one will be found praising his own pleasures and depreciating those of others. The money-maker will contrast the vanity of knowledge with the solid advantages of wealth. The ambitious man will despise knowledge which brings no honour; whereas the philosopher will regard only the fruition of truth, and will call other pleasures necessary rather than good. Now, how shall we decide between them? Is there any better criterion than experience and knowledge? And which of the three has the truest knowledge and the widest experience? The experience of youth makes the philosopher acquainted with the two kinds of desire, but the avaricious and the ambitious man never taste the pleasures of truth and wisdom. Honour he has equally with them; they are 'judged of him,' but he is 'not judged of them,' for they never attain to the knowledge of true being. And his instrument is reason, whereas their standard is only wealth and honour; and if by reason we are to judge, his good will be the truest. And so we arrive at the result that the pleasure of the rational part of the soul, and a life passed in such pleasure is the pleasantest. He who has a right to judge judges thus. Next comes the life of ambition, and, in the third place, that of money-making.

Twice has the just man overthrown the unjust—once more, as in an Olympian contest, first offering up a prayer to the saviour Zeus, let him try a fall. A wise man whispers to me that the pleasures of the wise are true and pure; all others are a shadow only. Let us examine this: Is not pleasure opposed to pain, and is there not a mean state which is neither? When a man is sick, nothing is more pleasant to him than health. But this he never found out while he was well. In pain he desires only to cease from pain; on the other hand, when he is in an ecstasy of pleasure, rest is painful to him. Thus rest or cessation is both pleasure and pain. But can that which is neither become both? Again, pleasure and pain are motions, and the absence of them is rest; but if so, how can the absence of either of them be the other? Thus we are led to infer that the contradiction is an appearance only, and witchery of the senses. And these are not the only pleasures, for there are others which have no preceding pains. Pure pleasure then is not the absence of pain, nor pure pain the absence of pleasure; although most of the pleasures which reach the mind through the body are reliefs of pain, and have not only their reactions when they depart, but their anticipations before they come. They can be best described in a simile. There is in nature an upper, lower, and middle region, and he who passes from the lower to the middle imagines that he is going up and is already in the upper world; and if he were taken back again would think, and truly think, that he was descending. All this arises out of his ignorance of the true upper, middle, and lower regions. And a like confusion happens with pleasure and pain, and with many other things. The man who compares grey with black, calls grey white; and the man who compares absence of pain with pain, calls the absence of pain pleasure. Again, hunger and thirst are inanitions of the body, ignorance and folly of the soul; and food is the satisfaction of the one, knowledge of the other. Now which is the purer satisfaction—that of eating and drinking, or that of knowledge? Consider the matter thus: The satisfaction of that which has more existence is truer than of that which has less. The invariable and immortal has a more real existence than the variable and mortal, and has a corresponding measure of knowledge and truth. The soul, again, has more existence and truth and knowledge than the body, and is therefore more really satisfied and has a more natural pleasure. Those who feast only on earthly food, are always going at random up to the middle and down again; but they never pass into the true upper world, or have a taste of true pleasure. They are like fatted beasts, full of gluttony and sensuality, and ready to kill one another by reason of their insatiable lust; for they are not filled with true being, and their vessel is leaky (Gorgias). Their pleasures are mere shadows of pleasure, mixed with pain, coloured and intensified by contrast, and therefore intensely desired; and men go fighting about them, as Stesichorus says that the Greeks fought about the shadow of Helen at Troy, because they know not the truth.

The same may be said of the passionate element:—the desires of the ambitious soul, as well as of the covetous, have an inferior satisfaction. Only when under the guidance of reason do either of the other principles do their own business or attain the pleasure which is natural to them. When not attaining, they compel the other parts of the soul to pursue a shadow of pleasure which is not theirs. And the more distant they are from philosophy and reason, the more distant they will be from law and order, and the more illusive will be their pleasures. The desires of love and tyranny are the farthest from law, and those of the king are nearest to it. There is one genuine pleasure, and two spurious ones: the tyrant goes beyond even the latter; he has run away altogether from law and reason. Nor can the measure of his inferiority be told, except in a figure. The tyrant is the third removed from the oligarch, and has therefore, not a shadow of his pleasure, but the shadow of a shadow only. The oligarch, again, is thrice removed from the king, and thus we get the formula 3×3, which is the number of a surface, representing the shadow which is the tyrant's pleasure, and if you like to cube this 'number of the beast,' you will find that the measure of the difference amounts to 729; the king is 729 times more happy than the tyrant. And this extraordinary number is NEARLY equal to the number of days and nights in a year ($365 \times 2 = 730$); and is therefore concerned with human life. This is the interval between a good and bad man in happiness only: what must be the difference between them in comeliness of life and virtue!

Perhaps you may remember some one saying at the beginning of our discussion that the unjust man was profited if he had the reputation of justice. Now that we know the nature of justice and injustice, let us make an image of the soul, which will personify his words. First of all, fashion a multitudinous beast, having a ring of heads of all manner of animals, tame and wild, and able to produce and change them at pleasure. Suppose now another form of a lion, and another of a man; the second smaller than the first, the third than the second; join them together and cover them with a human skin, in which they are completely concealed. When this has been done, let us tell the supporter of injustice that he is feeding up the beasts and starving the man. The maintainer of justice, on the other hand, is trying to strengthen the man; he is nourishing the gentle principle within him, and making an alliance with the lion heart, in order that he may be able to keep down the many-headed hydra, and bring all into unity with each other and with themselves. Thus in every point of view, whether in relation to pleasure, honour, or advantage, the just man is right, and the unjust wrong.

But now, let us reason with the unjust, who is not intentionally in error. Is not the noble that which subjects the beast to the man, or rather to the God in man; the ignoble, that which subjects the man to the beast? And if so, who would receive gold on condition that he was to degrade the noblest part of himself under the worst?—who would sell his son or daughter into the hands of brutal and evil men, for any amount of money? And will he sell his own fairer and diviner part without any compunction to the most godless and foul? Would he not be worse than Eriphyle, who sold her husband's life for a necklace? And intemperance is the letting loose of the multiform monster, and pride and sullenness are the growth and increase of the lion and serpent element, while luxury and effeminacy are caused by a too great relaxation of spirit. Flattery and meanness again arise when the spirited element is subjected to avarice, and the lion is habituated to become a monkey. The real disgrace of handicraft arts is, that those who are engaged in them have to flatter, instead of mastering their desires; therefore we say that they should be placed under the control of the better principle in another because they have none in themselves; not, as Thrasymachus imagined, to the injury of the subjects, but for their good. And our intention in educating the young, is to give them self-control; the law desires to nurse up in them a higher principle, and when they have acquired this, they may go their ways.

'What, then, shall a man profit, if he gain the whole world' and become more and more wicked? Or what shall he profit by escaping discovery, if the concealment of evil prevents the cure? If he had been punished, the brute within him would have been silenced, and the gentler element liberated; and he would have united temperance, justice, and wisdom in his soul—a union better far than any combination of bodily gifts. The man of understanding will honour knowledge above all; in the next place he will keep under his body, not only for the sake of health and strength, but in order to attain the most perfect harmony of body and soul. In the acquisition of riches, too, he will aim at order and harmony; he will not desire to heap up wealth without measure, but he will fear that the increase of wealth will disturb the constitution of his own soul. For the same reason he will only accept such honours as will make him a better man; any others he will decline. 'In that case,' said he, 'he will never be a politician.' Yes, but he will, in his own city; though probably not in his native country, unless by some divine accident. 'You mean that he will be a citizen of the ideal city, which has no place upon earth.' But in heaven, I replied, there is a pattern of such a city, and he who wishes may order his life after that image. Whether such a state is or ever will be matters not; he will act according to that pattern and no other...

The most noticeable points in the 9th Book of the Republic are:—(1) the account of pleasure; (2) the number of the interval which divides the king from the tyrant; (3) the pattern which is in heaven.

1. Plato's account of pleasure is remarkable for moderation, and in this respect contrasts with the later Platonists and the views which are attributed to them by Aristotle. He is not, like the Cynics, opposed to all pleasure, but rather desires that the several parts of the soul shall have their natural satisfaction; he even agrees with the Epicureans in describing pleasure as something more than the absence of pain. This is proved by the circumstance that there are pleasures which have no antecedent pains (as he also remarks in the Philebus), such as the pleasures of smell, and also the pleasures of hope and anticipation. In the previous book he had made the distinction between necessary and unnecessary pleasure, which

is repeated by Aristotle, and he now observes that there are a further class of 'wild beast' pleasures, corresponding to Aristotle's (Greek). He dwells upon the relative and unreal character of sensual pleasures and the illusion which arises out of the contrast of pleasure and pain, pointing out the superiority of the pleasures of reason, which are at rest, over the fleeting pleasures of sense and emotion. The pre-eminence of royal pleasure is shown by the fact that reason is able to form a judgment of the lower pleasures, while the two lower parts of the soul are incapable of judging the pleasures of reason. Thus, in his treatment of pleasure, as in many other subjects, the philosophy of Plato is 'sawn up into quantities' by Aristotle; the analysis which was originally made by him became in the next generation the foundation of further technical distinctions. Both in Plato and Aristotle we note the illusion under which the ancients fell of regarding the transience of pleasure as a proof of its unreality, and of confounding the permanence of the intellectual pleasures with the unchangeableness of the knowledge from which they are derived. Neither do we like to admit that the pleasures of knowledge, though more elevating, are not more lasting than other pleasures, and are almost equally dependent on the accidents of our bodily state (Introduction to Philebus).

2. The number of the interval which separates the king from the tyrant, and royal from tyrannical pleasures, is 729, the cube of 9. Which Plato characteristically designates as a number concerned with human life, because NEARLY equivalent to the number of days and nights in the year. He is desirous of proclaiming that the interval between them is immeasurable, and invents a formula to give expression to his idea. Those who spoke of justice as a cube, of virtue as an art of measuring (Prot.), saw no inappropriateness in conceiving the soul under the figure of a line, or the pleasure of the tyrant as separated from the pleasure of the king by the numerical interval of 729. And in modern times we sometimes use metaphorically what Plato employed as a philosophical formula. 'It is not easy to estimate the loss of the tyrant, except perhaps in this way,' says Plato. So we might say, that although the life of a good man is not to be compared to that of a bad man, yet you may measure the difference between them

by valuing one minute of the one at an hour of the other ('One day in thy courts is better than a thousand'), or you might say that 'there is an infinite difference.' But this is not so much as saying, in homely phrase, 'They are a thousand miles asunder.' And accordingly Plato finds the natural vehicle of his thoughts in a progression of numbers; this arithmetical formula he draws out with the utmost seriousness, and both here and in the number of generation seems to find an additional proof of the truth of his speculation in forming the number into a geometrical figure; just as persons in our own day are apt to fancy that a statement is verified when it has been only thrown into an abstract form. In speaking of the number 729 as proper to human life, he probably intended to intimate that one year of the tyrannical = 12 hours of the royal life.

The simple observation that the comparison of two similar solids is effected by the comparison of the cubes of their sides, is the mathematical groundwork of this fanciful expression. There is some difficulty in explaining the steps by which the number 729 is obtained; the oligarch is removed in the third degree from the royal and aristocratical, and the tyrant in the third degree from the oligarchical; but we have to arrange the terms as the sides of a square and to count the oligarch twice over, thus reckoning them not as = 5 but as = 9. The square of 9 is passed lightly over as only a step towards the cube.

3. Towards the close of the Republic, Plato seems to be more and more convinced of the ideal character of his own speculations. At the end of the 9th Book the pattern which is in heaven takes the place of the city of philosophers on earth. The vision which has received form and substance at his hands, is now discovered to be at a distance. And yet this distant kingdom is also the rule of man's life. ('Say not lo! here, or lo! there, for the kingdom of God is within you.') Thus a note is struck which prepares for the revelation of a future life in the following Book. But the future life is present still; the ideal of politics is to be realized in the individual.

Book X - Introduction & Analysis
Recompense of Life

Many things pleased me in the order of our State, but there was nothing which I liked better than the regulation about poetry. The division of the soul throws a new light on our exclusion of imitation. I do not mind telling you in confidence that all poetry is an outrage on the understanding, unless the hearers have that balm of knowledge which heals error. I have loved Homer ever since I was a boy, and even now he appears to me to be the great master of tragic poetry. But much as I love the man, I love truth more, and therefore I must speak out: and first of all, will you explain what is imitation, for really I do not understand? 'How likely then that I should understand!' That might very well be, for the duller often sees better than the keener eye. 'True, but in your presence I can hardly venture to say what I think.' Then suppose that we begin in our old fashion, with the doctrine of universals. Let us assume the existence of beds and tables. There is one idea of a bed, or of a table, which the maker of each had in his mind when making them; he did not make the ideas of beds and tables, but he made beds and tables according to the ideas. And is there not a maker of the works of all workmen, who makes not only vessels but plants and animals, himself, the earth and heaven, and things in heaven and under the earth? He makes the Gods also. 'He must be a wizard indeed!' But do you not see that there is a sense in which you could do the same? You have only to take a mirror, and catch the reflection of the sun, and the earth, or anything else—there now you have made them. 'Yes, but only in appearance.' Exactly so; and the painter is such a creator as you are with the mirror, and he is even more unreal than the carpenter; although neither the carpenter nor any other artist can be supposed to make the absolute bed. 'Not if philosophers may be believed.' Nor need we wonder that his bed has but an imperfect relation to the truth. Reflect:—Here are three beds; one in nature, which is made by God; another, which is made by the carpenter; and the third, by the painter. God only made one, nor could he have made more than one; for if there had been two, there would always have been a third—more absolute and abstract than either, under which they would have been included. We may therefore conceive God to be the natural maker of the bed, and in a lower sense the carpenter is also the maker; but the painter is rather the imitator of what the other two make; he has to do with a creation which is thrice removed from reality. And the tragic poet is an imitator, and, like every other imitator, is thrice removed from the king and from the truth. The painter imitates not the original bed, but the bed made by the carpenter. And this, without being really different, appears to be different, and has many points of view, of which only one is caught by the painter, who represents everything because he represents a piece of everything, and that piece an image. And he can paint any other artist, although he knows nothing of their arts; and this with sufficient skill to deceive children or simple people. Suppose now that somebody came to us and told us, how he had met a man who knew all that everybody knows, and better than anybody:—should we not infer him to be a simpleton who, having no discernment of truth and falsehood, had met with a wizard or enchanter, whom he fancied to be all-wise? And when we hear persons saying that Homer and the tragedians know all the arts and all the virtues, must we not infer that they are under a similar delusion? they do not see that the poets are imitators, and that their creations are only imitations. 'Very true.' But if a person could create as well as imitate, he would rather leave some permanent work and not an imitation only; he would rather be the receiver than the giver of praise? 'Yes, for then he would have more honour and advantage.'

Let us now interrogate Homer and the poets. Friend Homer, say I to him, I am not going to ask you about medicine, or any art to which your poems incidentally refer, but about their main subjects—war, military tactics, politics. If you are only twice and not thrice removed from the truth—not an imitator or an image-maker, please to inform us what good you have ever done to mankind? Is there any city which professes to have received laws from you, as Sicily and Italy have from Charondas, Sparta from Lycurgus, Athens from Solon? Or was any war ever carried on by your counsels? or is any invention attributed to you, as there is to Thales and Anacharsis? Or is there any Homeric way of life, such as the Pythagorean was, in which you instructed men, and which is called after you? 'No, indeed; and Creophylus (Flesh-child) was even more unfortunate in his breeding than he was in his name, if, as tradition says, Homer in his lifetime was allowed by him and his other friends to starve.' Yes, but could this ever have happened if Homer had really been the educator of Hellas? Would he not have had many devoted followers? If Protagoras and Prodicus can persuade their contemporaries that no one can manage house or State without them, is it likely that Homer and Hesiod would have been allowed to go about as beggars—I mean if they had really been able to do the world any good?—would not men have compelled them to stay where they were, or have followed them about in order to get education? But they did not; and therefore we may infer that Homer and all the poets are only imitators, who do but imitate the appearances of things. For as a painter by a knowledge of figure and colour can paint a cobbler without any practice in cobbling, so the poet can delineate any art in the colours of language, and give harmony and rhythm to the cobbler and also to the general; and you know how mere narration, when deprived of the ornaments of metre, is like a face which has lost the beauty of youth and never had any other. Once more, the imitator has no knowledge of reality, but only of appearance. The painter paints, and the artificer makes a bridle and reins, but neither understands the use of them—the knowledge of this is confined to the horseman; and so of other things. Thus we have three arts: one of use, another of invention, a third of imitation; and the user furnishes the rule to the two others. The flute-player will know the good and bad flute, and the maker will put faith in him; but the imitator will neither know nor have faith—neither science nor true opinion can be ascribed to him. Imitation, then, is devoid of knowledge, being only a kind of play or sport, and the tragic and epic poets are imitators in the highest degree.

And now let us enquire, what is the faculty in man which answers to imitation. Allow me to explain my meaning: Objects are differently seen when in the water and when out of the water, when near and when at a distance; and the painter or juggler makes use of this variation to impose upon us. And the art of measuring and weighing and calculating comes in to save our bewildered minds from the power of appearance; for, as we were saying, two contrary opinions of the same about the same and at the same time, cannot both of them be true. But which of them is true is determined by the art of calculation; and this is allied to the better faculty in the soul, as the arts of imitation are to the worse. And the same holds of the ear as well as of the eye, of poetry as well as painting. The imitation is of actions voluntary or involuntary, in which there is an expectation of a good or bad result, and present experience of pleasure and pain. But is a man in harmony with himself when he is the subject of these conflicting influences? Is there not rather a contradiction in him? Let me further ask, whether he is more likely to control sorrow when he is alone or when he is in company. 'In the latter case.' Feeling would lead him to indulge his sorrow, but reason and law control him and enjoin patience; since he cannot know whether his affliction is good or evil, and no human thing is of any great consequence, while sorrow is certainly a hindrance to good counsel. For when we stumble, we should not, like children, make an uproar; we should take the measures which reason prescribes, not raising a lament, but finding a cure. And the better part of us is ready to follow reason, while the irrational principle is full of sorrow and distraction at the recollection of our troubles. Unfortunately, however, this latter furnishes the chief materials of the imitative arts. Whereas reason is ever in repose and cannot easily be displayed, especially to a mixed multitude who have no experience of her. Thus the poet is like the painter in two ways: first he paints an inferior degree of truth, and secondly, he is concerned with an inferior part of the soul. He indulges the feelings, while he enfeebles the reason; and we refuse to allow him to have authority over the mind of man; for he has no measure of greater and less, and is a maker of images and very far gone from truth.

But we have not yet mentioned the heaviest count in the indictment—the power which poetry has of injuriously exciting the feelings. When we hear some passage in which a hero laments his sufferings at tedious length, you know that we sympathize with him and praise the poet; and yet in our own sorrows such an exhibition of feeling is regarded as effeminate and unmanly (Ion). Now, ought a man to feel pleasure in seeing another do what he hates and abominates in himself? Is he not giving way to a sentiment which in his own case he would control?—he is off his guard because the sorrow is another's; and he thinks that he may indulge his feelings without disgrace, and will be the gainer by the pleasure. But the inevitable consequence is that he who begins by weeping at the sorrows of others, will end by weeping at his own. The same is true of comedy,—you may often laugh at buffoonery which you would be ashamed to utter, and the love of coarse merriment on the stage will at last turn you into a buffoon at home. Poetry feeds and waters the passions and desires; she lets them rule instead of ruling them. And therefore, when we hear the encomiasts of Homer affirming that he is the educator of Hellas, and that all life should be regulated by his precepts, we may allow the excellence of their intentions, and agree with them in thinking Homer a great poet and tragedian. But we shall continue to prohibit all poetry which goes beyond hymns to the Gods and praises of famous men. Not pleasure and pain, but law and reason shall rule in our State.

These are our grounds for expelling poetry; but lest she should charge us with discourtesy, let us also make an apology to her. We will remind her that there is an ancient quarrel between poetry and philosophy, of which there are many traces in the writings of the poets, such as the saying of 'the she-dog, yelping at her mistress,' and 'the philosophers who are ready to circumvent Zeus,' and 'the philosophers who are paupers.' Nevertheless we bear her no ill-will, and will gladly allow her to return upon condition that she makes a defence of herself in verse; and her supporters who are not poets may speak in prose. We confess her charms; but if she cannot show that she is useful as well as delightful, like rational lovers, we must renounce our love, though endeared to us by early associations. Having come to years of discretion, we know that poetry is not truth, and that a man should be careful how he introduces her to that state or constitution which he himself is; for there is a mighty issue at stake—no less than the good or evil of a human soul. And it is not worth while to forsake justice and virtue for the attractions of poetry, any more than for the sake of honour or wealth. 'I agree with you.'

And yet the rewards of virtue are greater far than I have described. 'And can we conceive things greater still?' Not, perhaps, in this brief span of life: but should an immortal being care about anything short of eternity? 'I do not understand what you mean?' Do you not know that the soul is immortal? 'Surely you are not prepared to prove that?' Indeed I am. 'Then let me hear this argument, of which you make so light.'

You would admit that everything has an element of good and of evil. In all things there is an inherent corruption; and if this cannot destroy them, nothing else will. The soul too has her own corrupting principles, which are injustice, intemperance, cowardice, and the like. But none of these destroy the soul in the same sense that disease destroys the body. The soul may be full of all iniquities, but is not, by reason of them, brought any nearer to death. Nothing which was not destroyed from within ever perished by external affection of evil. The body, which is one thing, cannot be destroyed by food, which is another, unless the badness of the food is communicated to the body. Neither can the soul, which is one thing, be corrupted by the body, which is another, unless she herself is infected. And as no bodily evil can infect the soul, neither can any bodily evil, whether disease or violence, or any other destroy the soul, unless it can be shown to render her unholy and unjust. But no one will ever prove that the souls of men become more unjust when they die. If a person has the audacity to say the contrary, the answer is—Then why do criminals require the hand of the

executioner, and not die of themselves? 'Truly,' he said, 'injustice would
not be very terrible if it brought a cessation of evil; but I rather believe that
the injustice which murders others may tend to quicken and stimulate the
life of the unjust.' You are quite right. If sin which is her own natural and
inherent evil cannot destroy the soul, hardly will anything else destroy her.
But the soul which cannot be destroyed either by internal or external evil
must be immortal and everlasting. And if this be true, souls will always
exist in the same number. They cannot diminish, because they cannot be
destroyed; nor yet increase, for the increase of the immortal must come
from something mortal, and so all would end in immortality. Neither is
the soul variable and diverse; for that which is immortal must be of the
fairest and simplest composition. If we would conceive her truly, and so
behold justice and injustice in their own nature, she must be viewed by the
light of reason pure as at birth, or as she is reflected in philosophy when
holding converse with the divine and immortal and eternal. In her present
condition we see her only like the sea-god Glaucus, bruised and maimed
in the sea which is the world, and covered with shells and stones which are
incrusted upon her from the entertainments of earth.

Thus far, as the argument required, we have said nothing of the rewards
and honours which the poets attribute to justice; we have contented
ourselves with showing that justice in herself is best for the soul in herself,
even if a man should put on a Gyges' ring and have the helmet of Hades too.
And now you shall repay me what you borrowed; and I will enumerate the
rewards of justice in life and after death. I granted, for the sake of argument,
as you will remember, that evil might perhaps escape the knowledge of
Gods and men, although this was really impossible. And since I have
shown that justice has reality, you must grant me also that she has the palm
of appearance. In the first place, the just man is known to the Gods, and he
is therefore the friend of the Gods, and he will receive at their hands every
good, always excepting such evil as is the necessary consequence of former
sins. All things end in good to him, either in life or after death, even what
appears to be evil; for the Gods have a care of him who desires to be in their
likeness. And what shall we say of men? Is not honesty the best policy? The

clever rogue makes a great start at first, but breaks down before he reaches the goal, and slinks away in dishonour; whereas the true runner perseveres to the end, and receives the prize. And you must allow me to repeat all the blessings which you attributed to the fortunate unjust—they bear rule in the city, they marry and give in marriage to whom they will; and the evils which you attributed to the unfortunate just, do really fall in the end on the unjust, although, as you implied, their sufferings are better veiled in silence.

But all the blessings of this present life are as nothing when compared with those which await good men after death. 'I should like to hear about them.' Come, then, and I will tell you the story of Er, the son of Armenius, a valiant man. He was supposed to have died in battle, but ten days afterwards his body was found untouched by corruption and sent home for burial. On the twelfth day he was placed on the funeral pyre and there he came to life again, and told what he had seen in the world below. He said that his soul went with a great company to a place, in which there were two chasms near together in the earth beneath, and two corresponding chasms in the heaven above. And there were judges sitting in the intermediate space, bidding the just ascend by the heavenly way on the right hand, having the seal of their judgment set upon them before, while the unjust, having the seal behind, were bidden to descend by the way on the left hand. Him they told to look and listen, as he was to be their messenger to men from the world below. And he beheld and saw the souls departing after judgment at either chasm; some who came from earth, were worn and travel-stained; others, who came from heaven, were clean and bright. They seemed glad to meet and rest awhile in the meadow; here they discoursed with one another of what they had seen in the other world. Those who came from earth wept at the remembrance of their sorrows, but the spirits from above spoke of glorious sights and heavenly bliss. He said that for every evil deed they were punished tenfold—now the journey was of a thousand years' duration, because the life of man was reckoned as a hundred years—and the rewards of virtue were in the same proportion. He added something hardly worth repeating about infants dying almost as soon as they were born. Of parricides and other murderers he had tortures still more terrible to narrate. He was present when one of the spirits asked—Where is Ardiaeus the Great? (This Ardiaeus was a cruel tyrant, who had murdered his father, and his elder brother, a thousand years before.) Another spirit answered, 'He comes not hither, and will never come. And I myself,' he added, 'actually saw this terrible sight. At the entrance of the chasm, as we were about to reascend, Ardiaeus appeared, and some other sinners—most of whom had been tyrants, but not all—and just as they fancied that they were returning to life, the chasm gave a roar, and then wild, fiery-looking men who knew the meaning of the sound, seized him and several others, and bound them hand and foot and threw them down, and dragged them along at the side of the road, lacerating them and carding them like wool, and explaining to the passers-by, that they were going to be cast into hell.' The greatest terror of the pilgrims ascending was lest they should hear the voice, and when there was silence one by one they passed up with joy. To these sufferings there were corresponding delights.

On the eighth day the souls of the pilgrims resumed their journey, and in four days came to a spot whence they looked down upon a line of light, in colour like a rainbow, only brighter and clearer. One day more brought them to the place, and they saw that this was the column of light which binds together the whole universe. The ends of the column were fastened to heaven, and from them hung the distaff of Necessity, on which all the heavenly bodies turned—the hook and spindle were of adamant, and the whorl of a mixed substance. The whorl was in form like a number of boxes fitting into one another with their edges turned upwards, making together a single whorl which was pierced by the spindle. The outermost had the rim broadest, and the inner whorls were smaller and smaller, and had their rims narrower. The largest (the fixed stars) was spangled—the seventh (the sun) was brightest—the eighth (the moon) shone by the light of the seventh—the second and fifth (Saturn and Mercury) were most like one another and yellower than the eighth—the third (Jupiter) had the whitest light—the fourth (Mars) was red—the sixth (Venus) was in whiteness second. The whole had one motion, but while this was revolving in one direction the seven inner circles were moving in the opposite, with various degrees of swiftness and slowness. The spindle turned on the knees of Necessity, and a Siren stood hymning upon each circle, while Lachesis, Clotho, and Atropos, the daughters of Necessity, sat on thrones at equal intervals, singing of past, present, and future, responsive to the music of the Sirens; Clotho from time to time guiding the outer circle with a touch of her right hand; Atropos with her left hand touching and guiding the inner circles; Lachesis in turn putting forth her hand from time to time to guide both of them. On their arrival the pilgrims went to Lachesis, and there was an interpreter who arranged them, and taking from her knees lots, and samples of lives, got up into a pulpit and said: 'Mortal souls, hear the words of Lachesis, the daughter of Necessity. A new period of mortal life has begun, and you may choose what divinity you please; the responsibility of choosing is with you—God is blameless.' After speaking thus, he cast the lots among them and each one took up the lot which fell near him. He then placed on the ground before them the samples of lives, many more than the souls present; and there were all sorts of lives, of men and of animals. There were tyrannies ending in misery and exile, and lives of men and women famous for their different qualities; and also mixed lives, made up of wealth and poverty, sickness and health. Here, Glaucon, is the great risk of human life, and therefore the whole of education should be directed to the acquisition of such a knowledge as will teach a man to refuse the evil and choose the good. He should know all the combinations which occur in life—of beauty with poverty or with wealth,—of knowledge with external goods,—and at last choose with reference to the nature of the soul, regarding that only as the better life which makes men better, and leaving the rest. And a man must take with him an iron sense of truth and right into the world below, that there too he may remain undazzled by wealth or the allurements of evil, and be determined to avoid the extremes and choose the mean. For this, as the messenger reported the interpreter to have said, is the true happiness of man; and any one, as he proclaimed, may, if he choose with understanding, have a good lot, even though he come last.

'Let not the first be careless in his choice, nor the last despair.' He spoke; and when he had spoken, he who had drawn the first lot chose a tyranny: he did not see that he was fated to devour his own children—and when he discovered his mistake, he wept and beat his breast, blaming chance and the Gods and anybody rather than himself. He was one of those who had come from heaven, and in his previous life had been a citizen of a well-ordered State, but he had only habit and no philosophy. Like many another, he made a bad choice, because he had no experience of life; whereas those who came from earth and had seen trouble were not in such a hurry to choose. But if a man had followed philosophy while upon earth, and had been moderately fortunate in his lot, he might not only be happy here, but his pilgrimage both from and to this world would be smooth and heavenly. Nothing was more curious than the spectacle of the choice, at once sad and laughable and wonderful; most of the souls only seeking to avoid their own condition in a previous life. He saw the soul of Orpheus changing into a swan because he would not be born of a woman; there was Thamyras becoming a nightingale; musical birds, like the swan, choosing to be men; the twentieth soul, which was that of Ajax, preferring the life of a lion to that of a man, in remembrance of the injustice which was done to him in the judgment of the arms; and Agamemnon, from a like enmity to human nature, passing into an eagle. About the middle was the soul of Atalanta choosing the honours of an athlete, and next to her Epeus taking the nature of a workwoman; among the last was Thersites, who was changing himself into a monkey. Thither, the last of all, came Odysseus, and sought the lot of a private man, which lay neglected and despised, and when he found it he went away rejoicing, and said that if he had been first instead of last, his choice would have been the same. Men, too, were seen passing into animals, and wild and tame animals changing into one another.

When all the souls had chosen they went to Lachesis, who sent with each of them their genius or attendant to fulfil their lot. He first of all brought them under the hand of Clotho, and drew them within the revolution of the spindle impelled by her hand; from her they were carried to Atropos, who made the threads irreversible; whence, without turning round, they passed beneath the throne of Necessity; and when they had all passed, they moved on in scorching heat to the plain of Forgetfulness and rested at evening by the river Unmindful, whose water could not be retained in any vessel; of this they had all to drink a certain quantity—some of them drank more than was required, and he who drank forgot all things. Er himself was prevented from drinking. When they had gone to rest, about the middle of the night there were thunderstorms and earthquakes, and suddenly they were all driven divers ways, shooting like stars to their birth. Concerning his return to the body, he only knew that awaking suddenly in the morning he found himself lying on the pyre.

Thus, Glaucon, the tale has been saved, and will be our salvation, if we believe that the soul is immortal, and hold fast to the heavenly way of Justice and Knowledge. So shall we pass undefiled over the river of Forgetfulness, and be dear to ourselves and to the Gods, and have a crown of reward and happiness both in this world and also in the millennial pilgrimage of the other.

The Tenth Book of the Republic of Plato falls into two divisions: first, resuming an old thread which has been interrupted, Socrates assails the poets, who, now that the nature of the soul has been analyzed, are seen to be very far gone from the truth; and secondly, having shown the reality of the happiness of the just, he demands that appearance shall be restored to him, and then proceeds to prove the immortality of the soul. The argument, as in the Phaedo and Gorgias, is supplemented by the vision of a future life.

Why Plato, who was himself a poet, and whose dialogues are poems and dramas, should have been hostile to the poets as a class, and especially to the dramatic poets; why he should not have seen that truth may be embodied in verse as well as in prose, and that there are some indefinable lights and shadows of human life which can only be expressed in poetry—some elements of imagination which always entwine with reason; why he should have supposed epic verse to be inseparably associated with the impurities of the old Hellenic mythology; why he should try Homer and Hesiod by the unfair and prosaic test of utility,—are questions which have always been debated amongst students of Plato. Though unable to give a complete answer to them, we may show—first, that his views arose naturally out of the circumstances of his age; and secondly, we may elicit the truth as well as the error which is contained in them.

He is the enemy of the poets because poetry was declining in his own lifetime, and a theatrocracy, as he says in the Laws, had taken the place of an intellectual aristocracy. Euripides exhibited the last phase of the tragic drama, and in him Plato saw the friend and apologist of tyrants, and the Sophist of tragedy. The old comedy was almost extinct; the new had not yet arisen. Dramatic and lyric poetry, like every other branch of Greek literature, was falling under the power of rhetoric. There was no 'second or third' to Aeschylus and Sophocles in the generation which followed them. Aristophanes, in one of his later comedies (Frogs), speaks of 'thousands of tragedy-making prattlers,' whose attempts at poetry he compares to the chirping of swallows; 'their garrulity went far beyond Euripides,'—'they appeared once upon the stage, and there was an end of them.' To a man of genius who had a real appreciation of the godlike Aeschylus and the noble and gentle Sophocles, though disagreeing with some parts of their 'theology' (Rep.), these 'minor poets' must have been contemptible and intolerable. There is no feeling stronger in the dialogues of Plato than a sense of the decline and decay both in literature and in politics which marked his own age. Nor can he have been expected to look with favour on the licence of Aristophanes, now at the end of his career, who had begun by satirizing Socrates in the Clouds, and in a similar spirit forty years afterwards had satirized the founders of ideal commonwealths in his Eccleziazusae, or Female Parliament (Laws).

There were other reasons for the antagonism of Plato to poetry. The profession of an actor was regarded by him as a degradation of human nature, for 'one man in his life' cannot 'play many parts;' the characters which the actor performs seem to destroy his own character, and to leave nothing which can be truly called himself. Neither can any man live his life and act it. The actor is the slave of his art, not the master of it. Taking this view Plato is more decided in his expulsion of the dramatic than of the epic poets, though he must have known that the Greek tragedians afforded noble lessons and examples of virtue and patriotism, to which nothing in Homer can be compared. But great dramatic or even great rhetorical power is hardly consistent with firmness or strength of mind, and dramatic talent is often incidentally associated with a weak or dissolute character.

In the Tenth Book Plato introduces a new series of objections. First, he says that the poet or painter is an imitator, and in the third degree removed from the truth. His creations are not tested by rule and measure; they are only appearances. In modern times we should say that art is not merely imitation, but rather the expression of the ideal in forms of sense. Even adopting the humble image of Plato, from which his argument derives a colour, we should maintain that the artist may ennoble the bed which he paints by the folds of the drapery, or by the feeling of home which he introduces; and there have been modern painters who have imparted such an ideal interest to a blacksmith's or a carpenter's shop. The eye or mind which feels as well as sees can give dignity and pathos to a ruined mill, or a straw-built shed (Rembrandt), to the hull of a vessel 'going to its last home' (Turner). Still more would this apply to the greatest works of art, which seem to be the visible embodiment of the divine. Had Plato been asked whether the Zeus or Athene of Pheidias was the imitation of an imitation only, would he not have been compelled to admit that something more was to be found in them than in the form of any mortal; and that the rule of proportion to which they conformed was 'higher far than any geometry or arithmetic could express?' (Statesman.)

Again, Plato objects to the imitative arts that they express the emotional rather than the rational part of human nature. He does not admit Aristotle's theory, that tragedy or other serious imitations are a purgation of the passions by pity and fear; to him they appear only to afford the opportunity of indulging them. Yet we must acknowledge that we may sometimes cure disordered emotions by giving expression to them; and that they often gain strength when pent up within our own breast. It is not every indulgence of the feelings which is to be condemned. For there may be a gratification of the higher as well as of the lower—thoughts which are too deep or too sad to be expressed by ourselves, may find an utterance in the words of poets. Every one would acknowledge that there have been times when they were consoled and elevated by beautiful music or by the sublimity of architecture or by the peacefulness of nature. Plato has himself admitted, in the earlier part of the Republic, that the arts might have the effect of harmonizing as well as of enervating the mind; but in the Tenth Book he regards them through a Stoic or Puritan medium. He asks only 'What good have they done?' and is not satisfied with the reply, that 'They have given innocent pleasure to mankind.'

He tells us that he rejoices in the banishment of the poets, since he has found by the analysis of the soul that they are concerned with the inferior faculties. He means to say that the higher faculties have to do with universals, the lower with particulars of sense. The poets are on a level with their own age, but not on a level with Socrates and Plato; and he was well aware that Homer and Hesiod could not be made a rule of life by any process of legitimate interpretation; his ironical use of them is in fact a denial of their authority; he saw, too, that the poets were not critics—as he says in the Apology, 'Any one was a better interpreter of their writings than they were themselves. He himself ceased to be a poet when he became a disciple of Socrates; though, as he tells us of Solon, 'he might have been one of the greatest of them, if he had not been deterred by other pursuits' (Tim.) Thus from many points of view there is an antagonism between Plato and the poets, which was foreshadowed to him in the old quarrel between philosophy and poetry. The poets, as he says in the Protagoras, were the Sophists of their day; and his dislike of the one class is reflected on the other. He regards them both as the enemies of reasoning and abstraction, though in the case of Euripides more with reference to his immoral sentiments about tyrants and the like. For Plato is the prophet who 'came into the world to convince men'—first of the fallibility of sense and opinion, and secondly of the reality of abstract ideas. Whatever strangeness there may be in modern times in opposing philosophy to poetry, which to us seem to have so many elements in common, the strangeness will disappear if we conceive of poetry as allied to sense, and of philosophy as equivalent to thought and abstraction. Unfortunately the very word 'idea,' which to Plato is expressive of the most real of all things, is associated in our minds with an element of subjectiveness and unreality. We may note also how he differs from Aristotle who declares poetry to be truer than history, for the opposite reason, because it is concerned with universals, not like history, with particulars (Poet).

The things which are seen are opposed in Scripture to the things which are unseen—they are equally opposed in Plato to universals and ideas. To him all particulars appear to be floating about in a world of sense; they have a taint of error or even of evil. There is no difficulty in seeing that this is an illusion; for there is no more error or variation in an individual man, horse, bed, etc., than in the class man, horse, bed, etc.; nor is the truth which is displayed in individual instances less certain than that which is conveyed through the medium of ideas. But Plato, who is deeply impressed with the real importance of universals as instruments of thought, attributes to them an essential truth which is imaginary and unreal; for universals may be often false and particulars true. Had he attained to any clear conception of the individual, which is the synthesis of the universal and the particular; or had he been able to distinguish between opinion and sensation, which the ambiguity of the words (Greek) and the like, tended to confuse, he would not have denied truth to the particulars of sense.

But the poets are also the representatives of falsehood and feigning in all departments of life and knowledge, like the sophists and rhetoricians of the Gorgias and Phaedrus; they are the false priests, false prophets, lying spirits, enchanters of the world. There is another count put into the indictment against them by Plato, that they are the friends of the tyrant, and bask in the sunshine of his patronage. Despotism in all ages has had an apparatus of false ideas and false teachers at its service—in the history of Modern Europe as well as of Greece and Rome. For no government of men depends solely upon force; without some corruption of literature and morals—some appeal to the imagination of the masses—some pretence to the favour of heaven—some element of good giving power to evil, tyranny, even for a short time, cannot be maintained. The Greek tyrants were not insensible to the importance of awakening in their cause a Pseudo-Hellenic feeling; they were proud of successes at the Olympic games; they were not devoid of the love of literature and art. Plato is thinking in the first instance of Greek poets who had graced the courts of Dionysius or Archelaus: and the old spirit of freedom is roused within him at their prostitution of the Tragic Muse in the praises of tyranny. But his prophetic eye extends beyond them to the false teachers of other ages who are the creatures of the government under which they live. He compares the corruption of his contemporaries with the idea of a perfect society, and gathers up into one mass of evil the evils and errors of mankind; to him they are personified in the rhetoricians, sophists, poets, rulers who deceive and govern the world.

A further objection which Plato makes to poetry and the imitative arts is that they excite the emotions. Here the modern reader will be disposed to introduce a distinction which appears to have escaped him. For the emotions are neither bad nor good in themselves, and are not most likely to be controlled by the attempt to eradicate them, but by the moderate indulgence of them. And the vocation of art is to present thought in the form of feeling, to enlist the feelings on the side of reason, to inspire even for a moment courage or resignation; perhaps to suggest a sense of infinity and eternity in a way which mere language is incapable of attaining. True, the same power which in the purer age of art embodies gods and heroes only, may be made to express the voluptuous image of a Corinthian courtezan. But this only shows that art, like other outward things, may be turned to good and also to evil, and is not more closely connected with the higher than with the lower part of the soul. All imitative art is subject to certain limitations, and therefore necessarily partakes of the nature of a compromise. Something of ideal truth is sacrificed for the sake of the representation, and something in the exactness of the representation is sacrificed to the ideal. Still, works of art have a permanent element; they idealize and detain the passing thought, and are the intermediates between sense and ideas.

In the present stage of the human mind, poetry and other forms of fiction may certainly be regarded as a good. But we can also imagine the existence of an age in which a severer conception of truth has either banished or transformed them. At any rate we must admit that they hold a different place at different periods of the world's history. In the infancy of mankind, poetry, with the exception of proverbs, is the whole of literature, and the only instrument of intellectual culture; in modern times she is the shadow or echo of her former self, and appears to have a precarious existence. Milton in his day doubted whether an epic poem was any longer possible. At the same time we must remember, that what Plato would have called the charms of poetry have been partly transferred to prose; he himself (Statesman) admits rhetoric to be the handmaiden of Politics, and proposes to find in the strain of law (Laws) a substitute for the old poets. Among ourselves the creative power seems often to be growing weaker, and scientific fact to be more engrossing and overpowering to the mind than formerly. The illusion of the feelings commonly called love, has hitherto been the inspiring influence of modern poetry and romance, and has exercised a humanizing if not a strengthening influence on the world. But may not the stimulus which love has given to fancy be some day exhausted? The modern English novel which is the most popular of all forms of reading is not more than a century or two old: will the tale of love a hundred years hence, after so many thousand variations of the same theme, be still received with unabated interest?

Art cannot claim to be on a level with philosophy or religion, and may often corrupt them. It is possible to conceive a mental state in which all artistic representations are regarded as a false and imperfect expression, either of the religious ideal or of the philosophical ideal. The fairest forms may be revolting in certain moods of mind, as is proved by the fact that the Mahometans, and many sects of Christians, have renounced the use of pictures and images. The beginning of a great religion, whether Christian or Gentile, has not been 'wood or stone,' but a spirit moving in the hearts of men. The disciples have met in a large upper room or in 'holes and caves of the earth'; in the second or third generation, they have had mosques, temples, churches, monasteries. And the revival or reform of religions,

like the first revelation of them, has come from within and has generally
disregarded external ceremonies and accompaniments.

But poetry and art may also be the expression of the highest truth and
the purest sentiment. Plato himself seems to waver between two opposite
views—when, as in the third Book, he insists that youth should be brought
up amid wholesome imagery; and again in Book X, when he banishes
the poets from his Republic. Admitting that the arts, which some of us
almost deify, have fallen short of their higher aim, we must admit on the
other hand that to banish imagination wholly would be suicidal as well
as impossible. For nature too is a form of art; and a breath of the fresh
air or a single glance at the varying landscape would in an instant revive
and reillumine the extinguished spark of poetry in the human breast. In
the lower stages of civilization imagination more than reason distinguishes
man from the animals; and to banish art would be to banish thought, to
banish language, to banish the expression of all truth. No religion is wholly
devoid of external forms; even the Mahometan who renounces the use of
pictures and images has a temple in which he worships the Most High, as
solemn and beautiful as any Greek or Christian building. Feeling too and
thought are not really opposed; for he who thinks must feel before he can
execute. And the highest thoughts, when they become familiarized to us,
are always tending to pass into the form of feeling.

Plato does not seriously intend to expel poets from life and society. But
he feels strongly the unreality of their writings; he is protesting against
the degeneracy of poetry in his own day as we might protest against the
want of serious purpose in modern fiction, against the unseemliness or
extravagance of some of our poets or novelists, against the time-serving
of preachers or public writers, against the regardlessness of truth which
to the eye of the philosopher seems to characterize the greater part of the
world. For we too have reason to complain that our poets and novelists
'paint inferior truth' and 'are concerned with the inferior part of the
soul'; that the readers of them become what they read and are injuriously
affected by them. And we look in vain for that healthy atmosphere of
which Plato speaks,—'the beauty which meets the sense like a breeze and

imperceptibly draws the soul, even in childhood, into harmony with the beauty of reason.'

For there might be a poetry which would be the hymn of divine perfection, the harmony of goodness and truth among men: a strain which should renew the youth of the world, and bring back the ages in which the poet was man's only teacher and best friend,—which would find materials in the living present as well as in the romance of the past, and might subdue to the fairest forms of speech and verse the intractable materials of modern civilisation,—which might elicit the simple principles, or, as Plato would have called them, the essential forms, of truth and justice out of the variety of opinion and the complexity of modern society,—which would preserve all the good of each generation and leave the bad unsung,—which should be based not on vain longings or faint imaginings, but on a clear insight into the nature of man. Then the tale of love might begin again in poetry or prose, two in one, united in the pursuit of knowledge, or the service of God and man; and feelings of love might still be the incentive to great thoughts and heroic deeds as in the days of Dante or Petrarch; and many types of manly and womanly beauty might appear among us, rising above the ordinary level of humanity, and many lives which were like poems (Laws), be not only written, but lived by us. A few such strains have been heard among men in the tragedies of Aeschylus and Sophocles, whom Plato quotes, not, as Homer is quoted by him, in irony, but with deep and serious approval,—in the poetry of Milton and Wordsworth, and in passages of other English poets,—first and above all in the Hebrew prophets and psalmists. Shakespeare has taught us how great men should speak and act; he has drawn characters of a wonderful purity and depth; he has ennobled the human mind, but, like Homer (Rep.), he 'has left no way of life.' The next greatest poet of modern times, Goethe, is concerned with 'a lower degree of truth'; he paints the world as a stage on which 'all the men and women are merely players'; he cultivates life as an art, but he furnishes no ideals of truth and action. The poet may rebel against any attempt to set limits to his fancy; and he may argue truly that moralizing in verse is not poetry. Possibly, like Mephistopheles in Faust, he may retaliate on his adversaries. But the philosopher will still be justified in asking, 'How may the heavenly gift of poesy be devoted to the good of mankind?'

Returning to Plato, we may observe that a similar mixture of truth and error appears in other parts of the argument. He is aware of the absurdity of mankind framing their whole lives according to Homer; just as in the Phaedrus he intimates the absurdity of interpreting mythology upon rational principles; both these were the modern tendencies of his own age, which he deservedly ridicules. On the other hand, his argument that Homer, if he had been able to teach mankind anything worth knowing, would not have been allowed by them to go about begging as a rhapsodist, is both false and contrary to the spirit of Plato (Rep.). It may be compared with those other paradoxes of the Gorgias, that 'No statesman was ever unjustly put to death by the city of which he was the head'; and that 'No Sophist was ever defrauded by his pupils' (Gorg.)...

The argument for immortality seems to rest on the absolute dualism of soul and body. Admitting the existence of the soul, we know of no force which is able to put an end to her. Vice is her own proper evil; and if she cannot be destroyed by that, she cannot be destroyed by any other. Yet Plato has acknowledged that the soul may be so overgrown by the incrustations of earth as to lose her original form; and in the Timaeus he recognizes more strongly than in the Republic the influence which the body has over the mind, denying even the voluntariness of human actions, on the ground that they proceed from physical states (Tim.). In the Republic, as elsewhere, he wavers between the original soul which has to be restored, and the character which is developed by training and education...

The vision of another world is ascribed to Er, the son of Armenius, who is said by Clement of Alexandria to have been Zoroaster. The tale has certainly an oriental character, and may be compared with the pilgrimages of the soul in the Zend Avesta (Haug, Avesta). But no trace of acquaintance with Zoroaster is found elsewhere in Plato's writings, and there is no reason for giving him the name of Er the Pamphylian. The philosophy of Heracleitus cannot be shown to be borrowed from Zoroaster, and still less the myths of Plato.

The local arrangement of the vision is less distinct than that of the Phaedrus and Phaedo. Astronomy is mingled with symbolism and mythology; the great sphere of heaven is represented under the symbol of a cylinder or box, containing the seven orbits of the planets and the fixed stars; this is suspended from an axis or spindle which turns on the knees of Necessity; the revolutions of the seven orbits contained in the cylinder are guided by the fates, and their harmonious motion produces the music of the spheres. Through the innermost or eighth of these, which is the moon, is passed the spindle; but it is doubtful whether this is the continuation of the column of light, from which the pilgrims contemplate the heavens; the words of Plato imply that they are connected, but not the same. The column itself is clearly not of adamant. The spindle (which is of adamant) is fastened to the ends of the chains which extend to the middle of the column of light—this column is said to hold together the heaven; but whether it hangs from the spindle, or is at right angles to it, is not explained. The cylinder containing the orbits of the stars is almost as much a symbol as the figure of Necessity turning the spindle;—for the outermost rim is the sphere of the fixed stars, and nothing is said about the intervals of space which divide the paths of the stars in the heavens. The description is both a picture and an orrery, and therefore is necessarily inconsistent with itself. The column of light is not the Milky Way—which is neither straight, nor like a rainbow—but the imaginary axis of the earth. This is compared to the rainbow in respect not of form but of colour, and not to the undergirders of a trireme, but to the straight rope running from prow to stern in which the undergirders meet.

The orrery or picture of the heavens given in the Republic differs in its mode of representation from the circles of the same and of the other in the Timaeus. In both the fixed stars are distinguished from the planets, and they move in orbits without them, although in an opposite direction: in the Republic as in the Timaeus they are all moving round the axis of the world. But we are not certain that in the former they are moving round the earth. No distinct mention is made in the Republic of the circles of the same and other; although both in the Timaeus and in the Republic the motion of the fixed stars is supposed to coincide with the motion of the whole. The relative thickness of the rims is perhaps designed to express the relative distances of the planets. Plato probably intended to represent the earth, from which Er and his companions are viewing the heavens, as stationary in place; but whether or not herself revolving, unless this is implied in the revolution of the axis, is uncertain (Timaeus). The spectator may be supposed to look at the heavenly bodies, either from above or below. The earth is a sort of earth and heaven in one, like the heaven of the Phaedrus, on the back of which the spectator goes out to take a peep at the stars and is borne round in the revolution. There is no distinction between the equator and the ecliptic. But Plato is no doubt led to imagine that the planets have an opposite motion to that of the fixed stars, in order to account for their appearances in the heavens. In the description of the meadow, and the retribution of the good and evil after death, there are traces of Homer.

The description of the axis as a spindle, and of the heavenly bodies as forming a whole, partly arises out of the attempt to connect the motions of the heavenly bodies with the mythological image of the web, or weaving of the Fates. The giving of the lots, the weaving of them, and the making of them irreversible, which are ascribed to the three Fates—Lachesis, Clotho, Atropos, are obviously derived from their names. The element of chance in human life is indicated by the order of the lots. But chance, however adverse, may be overcome by the wisdom of man, if he knows how to choose aright; there is a worse enemy to man than chance; this enemy is himself. He who was moderately fortunate in the number of the lot—even the very last comer—might have a good life if he chose with wisdom. And as Plato does not like to make an assertion which is unproven, he more than confirms this statement a few sentences afterwards by the example of Odysseus, who chose last. But the virtue which is founded on habit is not sufficient to enable a man to choose; he must add to virtue knowledge, if he is to act rightly when placed in new circumstances. The routine of good actions and good habits is an inferior sort of goodness; and, as Coleridge says, 'Common sense is intolerable which is not based on metaphysics,' so Plato would have said, 'Habit is worthless which is not based upon philosophy.'

The freedom of the will to refuse the evil and to choose the good is distinctly asserted. 'Virtue is free, and as a man honours or dishonours her he will have more or less of her.' The life of man is 'rounded' by necessity; there are circumstances prior to birth which affect him (Pol.). But within the walls of necessity there is an open space in which he is his own master, and can study for himself the effects which the variously compounded gifts of nature or fortune have upon the soul, and act accordingly. All men cannot have the first choice in everything. But the lot of all men is good enough, if they choose wisely and will live diligently.

The verisimilitude which is given to the pilgrimage of a thousand years, by the intimation that Ardiaeus had lived a thousand years before; the coincidence of Er coming to life on the twelfth day after he was supposed to have been dead with the seven days which the pilgrims passed in the meadow, and the four days during which they journeyed to the column of light; the precision with which the soul is mentioned who chose the twentieth lot; the passing remarks that there was no definite character among the souls, and that the souls which had chosen ill blamed any one rather than themselves; or that some of the souls drank more than was necessary of the waters of Forgetfulness, while Er himself was hindered from drinking; the desire of Odysseus to rest at last, unlike the conception of him in Dante and Tennyson; the feigned ignorance of how Er returned to the body, when the other souls went shooting like stars to their birth,—add greatly to the probability of the narrative. They are such touches of nature as the art of Defoe might have introduced when he wished to win credibility for marvels and apparitions.

There still remain to be considered some points which have been intentionally reserved to the end: (1) the Janus-like character of the Republic, which presents two faces—one an Hellenic state, the other a kingdom of philosophers. Connected with the latter of the two aspects are (2) the paradoxes of the Republic, as they have been termed by Morgenstern: (a) the community of property; (b) of families; (c) the rule of philosophers; (d) the analogy of the individual and the State, which, like some other analogies in the Republic, is carried too far. We may then proceed to consider (3) the subject of education as conceived by Plato, bringing together in a general view the education of youth and the education of after-life; (4) we may note further some essential differences between ancient and modern politics which are suggested by the Republic; (5) we may compare the Politicus and the Laws; (6) we may observe the influence exercised by Plato on his imitators; and (7) take occasion to consider the nature and value of political, and (8) of religious ideals.

1. Plato expressly says that he is intending to found an Hellenic State (Book V). Many of his regulations are characteristically Spartan; such as the prohibition of gold and silver, the common meals of the men, the military training of the youth, the gymnastic exercises of the women. The life of Sparta was the life of a camp (Laws), enforced even more rigidly in time of peace than in war; the citizens of Sparta, like Plato's, were forbidden to trade—they were to be soldiers and not shopkeepers. Nowhere else in Greece was the individual so completely subjected to the State; the time when he was to marry, the education of his children, the clothes which he was to wear, the food which he was to eat, were all prescribed by law. Some of the best enactments in the Republic, such as the reverence to be paid to parents and elders, and some of the worst, such as the exposure of deformed children, are borrowed from the practice of Sparta. The encouragement of friendships between men and youths, or of men with one another, as affording incentives to bravery, is also Spartan; in Sparta too a nearer approach was made than in any other Greek State to equality of the sexes, and to community of property; and while there was probably less of licentiousness in the sense of immorality, the tie of marriage was regarded more lightly than in the rest of Greece. The 'suprema lex' was the preservation of the family, and the interest of the State. The coarse strength of a military government was not favourable to purity and refinement; and the excessive strictness of some regulations seems to have produced a reaction. Of all Hellenes the Spartans were most accessible to bribery; several of the greatest of them might be described in the words of Plato as

having a 'fierce secret longing after gold and silver.' Though not in the strict sense communists, the principle of communism was maintained among them in their division of lands, in their common meals, in their slaves, and in the free use of one another's goods. Marriage was a public institution: and the women were educated by the State, and sang and danced in public with the men.

Many traditions were preserved at Sparta of the severity with which the magistrates had maintained the primitive rule of music and poetry; as in the Republic of Plato, the new-fangled poet was to be expelled. Hymns to the Gods, which are the only kind of music admitted into the ideal State, were the only kind which was permitted at Sparta. The Spartans, though an unpoetical race, were nevertheless lovers of poetry; they had been stirred by the Elegiac strains of Tyrtaeus, they had crowded around Hippias to hear his recitals of Homer; but in this they resembled the citizens of the timocratic rather than of the ideal State. The council of elder men also corresponds to the Spartan gerousia; and the freedom with which they are permitted to judge about matters of detail agrees with what we are told of that institution. Once more, the military rule of not spoiling the dead or offering arms at the temples; the moderation in the pursuit of enemies; the importance attached to the physical well-being of the citizens; the use of warfare for the sake of defence rather than of aggression—are features probably suggested by the spirit and practice of Sparta.

To the Spartan type the ideal State reverts in the first decline; and the character of the individual timocrat is borrowed from the Spartan citizen. The love of Lacedaemon not only affected Plato and Xenophon, but was shared by many undistinguished Athenians; there they seemed to find a principle which was wanting in their own democracy. The (Greek) of the Spartans attracted them, that is to say, not the goodness of their laws, but the spirit of order and loyalty which prevailed. Fascinated by the idea, citizens of Athens would imitate the Lacedaemonians in their dress and manners; they were known to the contemporaries of Plato as 'the persons who had their ears bruised,' like the Roundheads of the Commonwealth. The love of another church or country when seen at a distance only, the

longing for an imaginary simplicity in civilized times, the fond desire of a
past which never has been, or of a future which never will be,—these are
aspirations of the human mind which are often felt among ourselves. Such
feelings meet with a response in the Republic of Plato.

But there are other features of the Platonic Republic, as, for example,
the literary and philosophical education, and the grace and beauty of life,
which are the reverse of Spartan. Plato wishes to give his citizens a taste of
Athenian freedom as well as of Lacedaemonian discipline. His individual
genius is purely Athenian, although in theory he is a lover of Sparta; and
he is something more than either—he has also a true Hellenic feeling. He
is desirous of humanizing the wars of Hellenes against one another; he
acknowledges that the Delphian God is the grand hereditary interpreter
of all Hellas. The spirit of harmony and the Dorian mode are to prevail,
and the whole State is to have an external beauty which is the reflex of
the harmony within. But he has not yet found out the truth which he
afterwards enunciated in the Laws—that he was a better legislator who
made men to be of one mind, than he who trained them for war. The
citizens, as in other Hellenic States, democratic as well as aristocratic, are
really an upper class; for, although no mention is made of slaves, the lower
classes are allowed to fade away into the distance, and are represented in
the individual by the passions. Plato has no idea either of a social State
in which all classes are harmonized, or of a federation of Hellas or the
world in which different nations or States have a place. His city is equipped
for war rather than for peace, and this would seem to be justified by the
ordinary condition of Hellenic States. The myth of the earth-born men is
an embodiment of the orthodox tradition of Hellas, and the allusion to the
four ages of the world is also sanctioned by the authority of Hesiod and the
poets. Thus we see that the Republic is partly founded on the ideal of the
old Greek polis, partly on the actual circumstances of Hellas in that age.
Plato, like the old painters, retains the traditional form, and like them he
has also a vision of a city in the clouds.

There is yet another thread which is interwoven in the texture of the
work; for the Republic is not only a Dorian State, but a Pythagorean

league. The 'way of life' which was connected with the name of
Pythagoras, like the Catholic monastic orders, showed the power which
the mind of an individual might exercise over his contemporaries, and may
have naturally suggested to Plato the possibility of reviving such 'mediaeval
institutions.' The Pythagoreans, like Plato, enforced a rule of life and a
moral and intellectual training. The influence ascribed to music, which to
us seems exaggerated, is also a Pythagorean feature; it is not to be regarded
as representing the real influence of music in the Greek world. More nearly
than any other government of Hellas, the Pythagorean league of three
hundred was an aristocracy of virtue. For once in the history of mankind
the philosophy of order or (Greek), expressing and consequently enlisting
on its side the combined endeavours of the better part of the people,
obtained the management of public affairs and held possession of it for a
considerable time (until about B.C. 500). Probably only in States prepared
by Dorian institutions would such a league have been possible. The rulers,
like Plato's (Greek), were required to submit to a severe training in order to
prepare the way for the education of the other members of the community.
Long after the dissolution of the Order, eminent Pythagoreans, such as
Archytas of Tarentum, retained their political influence over the cities of
Magna Graecia. There was much here that was suggestive to the kindred
spirit of Plato, who had doubtless meditated deeply on the 'way of life of
Pythagoras' (Rep.) and his followers. Slight traces of Pythagoreanism are
to be found in the mystical number of the State, in the number which
expresses the interval between the king and the tyrant, in the doctrine of
transmigration, in the music of the spheres, as well as in the great though
secondary importance ascribed to mathematics in education.

But as in his philosophy, so also in the form of his State, he goes
far beyond the old Pythagoreans. He attempts a task really impossible,
which is to unite the past of Greek history with the future of philosophy,
analogous to that other impossibility, which has often been the dream of
Christendom, the attempt to unite the past history of Europe with the
kingdom of Christ. Nothing actually existing in the world at all resembles
Plato's ideal State; nor does he himself imagine that such a State is possible.

This he repeats again and again; e.g. in the Republic, or in the Laws where, casting a glance back on the Republic, he admits that the perfect state of communism and philosophy was impossible in his own age, though still to be retained as a pattern. The same doubt is implied in the earnestness with which he argues in the Republic that ideals are none the worse because they cannot be realized in fact, and in the chorus of laughter, which like a breaking wave will, as he anticipates, greet the mention of his proposals; though like other writers of fiction, he uses all his art to give reality to his inventions. When asked how the ideal polity can come into being, he answers ironically, 'When one son of a king becomes a philosopher'; he designates the fiction of the earth-born men as 'a noble lie'; and when the structure is finally complete, he fairly tells you that his Republic is a vision only, which in some sense may have reality, but not in the vulgar one of a reign of philosophers upon earth. It has been said that Plato flies as well as walks, but this falls short of the truth; for he flies and walks at the same time, and is in the air and on firm ground in successive instants.

Niebuhr has asked a trifling question, which may be briefly noticed in this place—Was Plato a good citizen? If by this is meant, Was he loyal to Athenian institutions?—he can hardly be said to be the friend of democracy: but neither is he the friend of any other existing form of government; all of them he regarded as 'states of faction' (Laws); none attained to his ideal of a voluntary rule over voluntary subjects, which seems indeed more nearly to describe democracy than any other; and the worst of them is tyranny. The truth is, that the question has hardly any meaning when applied to a great philosopher whose writings are not meant for a particular age and country, but for all time and all mankind. The decline of Athenian politics was probably the motive which led Plato to frame an ideal State, and the Republic may be regarded as reflecting the departing glory of Hellas. As well might we complain of St. Augustine, whose great work 'The City of God' originated in a similar motive, for not being loyal to the Roman Empire. Even a nearer parallel might be afforded by the first Christians, who cannot fairly be charged with being bad citizens because, though 'subject to the higher powers,' they were looking forward to a city which is in heaven.

2. The idea of the perfect State is full of paradox when judged of according to the ordinary notions of mankind. The paradoxes of one age have been said to become the commonplaces of the next; but the paradoxes of Plato are at least as paradoxical to us as they were to his contemporaries. The modern world has either sneered at them as absurd, or denounced them as unnatural and immoral; men have been pleased to find in Aristotle's criticisms of them the anticipation of their own good sense. The wealthy and cultivated classes have disliked and also dreaded them; they have pointed with satisfaction to the failure of efforts to realize them in practice. Yet since they are the thoughts of one of the greatest of human intelligences, and of one who had done most to elevate morality and religion, they seem to deserve a better treatment at our hands. We may have to address the public, as Plato does poetry, and assure them that we mean no harm to existing institutions. There are serious errors which have a side of truth and which therefore may fairly demand a careful consideration: there are truths mixed with error of which we may indeed say, 'The half is better than the whole.' Yet 'the half' may be an important contribution to the study of human nature.

(a) The first paradox is the community of goods, which is mentioned slightly at the end of the third Book, and seemingly, as Aristotle observes, is confined to the guardians; at least no mention is made of the other classes. But the omission is not of any real significance, and probably arises out of the plan of the work, which prevents the writer from entering into details.

Aristotle censures the community of property much in the spirit of modern political economy, as tending to repress industry, and as doing away with the spirit of benevolence. Modern writers almost refuse to consider the subject, which is supposed to have been long ago settled by the common opinion of mankind. But it must be remembered that the sacredness of property is a notion far more fixed in modern than in ancient times. The world has grown older, and is therefore more conservative. Primitive society offered many examples of land held in common, either by a tribe or by a township, and such may probably have been the original form of landed tenure. Ancient legislators had invented various modes of dividing and preserving the divisions of land among the citizens; according to Aristotle there were nations who held the land in common and divided the produce, and there were others who divided the land and stored the produce in common. The evils of debt and the inequality of property were far greater in ancient than in modern times, and the accidents to which property was subject from war, or revolution, or taxation, or other legislative interference, were also greater. All these circumstances gave property a less fixed and sacred character. The early Christians are believed to have held their property in common, and the principle is sanctioned by the words of Christ himself, and has been maintained as a counsel of perfection in almost all ages of the Church. Nor have there been wanting instances of modern enthusiasts who have made a religion of communism; in every age of religious excitement notions like Wycliffe's 'inheritance of grace' have tended to prevail. A like spirit, but fiercer and more violent, has appeared in politics. 'The preparation of the Gospel of peace' soon becomes the red flag of Republicanism.

We can hardly judge what effect Plato's views would have upon his own contemporaries; they would perhaps have seemed to them only an exaggeration of the Spartan commonwealth. Even modern writers would acknowledge that the right of private property is based on expediency, and may be interfered with in a variety of ways for the public good. Any other mode of vesting property which was found to be more advantageous, would in time acquire the same basis of right; 'the most useful,' in Plato's words, 'would be the most sacred.' The lawyers and ecclesiastics of former ages would have spoken of property as a sacred institution. But they only meant by such language to oppose the greatest amount of resistance to any invasion of the rights of individuals and of the Church.

When we consider the question, without any fear of immediate application to practice, in the spirit of Plato's Republic, are we quite sure that the received notions of property are the best? Is the distribution of wealth which is customary in civilized countries the most favourable that can be conceived for the education and development of the mass of mankind? Can 'the spectator of all time and all existence' be quite convinced that one or two thousand years hence, great changes will not have taken place in the rights of property, or even that the very notion of property, beyond what is necessary for personal maintenance, may not have disappeared? This was a distinction familiar to Aristotle, though likely to be laughed at among ourselves. Such a change would not be greater than some other changes through which the world has passed in the transition from ancient to modern society, for example, the emancipation of the serfs in Russia, or the abolition of slavery in America and the West Indies; and not so great as the difference which separates the Eastern village community from the Western world. To accomplish such a revolution in the course of a few centuries, would imply a rate of progress not more rapid than has actually taken place during the last fifty or sixty years. The kingdom of Japan underwent more change in five or six years than Europe in five or six hundred. Many opinions and beliefs which have been cherished among ourselves quite as strongly as the sacredness of property have passed away; and the most untenable propositions respecting the right of bequests or entail have been maintained with as much fervour as the most moderate. Some one will be heard to ask whether a state of society can be final in which the interests of thousands are perilled on the life or character of a single person. And many will indulge the hope that our present condition may, after all, be only transitional, and may conduct to a higher, in which property, besides ministering to the enjoyment of the few, may also furnish the means of the highest culture to all, and will be a greater benefit to the public generally, and also more under the control of public authority. There may come a time when the saying, 'Have I not a right to do what I will with my own?' will appear to be a barbarous relic of individualism;—when the possession of a part may be a greater blessing to each and all than the possession of the whole is now to any one.

Such reflections appear visionary to the eye of the practical statesman, but they are within the range of possibility to the philosopher. He can imagine that in some distant age or clime, and through the influence of some individual, the notion of common property may or might have sunk as deep into the heart of a race, and have become as fixed to them, as private property is to ourselves. He knows that this latter institution is not more than four or five thousand years old: may not the end revert to the beginning? In our own age even Utopias affect the spirit of legislation, and an abstract idea may exercise a great influence on practical politics.

The objections that would be generally urged against Plato's community of property, are the old ones of Aristotle, that motives for exertion would be taken away, and that disputes would arise when each was dependent upon all. Every man would produce as little and consume as much as he liked. The experience of civilized nations has hitherto been adverse to Socialism. The effort is too great for human nature; men try to live in common, but the personal feeling is always breaking in. On the other hand it may be doubted whether our present notions of property are not conventional, for they differ in different countries and in different states of society. We boast of an individualism which is not freedom, but rather an artificial result of the industrial state of modern Europe. The individual is nominally free, but he is also powerless in a world bound hand and foot in the chains of economic necessity. Even if we cannot expect the mass of mankind to become disinterested, at any rate we observe in them a power of organization which fifty years ago would never have been suspected. The same forces which have revolutionized the political system of Europe, may effect a similar change in the social and industrial relations of mankind. And if we suppose the influence of some good as well as neutral motives working in the community, there will be no absurdity in expecting that the mass of mankind having power, and becoming enlightened about the higher possibilities of human life, when they learn how much more is attainable for all than is at present the possession of a favoured few, may pursue the common interest with an intelligence and persistency which mankind have hitherto never seen.

Now that the world has once been set in motion, and is no longer held fast under the tyranny of custom and ignorance; now that criticism has pierced the veil of tradition and the past no longer overpowers the

present,—the progress of civilization may be expected to be far greater
and swifter than heretofore. Even at our present rate of speed the point
at which we may arrive in two or three generations is beyond the power
of imagination to foresee. There are forces in the world which work, not
in an arithmetical, but in a geometrical ratio of increase. Education, to
use the expression of Plato, moves like a wheel with an ever-multiplying
rapidity. Nor can we say how great may be its influence, when it becomes
universal,—when it has been inherited by many generations,—when it is
freed from the trammels of superstition and rightly adapted to the wants
and capacities of different classes of men and women. Neither do we know
how much more the co-operation of minds or of hands may be capable of
accomplishing, whether in labour or in study. The resources of the natural
sciences are not half-developed as yet; the soil of the earth, instead of
growing more barren, may become many times more fertile than hitherto;
the uses of machinery far greater, and also more minute than at present.
New secrets of physiology may be revealed, deeply affecting human nature
in its innermost recesses. The standard of health may be raised and the lives
of men prolonged by sanitary and medical knowledge. There may be peace,
there may be leisure, there may be innocent refreshments of many kinds.
The ever-increasing power of locomotion may join the extremes of earth.
There may be mysterious workings of the human mind, such as occur
only at great crises of history. The East and the West may meet together,
and all nations may contribute their thoughts and their experience to the
common stock of humanity. Many other elements enter into a speculation
of this kind. But it is better to make an end of them. For such reflections
appear to the majority far-fetched, and to men of science, commonplace.

(b) Neither to the mind of Plato nor of Aristotle did the doctrine of
community of property present at all the same difficulty, or appear to be
the same violation of the common Hellenic sentiment, as the community
of wives and children. This paradox he prefaces by another proposal, that
the occupations of men and women shall be the same, and that to this end
they shall have a common training and education. Male and female animals
have the same pursuits—why not also the two sexes of man?

But have we not here fallen into a contradiction? for we were saying that different natures should have different pursuits. How then can men and women have the same? And is not the proposal inconsistent with our notion of the division of labour?—These objections are no sooner raised than answered; for, according to Plato, there is no organic difference between men and women, but only the accidental one that men beget and women bear children. Following the analogy of the other animals, he contends that all natural gifts are scattered about indifferently among both sexes, though there may be a superiority of degree on the part of the men. The objection on the score of decency to their taking part in the same gymnastic exercises, is met by Plato's assertion that the existing feeling is a matter of habit.

That Plato should have emancipated himself from the ideas of his own country and from the example of the East, shows a wonderful independence of mind. He is conscious that women are half the human race, in some respects the more important half (Laws); and for the sake both of men and women he desires to raise the woman to a higher level of existence. He brings, not sentiment, but philosophy to bear upon a question which both in ancient and modern times has been chiefly regarded in the light of custom or feeling. The Greeks had noble conceptions of womanhood in the goddesses Athene and Artemis, and in the heroines Antigone and Andromache. But these ideals had no counterpart in actual life. The Athenian woman was in no way the equal of her husband; she was not the entertainer of his guests or the mistress of his house, but only his housekeeper and the mother of his children. She took no part in military or political matters; nor is there any instance in the later ages of Greece of a woman becoming famous in literature. 'Hers is the greatest glory who has the least renown among men,' is the historian's conception of feminine excellence. A very different ideal of womanhood is held up by Plato to the world; she is to be the companion of the man, and to share with him in the toils of war and in the cares of government. She is to be similarly trained both in bodily and mental exercises. She is to lose as far as possible the incidents of maternity and the characteristics of the female sex.

The modern antagonist of the equality of the sexes would argue that the differences between men and women are not confined to the single point urged by Plato; that sensibility, gentleness, grace, are the qualities of women, while energy, strength, higher intelligence, are to be looked for in men. And the criticism is just: the differences affect the whole nature, and are not, as Plato supposes, confined to a single point. But neither can we say how far these differences are due to education and the opinions of mankind, or physically inherited from the habits and opinions of former generations. Women have been always taught, not exactly that they are slaves, but that they are in an inferior position, which is also supposed to have compensating advantages; and to this position they have conformed. It is also true that the physical form may easily change in the course of generations through the mode of life; and the weakness or delicacy, which was once a matter of opinion, may become a physical fact. The characteristics of sex vary greatly in different countries and ranks of society, and at different ages in the same individuals. Plato may have been right in denying that there was any ultimate difference in the sexes of man other than that which exists in animals, because all other differences may be conceived to disappear in other states of society, or under different circumstances of life and training.

The first wave having been passed, we proceed to the second—community of wives and children. 'Is it possible? Is it desirable?' For as Glaucon intimates, and as we far more strongly insist, 'Great doubts may be entertained about both these points.' Any free discussion of the question is impossible, and mankind are perhaps right in not allowing the ultimate bases of social life to be examined. Few of us can safely enquire into the things which nature hides, any more than we can dissect our own bodies. Still, the manner in which Plato arrived at his conclusions should be considered. For here, as Mr. Grote has remarked, is a wonderful thing, that one of the wisest and best of men should have entertained ideas of morality which are wholly at variance with our own. And if we would do Plato justice, we must examine carefully the character of his proposals. First, we may observe that the relations of the sexes supposed by him are the reverse of licentious: he seems rather to aim at an impossible strictness. Secondly, he conceives the family to be the natural enemy of the state; and he entertains the serious hope that an universal brotherhood may take the place of private interests—an aspiration which, although not justified by experience, has possessed many noble minds. On the other hand, there is no sentiment or imagination in the connections which men and women are supposed by him to form; human beings return to the level of the animals, neither exalting to heaven, nor yet abusing the natural instincts. All that world of poetry and fancy which the passion of love has called forth in modern literature and romance would have been banished by Plato. The arrangements of marriage in the Republic are directed to one object—the improvement of the race. In successive generations a great development both of bodily and mental qualities might be possible. The analogy of animals tends to show that mankind can within certain limits receive a change of nature. And as in animals we should commonly choose the best for breeding, and destroy the others, so there must be a selection made of the human beings whose lives are worthy to be preserved.

We start back horrified from this Platonic ideal, in the belief, first, that the higher feelings of humanity are far too strong to be crushed out; secondly, that if the plan could be carried into execution we should be poorly recompensed by improvements in the breed for the loss of the best things in life. The greatest regard for the weakest and meanest of human beings—the infant, the criminal, the insane, the idiot, truly seems to us one of the noblest results of Christianity. We have learned, though as yet imperfectly, that the individual man has an endless value in the sight of God, and that we honour Him when we honour the darkened and disfigured image of Him (Laws). This is the lesson which Christ taught in a parable when He said, 'Their angels do always behold the face of My Father which is in heaven.' Such lessons are only partially realized in any age; they were foreign to the age of Plato, as they have very different degrees of strength in different countries or ages of the Christian world. To the Greek the family was a religious and customary institution binding the members together by a tie inferior in strength to that of friendship, and having a less solemn and sacred sound than that of country. The relationship which existed on the lower level of custom, Plato imagined that he was raising to the higher level of nature and reason; while from the modern and Christian point of view we regard him as sanctioning murder and destroying the first principles of morality.

The great error in these and similar speculations is that the difference between man and the animals is forgotten in them. The human being is regarded with the eye of a dog- or bird-fancier, or at best of a slave-owner; the higher or human qualities are left out. The breeder of animals aims chiefly at size or speed or strength; in a few cases at courage or temper; most often the fitness of the animal for food is the great desideratum. But mankind are not bred to be eaten, nor yet for their superiority in fighting or in running or in drawing carts. Neither does the improvement of the human race consist merely in the increase of the bones and flesh, but in the growth and enlightenment of the mind. Hence there must be 'a marriage of true minds' as well as of bodies, of imagination and reason as well as of lusts and instincts. Men and women without feeling or imagination are justly called brutes; yet Plato takes away these qualities and puts nothing in their place, not even the desire of a noble offspring, since parents are not to know their own children. The most important transaction of social life, he who is the idealist philosopher converts into the most brutal. For the pair are to have no relation to one another, except at the hymeneal festival; their children are not theirs, but the state's; nor is any tie of affection to unite them. Yet here the analogy of the animals might have saved Plato from a gigantic error, if he had 'not lost sight of his own illustration.' For the 'nobler sort of birds and beasts' nourish and protect their offspring and are faithful to one another.

An eminent physiologist thinks it worth while 'to try and place life on a physical basis.' But should not life rest on the moral rather than upon the physical? The higher comes first, then the lower, first the human and rational, afterwards the animal. Yet they are not absolutely divided;

and in times of sickness or moments of self-indulgence they seem to be only different aspects of a common human nature which includes them both. Neither is the moral the limit of the physical, but the expansion and enlargement of it,—the highest form which the physical is capable of receiving. As Plato would say, the body does not take care of the body, and still less of the mind, but the mind takes care of both. In all human action not that which is common to man and the animals is the characteristic element, but that which distinguishes him from them. Even if we admit the physical basis, and resolve all virtue into health of body 'la facon que notre sang circule,' still on merely physical grounds we must come back to ideas. Mind and reason and duty and conscience, under these or other names, are always reappearing. There cannot be health of body without health of mind; nor health of mind without the sense of duty and the love of truth (Charm).

That the greatest of ancient philosophers should in his regulations about marriage have fallen into the error of separating body and mind, does indeed appear surprising. Yet the wonder is not so much that Plato should have entertained ideas of morality which to our own age are revolting, but that he should have contradicted himself to an extent which is hardly credible, falling in an instant from the heaven of idealism into the crudest animalism. Rejoicing in the newly found gift of reflection, he appears to have thought out a subject about which he had better have followed the enlightened feeling of his own age. The general sentiment of Hellas was opposed to his monstrous fancy. The old poets, and in later time the tragedians, showed no want of respect for the family, on which much of their religion was based. But the example of Sparta, and perhaps in some degree the tendency to defy public opinion, seems to have misled him. He will make one family out of all the families of the state. He will select the finest specimens of men and women and breed from these only.

Yet because the illusion is always returning (for the animal part of human nature will from time to time assert itself in the disguise of philosophy as well as of poetry), and also because any departure from established morality, even where this is not intended, is apt to be unsettling, it may be worth while to draw out a little more at length the objections to the Platonic marriage. In the first place, history shows that wherever polygamy has been largely allowed the race has deteriorated. One man to one woman is the law of God and nature. Nearly all the civilized peoples of the world at some period before the age of written records, have become monogamists; and the step when once taken has never been retraced. The exceptions occurring among Brahmins or Mahometans or the ancient Persians, are of that sort which may be said to prove the rule. The connexions formed between superior and inferior races hardly ever produce a noble offspring, because they are licentious; and because the children in such cases usually despise the mother and are neglected by the father who is ashamed of them. Barbarous nations when they are introduced by Europeans to vice die out; polygamist peoples either import and adopt children from other countries, or dwindle in numbers, or both. Dynasties and aristocracies which have disregarded the laws of nature have decreased in numbers and degenerated in stature; 'mariages de convenance' leave their enfeebling stamp on the offspring of them (King Lear). The marriage of near relations, or the marrying in and in of the same family tends constantly to weakness or idiocy in the children, sometimes assuming the form as they grow older of passionate licentiousness. The common prostitute rarely has any offspring. By such unmistakable evidence is the authority of morality asserted in the relations of the sexes: and so many more elements enter into this 'mystery' than are dreamed of by Plato and some other philosophers.

Recent enquirers have indeed arrived at the conclusion that among primitive tribes there existed a community of wives as of property, and that the captive taken by the spear was the only wife or slave whom any man was permitted to call his own. The partial existence of such customs among some of the lower races of man, and the survival of peculiar ceremonies in the marriages of some civilized nations, are thought to furnish a proof of similar institutions having been once universal. There can be no question that the study of anthropology has considerably changed our views respecting the first appearance of man upon the earth. We know more about the aborigines of the world than formerly, but our

increasing knowledge shows above all things how little we know. With
all the helps which written monuments afford, we do but faintly realize
the condition of man two thousand or three thousand years ago. Of what
his condition was when removed to a distance 200,000 or 300,000 years,
when the majority of mankind were lower and nearer the animals than any
tribe now existing upon the earth, we cannot even entertain conjecture.
Plato (Laws) and Aristotle (Metaph.) may have been more right than we
imagine in supposing that some forms of civilisation were discovered and
lost several times over. If we cannot argue that all barbarism is a degraded
civilization, neither can we set any limits to the depth of degradation to
which the human race may sink through war, disease, or isolation. And if
we are to draw inferences about the origin of marriage from the practice
of barbarous nations, we should also consider the remoter analogy of the
animals. Many birds and animals, especially the carnivorous, have only
one mate, and the love and care of offspring which seems to be natural
is inconsistent with the primitive theory of marriage. If we go back to an
imaginary state in which men were almost animals and the companions
of them, we have as much right to argue from what is animal to what is
human as from the barbarous to the civilized man. The record of animal
life on the globe is fragmentary,—the connecting links are wanting and
cannot be supplied; the record of social life is still more fragmentary and
precarious. Even if we admit that our first ancestors had no such institution
as marriage, still the stages by which men passed from outer barbarism to
the comparative civilization of China, Assyria, and Greece, or even of the
ancient Germans, are wholly unknown to us.

Such speculations are apt to be unsettling, because they seem to show
that an institution which was thought to be a revelation from heaven, is
only the growth of history and experience. We ask what is the origin of
marriage, and we are told that like the right of property, after many wars
and contests, it has gradually arisen out of the selfishness of barbarians. We
stand face to face with human nature in its primitive nakedness. We are
compelled to accept, not the highest, but the lowest account of the origin
of human society. But on the other hand we may truly say that every step

in human progress has been in the same direction, and that in the course of ages the idea of marriage and of the family has been more and more defined and consecrated. The civilized East is immeasurably in advance of any savage tribes; the Greeks and Romans have improved upon the East; the Christian nations have been stricter in their views of the marriage relation than any of the ancients. In this as in so many other things, instead of looking back with regret to the past, we should look forward with hope to the future. We must consecrate that which we believe to be the most holy, and that 'which is the most holy will be the most useful.' There is more reason for maintaining the sacredness of the marriage tie, when we see the benefit of it, than when we only felt a vague religious horror about the violation of it. But in all times of transition, when established beliefs are being undermined, there is a danger that in the passage from the old to the new we may insensibly let go the moral principle, finding an excuse for listening to the voice of passion in the uncertainty of knowledge, or the fluctuations of opinion. And there are many persons in our own day who, enlightened by the study of anthropology, and fascinated by what is new and strange, some using the language of fear, others of hope, are inclined to believe that a time will come when through the self-assertion of women, or the rebellious spirit of children, by the analysis of human relations, or by the force of outward circumstances, the ties of family life may be broken or greatly relaxed. They point to societies in America and elsewhere which tend to show that the destruction of the family need not necessarily involve the overthrow of all morality. Wherever we may think of such speculations, we can hardly deny that they have been more rife in this generation than in any other; and whither they are tending, who can predict?

To the doubts and queries raised by these 'social reformers' respecting the relation of the sexes and the moral nature of man, there is a sufficient answer, if any is needed. The difference about them and us is really one of fact. They are speaking of man as they wish or fancy him to be, but we are speaking of him as he is. They isolate the animal part of his nature; we regard him as a creature having many sides, or aspects, moving between good and evil, striving to rise above himself and to become 'a little lower than the angels.' We also, to use a Platonic formula, are not ignorant of the dissatisfactions and incompatibilities of family life, of the meannesses of trade, of the flatteries of one class of society by another, of the impediments which the family throws in the way of lofty aims and aspirations. But we are conscious that there are evils and dangers in the background greater still, which are not appreciated, because they are either concealed or suppressed. What a condition of man would that be, in which human passions were controlled by no authority, divine or human, in which there was no shame or decency, no higher affection overcoming or sanctifying the natural instincts, but simply a rule of health! Is it for this that we are asked to throw away the civilization which is the growth of ages?

For strength and health are not the only qualities to be desired; there are the more important considerations of mind and character and soul. We know how human nature may be degraded; we do not know how by artificial means any improvement in the breed can be effected. The problem is a complex one, for if we go back only four steps (and these at least enter into the composition of a child), there are commonly thirty progenitors to be taken into account. Many curious facts, rarely admitting of proof, are told us respecting the inheritance of disease or character from a remote ancestor. We can trace the physical resemblances of parents and children in the same family—

'Sic oculos, sic ille manus, sic ora ferebat';

but scarcely less often the differences which distinguish children both from their parents and from one another. We are told of similar mental peculiarities running in families, and again of a tendency, as in the animals, to revert to a common or original stock. But we have a difficulty in distinguishing what is a true inheritance of genius or other qualities, and what is mere imitation or the result of similar circumstances. Great men and great women have rarely had great fathers and mothers. Nothing that we know of in the circumstances of their birth or lineage will explain their appearance. Of the English poets of the last and two preceding centuries scarcely a descendant remains,—none have ever been distinguished. So deeply has nature hidden her secret, and so ridiculous is the fancy which has been entertained by some that we might in time by suitable marriage arrangements or, as Plato would have said, 'by an ingenious system of lots,' produce a Shakespeare or a Milton. Even supposing that we could breed men having the tenacity of bulldogs, or, like the Spartans, 'lacking the wit to run away in battle,' would the world be any the better? Many of the noblest specimens of the human race have been among the weakest physically. Tyrtaeus or Aesop, or our own Newton, would have been exposed at Sparta; and some of the fairest and strongest men and women have been among the wickedest and worst. Not by the Platonic device of uniting the strong and fair with the strong and fair, regardless of sentiment and morality, nor yet by his other device of combining dissimilar natures (Statesman), have mankind gradually passed from the brutality and licentiousness of primitive marriage to marriage Christian and civilized.

Few persons would deny that we bring into the world an inheritance of mental and physical qualities derived first from our parents, or through them from some remoter ancestor, secondly from our race, thirdly from the general condition of mankind into which we are born. Nothing is commoner than the remark, that 'So and so is like his father or his uncle'; and an aged person may not unfrequently note a resemblance in a youth to a long-forgotten ancestor, observing that 'Nature sometimes skips a generation.' It may be true also, that if we knew more about our ancestors, these similarities would be even more striking to us. Admitting the facts which are thus described in a popular way, we may however remark that there is no method of difference by which they can be defined or estimated, and that they constitute only a small part of each individual. The doctrine of heredity may seem to take out of our hands the conduct of our own lives, but it is the idea, not the fact, which is really terrible to us. For what we have received from our ancestors is only a fraction of what we are, or may become. The knowledge that drunkenness or insanity has been prevalent in a family may be the best safeguard against their recurrence in a future generation. The parent will be most awake to the vices or diseases in his child of which he is most sensible within himself. The whole of life may be directed to their prevention or cure. The traces of consumption may become fainter, or be wholly effaced: the inherent tendency to vice or crime may be eradicated. And so heredity, from being a curse, may become a blessing. We acknowledge that in the matter of our birth, as in our nature generally, there are previous circumstances which affect us. But upon this platform of circumstances or within this wall of necessity, we have still the power of creating a life for ourselves by the informing energy of the human will.

There is another aspect of the marriage question to which Plato is a stranger. All the children born in his state are foundlings. It never occurred to him that the greater part of them, according to universal experience, would have perished. For children can only be brought up in families. There is a subtle sympathy between the mother and the child which cannot be supplied by other mothers, or by 'strong nurses one or more' (Laws). If Plato's 'pen' was as fatal as the Creches of Paris, or the foundling hospital of Dublin, more than nine-tenths of his children would have perished. There would have been no need to expose or put out of the way the weaklier children, for they would have died of themselves. So emphatically does nature protest against the destruction of the family.

What Plato had heard or seen of Sparta was applied by him in a mistaken way to his ideal commonwealth. He probably observed that both the Spartan men and women were superior in form and strength to the other Greeks; and this superiority he was disposed to attribute to the laws and customs relating to marriage. He did not consider that the desire of a noble offspring was a passion among the Spartans, or that their physical superiority was to be attributed chiefly, not to their marriage customs, but to their temperance and training. He did not reflect that Sparta was great, not in consequence of the relaxation of morality, but in spite of it, by virtue of a political principle stronger far than existed in any other Grecian state. Least of all did he observe that Sparta did not really produce the finest specimens of the Greek race. The genius, the political inspiration of Athens, the love of liberty—all that has made Greece famous with posterity, were wanting among the Spartans. They had no Themistocles, or Pericles, or Aeschylus, or Sophocles, or Socrates, or Plato. The individual was not allowed to appear above the state; the laws were fixed, and he had no business to alter or reform them. Yet whence has the progress of cities and nations arisen, if not from remarkable individuals, coming into the world we know not how, and from causes over which we have no control? Something too much may have been said in modern times of the value of individuality. But we can hardly condemn too strongly a system which, instead of fostering the scattered seeds or sparks of genius and character, tends to smother and extinguish them.

Still, while condemning Plato, we must acknowledge that neither Christianity, nor any other form of religion and society, has hitherto been able to cope with this most difficult of social problems, and that the side from which Plato regarded it is that from which we turn away. Population is the most untameable force in the political and social world. Do we not find, especially in large cities, that the greatest hindrance to the amelioration of the poor is their improvidence in marriage?—a small fault truly, if not involving endless consequences. There are whole countries too, such as India, or, nearer home, Ireland, in which a right solution of the marriage question seems to lie at the foundation of the happiness of the community. There are too many people on a given space, or they marry too early and bring into the world a sickly and half-developed offspring; or owing to the very conditions of their existence, they become emaciated and hand on a similar life to their descendants. But who can oppose the voice of prudence to the 'mightiest passions of mankind' (Laws), especially when they have been licensed by custom and religion? In addition to the influences of education, we seem to require some new principles of right and wrong in these matters, some force of opinion, which may indeed be already heard whispering in private, but has never affected the moral sentiments of mankind in general. We unavoidably lose sight of the principle of utility, just in that action of our lives in which we have the most need of it. The influences which we can bring to bear upon this question are chiefly indirect. In a generation or two, education, emigration,

improvements in agriculture and manufactures, may have provided the
solution. The state physician hardly likes to probe the wound: it is beyond
his art; a matter which he cannot safely let alone, but which he dare not
touch:

'We do but skin and film the ulcerous place.'

When again in private life we see a whole family one by one dropping
into the grave under the Ate of some inherited malady, and the parents
perhaps surviving them, do our minds ever go back silently to that day
twenty-five or thirty years before on which under the fairest auspices, amid
the rejoicings of friends and acquaintances, a bride and bridegroom joined
hands with one another? In making such a reflection we are not opposing
physical considerations to moral, but moral to physical; we are seeking to
make the voice of reason heard, which drives us back from the extravagance
of sentimentalism on common sense. The late Dr. Combe is said by his
biographer to have resisted the temptation to marriage, because he knew
that he was subject to hereditary consumption. One who deserved to be
called a man of genius, a friend of my youth, was in the habit of wearing
a black ribbon on his wrist, in order to remind him that, being liable to
outbreaks of insanity, he must not give way to the natural impulses of
affection: he died unmarried in a lunatic asylum. These two little facts
suggest the reflection that a very few persons have done from a sense of duty
what the rest of mankind ought to have done under like circumstances,
if they had allowed themselves to think of all the misery which they were
about to bring into the world. If we could prevent such marriages without
any violation of feeling or propriety, we clearly ought; and the prohibition
in the course of time would be protected by a 'horror naturalis' similar to
that which, in all civilized ages and countries, has prevented the marriage
of near relations by blood. Mankind would have been the happier, if some
things which are now allowed had from the beginning been denied to
them; if the sanction of religion could have prohibited practices inimical
to health; if sanitary principles could in early ages have been invested with
a superstitious awe. But, living as we do far on in the world's history,
we are no longer able to stamp at once with the impress of religion a

new prohibition. A free agent cannot have his fancies regulated by law; and the execution of the law would be rendered impossible, owing to the uncertainty of the cases in which marriage was to be forbidden. Who can weigh virtue, or even fortune against health, or moral and mental qualities against bodily? Who can measure probabilities against certainties? There has been some good as well as evil in the discipline of suffering; and there are diseases, such as consumption, which have exercised a refining and softening influence on the character. Youth is too inexperienced to balance such nice considerations; parents do not often think of them, or think of them too late. They are at a distance and may probably be averted; change of place, a new state of life, the interests of a home may be the cure of them. So persons vainly reason when their minds are already made up and their fortunes irrevocably linked together. Nor is there any ground for supposing that marriages are to any great extent influenced by reflections of this sort, which seem unable to make any head against the irresistible impulse of individual attachment.

Lastly, no one can have observed the first rising flood of the passions in youth, the difficulty of regulating them, and the effects on the whole mind and nature which follow from them, the stimulus which is given to them by the imagination, without feeling that there is something unsatisfactory in our method of treating them. That the most important influence on human life should be wholly left to chance or shrouded in mystery, and instead of being disciplined or understood, should be required to conform only to an external standard of propriety—cannot be regarded by the philosopher as a safe or satisfactory condition of human things. And still those who have the charge of youth may find a way by watchfulness, by affection, by the manliness and innocence of their own lives, by occasional hints, by general admonitions which every one can apply for himself, to mitigate this terrible evil which eats out the heart of individuals and corrupts the moral sentiments of nations. In no duty towards others is there more need of reticence and self-restraint. So great is the danger lest he who would be the counsellor of another should reveal the secret prematurely, lest he should get another too much into his power; or fix the passing impression of evil by demanding the confession of it.

Nor is Plato wrong in asserting that family attachments may interfere with higher aims. If there have been some who 'to party gave up what was meant for mankind,' there have certainly been others who to family gave up what was meant for mankind or for their country. The cares of children, the necessity of procuring money for their support, the flatteries of the rich by the poor, the exclusiveness of caste, the pride of birth or wealth, the tendency of family life to divert men from the pursuit of the ideal or the heroic, are as lowering in our own age as in that of Plato. And if we prefer to look at the gentle influences of home, the development of the affections, the amenities of society, the devotion of one member of a family for the good of the others, which form one side of the picture, we must not quarrel with him, or perhaps ought rather to be grateful to him, for having presented to us the reverse. Without attempting to defend Plato on grounds of morality, we may allow that there is an aspect of the world which has not unnaturally led him into error.

We hardly appreciate the power which the idea of the State, like all other abstract ideas, exercised over the mind of Plato. To us the State seems to be built up out of the family, or sometimes to be the framework in which family and social life is contained. But to Plato in his present mood of mind the family is only a disturbing influence which, instead of filling up, tends to disarrange the higher unity of the State. No organization is needed except a political, which, regarded from another point of view, is a military one. The State is all-sufficing for the wants of man, and, like the idea of the Church in later ages, absorbs all other desires and affections. In time of war the thousand citizens are to stand like a rampart impregnable against the world or the Persian host; in time of peace the preparation for war and their duties to the State, which are also their duties to one another, take up their whole life and time. The only other interest which is allowed to them besides that of war, is the interest of philosophy. When they are too old to be soldiers they are to retire from active life and to have a second novitiate of study and contemplation. There is an element of monasticism even in Plato's communism. If he could have done without children, he might have converted his Republic into a religious order. Neither in the Laws, when the daylight of common sense breaks in upon him, does he retract his error. In the state of which he would be the founder, there is no marrying or giving in marriage: but because of the infirmity of mankind, he condescends to allow the law of nature to prevail.

(c) But Plato has an equal, or, in his own estimation, even greater paradox in reserve, which is summed up in the famous text, 'Until kings are philosophers or philosophers are kings, cities will never cease from ill.' And by philosophers he explains himself to mean those who are capable of apprehending ideas, especially the idea of good. To the attainment of this higher knowledge the second education is directed. Through a process of training which has already made them good citizens they are now to be made good legislators. We find with some surprise (not unlike the feeling which Aristotle in a well-known passage describes the hearers of Plato's lectures as experiencing, when they went to a discourse on the idea of good, expecting to be instructed in moral truths, and received instead of them arithmetical and mathematical formulae) that Plato does not propose for his future legislators any study of finance or law or military tactics, but only of abstract mathematics, as a preparation for the still more abstract conception of good. We ask, with Aristotle, What is the use of a man knowing the idea of good, if he does not know what is good for this individual, this state, this condition of society? We cannot understand how Plato's legislators or guardians are to be fitted for their work of statesmen by the study of the five mathematical sciences. We vainly search in Plato's own writings for any explanation of this seeming absurdity.

The discovery of a great metaphysical conception seems to ravish the mind with a prophetic consciousness which takes away the power of estimating its value. No metaphysical enquirer has ever fairly criticised his own speculations; in his own judgment they have been above criticism; nor has he understood that what to him seemed to be absolute truth may reappear in the next generation as a form of logic or an instrument of thought. And posterity have also sometimes equally misapprehended the real value of his speculations. They appear to them to have contributed nothing to the stock of human knowledge. The IDEA of good is apt to be regarded by the modern thinker as an unmeaning abstraction; but he forgets that this abstraction is waiting ready for use, and will hereafter be filled up by the divisions of knowledge. When mankind do not as yet know that the world is subject to law, the introduction of the mere conception of law or design or final cause, and the far-off anticipation of the harmony of knowledge, are great steps onward. Even the crude generalization of the unity of all things leads men to view the world with different eyes, and may easily affect their conception of human life and of politics, and also their own conduct and character (Tim). We can imagine how a great mind like that of Pericles might derive elevation from his intercourse with Anaxagoras (Phaedr.). To be struggling towards a higher but unattainable conception is a more favourable intellectual condition than to rest satisfied in a narrow portion of ascertained fact. And the earlier, which have sometimes been the greater ideas of science, are often lost sight of at a later period. How rarely can we say of any modern enquirer in the magnificent language of Plato, that 'He is the spectator of all time and of all existence!'

Nor is there anything unnatural in the hasty application of these vast metaphysical conceptions to practical and political life. In the first enthusiasm of ideas men are apt to see them everywhere, and to apply them in the most remote sphere. They do not understand that the experience of ages is required to enable them to fill up 'the intermediate axioms.' Plato himself seems to have imagined that the truths of psychology, like those of astronomy and harmonics, would be arrived at by a process of deduction, and that the method which he has pursued in the Fourth Book, of inferring them from experience and the use of language, was imperfect and only provisional. But when, after having arrived at the idea of good, which is the end of the science of dialectic, he is asked, What is the nature, and what are the divisions of the science? He refuses to answer, as if intending by the refusal to intimate that the state of knowledge which then existed was not such as would allow the philosopher to enter into his final rest. The previous sciences must first be studied, and will, we may add, continue to be studied tell the end of time, although in a sense different from any which Plato could have conceived. But we may observe, that while he is aware of the vacancy of his own ideal, he is full of enthusiasm in the contemplation of it. Looking into the orb of light, he sees nothing, but he is warmed and elevated. The Hebrew prophet believed that faith in God would enable him to govern the world; the Greek philosopher imagined that contemplation of the good would make a legislator. There is as much to be filled up in the one case as in the other, and the one mode of conception is to the Israelite what the other is to the Greek. Both find a repose in a divine perfection, which, whether in a more personal or impersonal form, exists without them and independently of them, as well as within them.

There is no mention of the idea of good in the Timaeus, nor of the divine Creator of the world in the Republic; and we are naturally led to ask in what relation they stand to one another. Is God above or below the idea of good? Or is the Idea of Good another mode of conceiving God? The latter appears to be the truer answer. To the Greek philosopher the perfection and unity of God was a far higher conception than his personality, which he hardly found a word to express, and which to him would have seemed to be borrowed from mythology. To the Christian, on the other hand, or to the modern thinker in general, it is difficult, if not impossible, to attach reality to what he terms mere abstraction; while to Plato this very abstraction is the truest and most real of all things. Hence, from a difference in forms of thought, Plato appears to be resting on a creation of his own mind only. But if we may be allowed to paraphrase the idea of good by the words 'intelligent principle of law and order in the universe, embracing equally man and nature,' we begin to find a meeting-point between him and ourselves.

The question whether the ruler or statesman should be a philosopher is one that has not lost interest in modern times. In most countries of Europe and Asia there has been some one in the course of ages who has truly united the power of command with the power of thought and reflection, as there have been also many false combinations of these qualities. Some kind of speculative power is necessary both in practical and political life; like the rhetorician in the Phaedrus, men require to have a conception of the varieties of human character, and to be raised on great occasions above the commonplaces of ordinary life. Yet the idea of the philosopher-statesman has never been popular with the mass of mankind; partly because he cannot take the world into his confidence or make them understand the motives from which he acts; and also because they are jealous of a power which they do not understand. The revolution which human nature desires to effect step by step in many ages is likely to be precipitated by him in a single year or life. They are afraid that in the pursuit of his greater aims he may disregard the common feelings of humanity, he is too apt to be looking into the distant future or back into the remote past, and unable to see actions or events which, to use an expression of Plato's 'are tumbling out at his feet.' Besides, as Plato would say, there are other corruptions of these philosophical statesmen. Either 'the native hue of resolution is sicklied o'er with the pale cast of thought,' and at the moment when action above all things is required he is undecided, or general principles are enunciated by him in order to cover some change of policy; or his ignorance of the world has made him more easily fall a prey to the arts of others; or in some cases he has been converted into a courtier, who enjoys the luxury of holding liberal opinions, but was never known to perform a liberal action. No wonder that mankind have been in the habit of calling statesmen of this class pedants, sophisters, doctrinaires, visionaries. For, as we may be allowed to say, a little parodying the words of Plato, 'they have seen bad imitations of the philosopher-statesman.' But a man in whom the power of thought and action are perfectly balanced, equal to the present, reaching forward to the future, 'such a one,' ruling in a constitutional state, 'they have never seen.'

But as the philosopher is apt to fail in the routine of political life, so the ordinary statesman is also apt to fail in extraordinary crises. When the face of the world is beginning to alter, and thunder is heard in the distance, he is still guided by his old maxims, and is the slave of his inveterate party prejudices; he cannot perceive the signs of the times; instead of looking forward he looks back; he learns nothing and forgets nothing; with 'wise saws and modern instances' he would stem the rising tide of revolution. He lives more and more within the circle of his own party, as the world without him becomes stronger. This seems to be the reason why the old order of things makes so poor a figure when confronted with the new, why churches can never reform, why most political changes are made blindly and convulsively. The great crises in the history of nations have often been met by an ecclesiastical positiveness, and a more obstinate reassertion of principles which have lost their hold upon a nation. The fixed ideas of a reactionary statesman may be compared to madness; they grow upon him, and he becomes possessed by them; no judgement of others is ever admitted by him to be weighed in the balance against his own.

(d) Plato, labouring under what, to modern readers, appears to have been a confusion of ideas, assimilates the state to the individual, and fails to distinguish Ethics from Politics. He thinks that to be most of a state which is most like one man, and in which the citizens have the greatest uniformity of character. He does not see that the analogy is partly fallacious, and that the will or character of a state or nation is really the balance or rather the surplus of individual wills, which are limited by the condition of having to act in common. The movement of a body of men can never have the pliancy or facility of a single man; the freedom of the individual, which is always limited, becomes still more straitened when transferred to a nation. The powers of action and feeling are necessarily weaker and more balanced when they are diffused through a community; whence arises the often discussed question, 'Can a nation, like an individual, have a conscience?' We hesitate to say that the characters of nations are nothing more than the sum of the characters of the individuals who compose them; because there may be tendencies in individuals which react upon one another. A whole nation may be wiser than any one man in it; or may be animated by some common opinion or feeling which could not equally have affected the mind of a single person, or may have been inspired by a leader of genius to perform acts more than human. Plato does not appear to have analysed the complications which arise out of the collective action of mankind. Neither is he capable of seeing that analogies, though specious as arguments, may often have no foundation in fact, or of distinguishing between what is intelligible or vividly present to the mind, and what is true. In this respect he is far below Aristotle, who is comparatively seldom imposed upon by false analogies. He cannot disentangle the arts from the virtues—at least he is always arguing from one to the other. His notion of music is transferred from harmony of sounds to harmony of life: in this he is assisted by the ambiguities of language as well as by the prevalence of Pythagorean notions. And having once assimilated the state to the individual, he imagines that he will find the succession of states paralleled in the lives of individuals.

Still, through this fallacious medium, a real enlargement of ideas is attained. When the virtues as yet presented no distinct conception to the mind, a great advance was made by the comparison of them with the arts; for virtue is partly art, and has an outward form as well as an inward principle. The harmony of music affords a lively image of the harmonies of the world and of human life, and may be regarded as a splendid illustration which was naturally mistaken for a real analogy. In the same way the identification of ethics with politics has a tendency to give definiteness to ethics, and also to elevate and ennoble men's notions of the aims of government and of the duties of citizens; for ethics from one point of view may be conceived as an idealized law and politics; and politics, as ethics reduced to the conditions of human society. There have been evils which have arisen out of the attempt to identify them, and this has led to the separation or antagonism of them, which has been introduced by modern political writers. But we may likewise feel that something has been lost in their separation, and that the ancient philosophers who estimated the moral and intellectual wellbeing of mankind first, and the wealth of nations and individuals second, may have a salutary influence on the speculations of modern times. Many political maxims originate in a reaction against an opposite error; and when the errors against which they were directed have passed away, they in turn become errors.

3. Plato's views of education are in several respects remarkable; like the rest of the Republic they are partly Greek and partly ideal, beginning with the ordinary curriculum of the Greek youth, and extending to after-life. Plato is the first writer who distinctly says that education is to comprehend the whole of life, and to be a preparation for another in which education begins again. This is the continuous thread which runs through the Republic, and which more than any other of his ideas admits of an application to modern life.

He has long given up the notion that virtue cannot be taught; and he is disposed to modify the thesis of the Protagoras, that the virtues are one and not many. He is not unwilling to admit the sensible world into his scheme of truth. Nor does he assert in the Republic the involuntariness of vice, which is maintained by him in the Timaeus, Sophist, and Laws (Protag., Apol., Gorg.). Nor do the so-called Platonic ideas recovered from a former state of existence affect his theory of mental improvement. Still we observe in him the remains of the old Socratic doctrine, that true knowledge must be elicited from within, and is to be sought for in ideas, not in particulars of sense. Education, as he says, will implant a principle of intelligence which is better than ten thousand eyes. The paradox that the virtues are one, and the kindred notion that all virtue is knowledge, are not entirely renounced; the first is seen in the supremacy given to justice over the rest; the second in the tendency to absorb the moral virtues in the intellectual, and to centre all goodness in the contemplation of the idea of good. The world of sense is still depreciated and identified with opinion, though admitted to be a shadow of the true. In the Republic he is evidently impressed with the conviction that vice arises chiefly from ignorance and may be cured by education; the multitude are hardly to be deemed responsible for what they do. A faint allusion to the doctrine of reminiscence occurs in the Tenth Book; but Plato's views of education have no more real connection with a previous state of existence than our own; he only proposes to elicit from the mind that which is there already. Education is represented by him, not as the filling of a vessel, but as the turning the eye of the soul towards the light.

He treats first of music or literature, which he divides into true and false, and then goes on to gymnastics; of infancy in the Republic he takes no notice, though in the Laws he gives sage counsels about the nursing of children and the management of the mothers, and would have an education which is even prior to birth. But in the Republic he begins with the age at which the child is capable of receiving ideas, and boldly asserts, in language which sounds paradoxical to modern ears, that he must be taught the false before he can learn the true. The modern and ancient philosophical world are not agreed about truth and falsehood; the one identifies truth almost exclusively with fact, the other with ideas. This is the difference between ourselves and Plato, which is, however, partly a difference of words. For we too should admit that a child must receive many lessons which he imperfectly understands; he must be taught some things in a figure only, some too which he can hardly be expected to believe when he grows older; but we should limit the use of fiction by the necessity of the case. Plato would draw the line differently; according to him the aim of early education is not truth as a matter of fact, but truth as a matter of principle; the child is to be taught first simple religious truths, and then simple moral truths, and insensibly to learn the lesson of good manners and good taste. He would make an entire reformation of the old mythology; like Xenophanes and Heracleitus he is sensible of the deep chasm which separates his own age from Homer and Hesiod, whom he quotes and invests with an imaginary authority, but only for his own purposes. The lusts and treacheries of the gods are to be banished; the terrors of the world below are to be dispelled; the misbehaviour of the Homeric heroes is not to be a model for youth. But there is another strain heard in Homer which may teach our youth endurance; and something may be learnt in medicine from the simple practice of the Homeric age. The principles on which religion is to be based are two only: first, that God is true; secondly, that he is good. Modern and Christian writers have often fallen short of these; they can hardly be said to have gone beyond them.

The young are to be brought up in happy surroundings, out of the way of sights or sounds which may hurt the character or vitiate the taste. They are to live in an atmosphere of health; the breeze is always to be wafting to them the impressions of truth and goodness. Could such an education be realized, or if our modern religious education could be bound up with truth and virtue and good manners and good taste, that would be the best hope of human improvement. Plato, like ourselves, is looking forward to changes in the moral and religious world, and is preparing for them. He recognizes the danger of unsettling young men's minds by sudden changes of laws and principles, by destroying the sacredness of one set of ideas when there is nothing else to take their place. He is afraid too of the influence of the drama, on the ground that it encourages false sentiment, and therefore he would not have his children taken to the theatre; he thinks that the effect on the spectators is bad, and on the actors still worse. His idea of education is that of harmonious growth, in which are insensibly learnt the lessons of temperance and endurance, and the body and mind develope in equal proportions. The first principle which runs through all art and nature is simplicity; this also is to be the rule of human life.

The second stage of education is gymnastic, which answers to the period of muscular growth and development. The simplicity which is enforced in music is extended to gymnastic; Plato is aware that the training of the body may be inconsistent with the training of the mind, and that bodily exercise may be easily overdone. Excessive training of the body is apt to give men a headache or to render them sleepy at a lecture on philosophy, and this they attribute not to the true cause, but to the nature of the subject. Two points are noticeable in Plato's treatment of gymnastic:—First, that the time of training is entirely separated from the time of literary education. He seems to have thought that two things of an opposite and different nature could not be learnt at the same time. Here we can hardly agree with him; and, if we may judge by experience, the effect of spending three years between the ages of fourteen and seventeen in mere bodily exercise would be far from improving to the intellect. Secondly, he affirms that music and gymnastic are not, as common opinion is apt to imagine, intended, the one for the cultivation of the mind and the other of the body, but that they are both equally designed for the improvement of the mind. The body, in his view, is the servant of the mind; the subjection of the lower to the higher is for the advantage of both. And doubtless the mind may exercise a very great and paramount influence over the body, if exerted not at particular moments and by fits and starts, but continuously, in making preparation for the whole of life. Other Greek writers saw the mischievous tendency of Spartan discipline (Arist. Pol; Thuc.). But only Plato recognized the fundamental error on which the practice was based.

The subject of gymnastic leads Plato to the sister subject of medicine, which he further illustrates by the parallel of law. The modern disbelief in medicine has led in this, as in some other departments of knowledge, to a demand for greater simplicity; physicians are becoming aware that they often make diseases 'greater and more complicated' by their treatment of them (Rep.). In two thousand years their art has made but slender progress; what they have gained in the analysis of the parts is in a great degree lost by their feebler conception of the human frame as a whole. They have attended more to the cure of diseases than to the conditions of health; and the improvements in medicine have been more than counterbalanced by the disuse of regular training. Until lately they have hardly thought of air and water, the importance of which was well understood by the ancients; as Aristotle remarks, 'Air and water, being the elements which we most use, have the greatest effect upon health' (Polit.). For ages physicians have been under the dominion of prejudices which have only recently given way; and now there are as many opinions in medicine as in theology, and an equal degree of scepticism and some want of toleration about both. Plato has several good notions about medicine; according to him, 'the eye cannot be cured without the rest of the body, nor the body without the mind' (Charm.). No man of sense, he says in the Timaeus, would take physic; and we heartily sympathize with him in the Laws when he declares that 'the limbs of the rustic worn with toil will derive more benefit from warm baths than from the prescriptions of a not over wise doctor.' But we can hardly praise him when, in obedience to the authority of Homer, he depreciates diet, or approve of the inhuman spirit in which he would get rid of invalid and useless lives by leaving them to die. He does not seem to have considered that the 'bridle of Theages' might be accompanied by qualities which were of far more value to the State than the health or strength of the citizens; or that the duty of taking care of the helpless might be an important element of education in a State. The physician himself (this is a delicate and subtle observation) should not be a man in robust health; he should have, in modern phraseology, a nervous temperament; he should have experience of disease in his own person, in order that his powers of observation may be quickened in the case of others.

The perplexity of medicine is paralleled by the perplexity of law; in which, again, Plato would have men follow the golden rule of simplicity. Greater matters are to be determined by the legislator or by the oracle of Delphi, lesser matters are to be left to the temporary regulation of the citizens themselves. Plato is aware that laissez faire is an important element of government. The diseases of a State are like the heads of a hydra; they multiply when they are cut off. The true remedy for them is not extirpation but prevention. And the way to prevent them is to take care of education, and education will take care of all the rest. So in modern times men have often felt that the only political measure worth having—the only one which would produce any certain or lasting effect, was a measure of national education. And in our own more than in any previous age the necessity has been recognized of restoring the ever-increasing confusion of law to simplicity and common sense.

When the training in music and gymnastic is completed, there follows the first stage of active and public life. But soon education is to begin again from a new point of view. In the interval between the Fourth and Seventh Books we have discussed the nature of knowledge, and have thence been led to form a higher conception of what was required of us. For true knowledge, according to Plato, is of abstractions, and has to do, not with particulars or individuals, but with universals only; not with the beauties of poetry, but with the ideas of philosophy. And the great aim of education is the cultivation of the habit of abstraction. This is to be acquired through the study of the mathematical sciences. They alone are capable of giving ideas of relation, and of arousing the dormant energies of thought.

Mathematics in the age of Plato comprehended a very small part of that which is now included in them; but they bore a much larger proportion to the sum of human knowledge. They were the only organon of thought which the human mind at that time possessed, and the only measure by which the chaos of particulars could be reduced to rule and order. The faculty which they trained was naturally at war with the poetical or imaginative; and hence to Plato, who is everywhere seeking for abstractions and trying to get rid of the illusions of sense, nearly the whole of education is contained in them. They seemed to have an inexhaustible application, partly because their true limits were not yet understood. These Plato himself is beginning to investigate; though not aware that number and figure are mere abstractions of sense, he recognizes that the forms used by geometry are borrowed from the sensible world. He seeks to find the ultimate ground of mathematical ideas in the idea of good, though he does not satisfactorily explain the connexion between them; and in his conception of the relation of ideas to numbers, he falls very far short of the definiteness attributed to him by Aristotle (Met.). But if he fails to recognize the true limits of mathematics, he also reaches a point beyond them; in his view, ideas of number become secondary to a higher conception of knowledge. The dialectician is as much above the mathematician as the mathematician is above the ordinary man. The one, the self-proving, the good which is the higher sphere of dialectic, is the perfect truth to which all things ascend, and in which they finally repose.

This self-proving unity or idea of good is a mere vision of which no distinct explanation can be given, relative only to a particular stage in Greek philosophy. It is an abstraction under which no individuals are comprehended, a whole which has no parts (Arist., Nic. Eth.). The vacancy of such a form was perceived by Aristotle, but not by Plato. Nor did he recognize that in the dialectical process are included two or more methods of investigation which are at variance with each other. He did not see that whether he took the longer or the shorter road, no advance could be made in this way. And yet such visions often have an immense effect; for although the method of science cannot anticipate science, the idea of science, not as it is, but as it will be in the future, is a great and inspiring principle. In the pursuit of knowledge we are always pressing forward to something beyond us; and as a false conception of knowledge, for example the scholastic philosophy, may lead men astray during many ages, so the true ideal, though vacant, may draw all their thoughts in a right direction. It makes a great difference whether the general expectation of knowledge, as this indefinite feeling may be termed, is based upon a sound judgment. For mankind may often entertain a true conception of what knowledge ought to be when they have but a slender experience of facts. The correlation of the sciences, the consciousness of the unity of nature, the idea of classification, the sense of proportion, the unwillingness to stop short of certainty or to confound probability with truth, are important principles of the higher education. Although Plato could tell us nothing, and perhaps knew that he could tell us nothing, of the absolute truth, he has exercised an influence on the human mind which even at the present day is not exhausted; and political and social questions may yet arise in which the thoughts of Plato may be read anew and receive a fresh meaning.

The Idea of good is so called only in the Republic, but there are traces of it in other dialogues of Plato. It is a cause as well as an idea, and from this point of view may be compared with the creator of the Timaeus, who out of his goodness created all things. It corresponds to a certain extent with the modern conception of a law of nature, or of a final cause, or of both in one, and in this regard may be connected with the measure and symmetry of the Philebus. It is represented in the Symposium under the aspect of beauty, and is supposed to be attained there by stages of initiation, as here by regular gradations of knowledge. Viewed subjectively, it is the process or science of dialectic. This is the science which, according to the Phaedrus, is the true basis of rhetoric, which alone is able to distinguish the natures and classes of men and things; which divides a whole into the natural parts, and reunites the scattered parts into a natural or organized whole; which defines the abstract essences or universal ideas of all things, and connects them; which pierces the veil of hypotheses and reaches the final cause or first principle of all; which regards the sciences in relation to the idea of good. This ideal science is the highest process of thought, and may be described as the soul conversing with herself or holding communion with eternal truth and beauty, and in another form is the everlasting question and answer—the ceaseless interrogative of Socrates. The dialogues of Plato are themselves examples of the nature and method of dialectic. Viewed objectively, the idea of good is a power or cause which makes the world without us correspond with the world within. Yet this world without us is still a world of ideas. With Plato the investigation of nature is another department of knowledge, and in this he seeks to attain only probable conclusions (Timaeus).

If we ask whether this science of dialectic which Plato only half explains to us is more akin to logic or to metaphysics, the answer is that in his mind the two sciences are not as yet distinguished, any more than the subjective and objective aspects of the world and of man, which German philosophy has revealed to us. Nor has he determined whether his science of dialectic is at rest or in motion, concerned with the contemplation of absolute being, or with a process of development and evolution. Modern metaphysics may be described as the science of abstractions, or as the science of the evolution of thought; modern logic, when passing beyond the bounds of mere Aristotelian forms, may be defined as the science of method. The germ of both of them is contained in the Platonic dialectic; all metaphysicians have something in common with the ideas of Plato; all logicians have derived something from the method of Plato. The nearest approach in modern philosophy to the universal science of Plato, is to be found in the Hegelian 'succession of moments in the unity of the idea.' Plato and Hegel alike seem to have conceived the world as the correlation of abstractions; and not impossibly they would have understood one another better than any of their commentators understand them (Swift's Voyage to Laputa. 'Having a desire to see those ancients who were most renowned for wit and learning, I set apart one day on purpose. I proposed that Homer and Aristotle might appear at the head of all their commentators; but these were so numerous that some hundreds were forced to attend in the court and outward rooms of the palace. I knew, and could distinguish these two heroes, at first sight, not only from the crowd, but from each other. Homer was the taller and comelier person of the two, walked very erect for one of his age, and his eyes were the most quick and piercing I ever beheld. Aristotle stooped much, and made use of a staff. His visage was meagre, his hair lank and thin, and his voice hollow. I soon discovered that both of them were perfect strangers to the rest of the company, and had never seen or heard of them before. And I had a whisper from a ghost, who shall be nameless, "That these commentators always kept in the most distant quarters from their principals, in the lower world, through a consciousness of shame and guilt, because they had so horribly misrepresented the meaning of these authors to posterity." I introduced Didymus and Eustathius to Homer, and prevailed on him to treat them better than perhaps they deserved, for he soon found they wanted a genius to enter into the spirit of a poet. But Aristotle was out of all patience with the account I gave him of Scotus and Ramus, as I presented them to him; and he asked them "whether the rest of the tribe were as great dunces as themselves?"'). There is, however, a difference between them: for whereas Hegel is thinking of all the minds of men as one mind, which developes the stages of the idea in different countries or at different times in the same country, with Plato these gradations are regarded only as an order of thought or ideas; the history of the human mind had not yet dawned upon him.

Many criticisms may be made on Plato's theory of education. While in some respects he unavoidably falls short of modern thinkers, in others he is in advance of them. He is opposed to the modes of education which prevailed in his own time; but he can hardly be said to have discovered new ones. He does not see that education is relative to the characters of individuals; he only desires to impress the same form of the state on the minds of all. He has no sufficient idea of the effect of literature on the formation of the mind, and greatly exaggerates that of mathematics. His aim is above all things to train the reasoning faculties; to implant in the mind the spirit and power of abstraction; to explain and define general notions, and, if possible, to connect them. No wonder that in the vacancy of actual knowledge his followers, and at times even he himself, should have fallen away from the doctrine of ideas, and have returned to that branch of knowledge in which alone the relation of the one and many can be truly seen—the science of number. In his views both of teaching and training he might be styled, in modern language, a doctrinaire; after the Spartan fashion he would have his citizens cast in one mould; he does not seem to consider that some degree of freedom, 'a little wholesome neglect,' is necessary to strengthen and develope the character and to give play to the individual nature. His citizens would not have acquired that knowledge which in the vision of Er is supposed to be gained by the pilgrims from their experience of evil.

On the other hand, Plato is far in advance of modern philosophers and theologians when he teaches that education is to be continued through life and will begin again in another. He would never allow education of some kind to cease; although he was aware that the proverbial saying of Solon, 'I grow old learning many things,' cannot be applied literally. Himself ravished with the contemplation of the idea of good, and delighting in solid geometry (Rep.), he has no difficulty in imagining that a lifetime might be passed happily in such pursuits. We who know how many more men of business there are in the world than real students or thinkers, are not equally sanguine. The education which he proposes for his citizens is really the ideal life of the philosopher or man of genius, interrupted, but only for a time, by practical duties,—a life not for the many, but for the few.

Yet the thought of Plato may not be wholly incapable of application to our own times. Even if regarded as an ideal which can never be realized, it may have a great effect in elevating the characters of mankind, and raising them above the routine of their ordinary occupation or profession. It is the best form under which we can conceive the whole of life. Nevertheless the idea of Plato is not easily put into practice. For the education of after life is necessarily the education which each one gives himself. Men and women cannot be brought together in schools or colleges at forty or fifty years of age; and if they could the result would be disappointing. The destination of most men is what Plato would call 'the Den' for the whole of life, and with that they are content. Neither have they teachers or advisers with whom they can take counsel in riper years. There is no 'schoolmaster abroad' who will tell them of their faults, or inspire them with the higher sense of duty, or with the ambition of a true success in life; no Socrates who will convict them of ignorance; no Christ, or follower of Christ, who will reprove them of sin. Hence they have a difficulty in receiving the first element of improvement, which is self-knowledge. The hopes of youth no longer stir them; they rather wish to rest than to pursue high objects. A few only who have come across great men and women, or eminent teachers of religion and morality, have received a second life from them, and have lighted a candle from the fire of their genius.

The want of energy is one of the main reasons why so few persons continue to improve in later years. They have not the will, and do not know the way. They 'never try an experiment,' or look up a point of interest for themselves; they make no sacrifices for the sake of knowledge; their minds, like their bodies, at a certain age become fixed. Genius has been defined as 'the power of taking pains'; but hardly any one keeps up his interest in knowledge throughout a whole life. The troubles of a family, the business of making money, the demands of a profession destroy the elasticity of the mind. The waxen tablet of the memory which was once capable of receiving 'true thoughts and clear impressions' becomes hard and crowded; there is not room for the accumulations of a long life (Theaet.). The student, as years advance, rather makes an exchange of knowledge than adds to his stores. There is no pressing necessity to learn; the stock of Classics or History or Natural Science which was enough for a man at twenty-five is enough for him at fifty. Neither is it easy to give a definite answer to any one who asks how he is to improve. For self-education consists in a thousand things, commonplace in themselves,—in adding to what we are by nature something of what we are not; in learning to see ourselves as others see us; in judging, not by opinion, but by the evidence of facts; in seeking out the society of superior minds; in a study of lives and writings of great men; in observation of the world and character; in receiving kindly the natural influence of different times of life; in any act or thought which is raised above the practice or opinions of mankind; in the pursuit of some new or original enquiry; in any effort of mind which calls forth some latent power.

If any one is desirous of carrying out in detail the Platonic education of after-life, some such counsels as the following may be offered to him:—That he shall choose the branch of knowledge to which his own mind most distinctly inclines, and in which he takes the greatest delight, either one which seems to connect with his own daily employment, or, perhaps, furnishes the greatest contrast to it. He may study from the speculative side the profession or business in which he is practically engaged. He may make Homer, Dante, Shakespeare, Plato, Bacon the friends and companions of his life. He may find opportunities of hearing the living voice of a great teacher. He may select for enquiry some point of history or some unexplained phenomenon of nature. An hour a day passed in such scientific or literary pursuits will furnish as many facts as the memory can retain, and will give him 'a pleasure not to be repented of' (Timaeus). Only let him beware of being the slave of crotchets, or of running after a Will o' the Wisp in his ignorance, or in his vanity of attributing to himself the gifts of a poet or assuming the air of a philosopher. He should know the limits of his own powers. Better to build up the mind by slow additions, to creep on quietly from one thing to another, to gain insensibly new powers and new interests in knowledge, than to form vast schemes which are never destined to be realized. But perhaps, as Plato would say, 'This is part of another subject' (Tim.); though we may also defend our digression by his example (Theaet.).

4. We remark with surprise that the progress of nations or the natural growth of institutions which fill modern treatises on political philosophy seem hardly ever to have attracted the attention of Plato and Aristotle. The ancients were familiar with the mutability of human affairs; they could moralize over the ruins of cities and the fall of empires (Plato, Statesman, and Sulpicius' Letter to Cicero); by them fate and chance were deemed to be real powers, almost persons, and to have had a great share in political events. The wiser of them like Thucydides believed that 'what had been

would be again,' and that a tolerable idea of the future could be gathered from the past. Also they had dreams of a Golden Age which existed once upon a time and might still exist in some unknown land, or might return again in the remote future. But the regular growth of a state enlightened by experience, progressing in knowledge, improving in the arts, of which the citizens were educated by the fulfilment of political duties, appears never to have come within the range of their hopes and aspirations. Such a state had never been seen, and therefore could not be conceived by them. Their experience (Aristot. Metaph.; Plato, Laws) led them to conclude that there had been cycles of civilization in which the arts had been discovered and lost many times over, and cities had been overthrown and rebuilt again and again, and deluges and volcanoes and other natural convulsions had altered the face of the earth. Tradition told them of many destructions of mankind and of the preservation of a remnant. The world began again after a deluge and was reconstructed out of the fragments of itself. Also they were acquainted with empires of unknown antiquity, like the Egyptian or Assyrian; but they had never seen them grow, and could not imagine, any more than we can, the state of man which preceded them. They were puzzled and awestricken by the Egyptian monuments, of which the forms, as Plato says, not in a figure, but literally, were ten thousand years old (Laws), and they contrasted the antiquity of Egypt with their own short memories.

The early legends of Hellas have no real connection with the later history: they are at a distance, and the intermediate region is concealed from view; there is no road or path which leads from one to the other. At the beginning of Greek history, in the vestibule of the temple, is seen standing first of all the figure of the legislator, himself the interpreter and servant of the God. The fundamental laws which he gives are not supposed to change with time and circumstances. The salvation of the state is held rather to depend on the inviolable maintenance of them. They were sanctioned by the authority of heaven, and it was deemed impiety to alter them. The desire to maintain them unaltered seems to be the origin of what at first sight is very surprising to us—the intolerant zeal of Plato

against innovators in religion or politics (Laws); although with a happy
inconsistency he is also willing that the laws of other countries should
be studied and improvements in legislation privately communicated to
the Nocturnal Council (Laws). The additions which were made to them
in later ages in order to meet the increasing complexity of affairs were
still ascribed by a fiction to the original legislator; and the words of such
enactments at Athens were disputed over as if they had been the words of
Solon himself. Plato hopes to preserve in a later generation the mind of the
legislator; he would have his citizens remain within the lines which he has
laid down for them. He would not harass them with minute regulations,
he would have allowed some changes in the laws: but not changes which
would affect the fundamental institutions of the state, such for example
as would convert an aristocracy into a timocracy, or a timocracy into a
popular form of government.

Passing from speculations to facts, we observe that progress has been
the exception rather than the law of human history. And therefore we are
not surprised to find that the idea of progress is of modern rather than
of ancient date; and, like the idea of a philosophy of history, is not more
than a century or two old. It seems to have arisen out of the impression
left on the human mind by the growth of the Roman Empire and of the
Christian Church, and to be due to the political and social improvements
which they introduced into the world; and still more in our own century to
the idealism of the first French Revolution and the triumph of American
Independence; and in a yet greater degree to the vast material prosperity
and growth of population in England and her colonies and in America. It
is also to be ascribed in a measure to the greater study of the philosophy
of history. The optimist temperament of some great writers has assisted
the creation of it, while the opposite character has led a few to regard the
future of the world as dark. The 'spectator of all time and of all existence'
sees more of 'the increasing purpose which through the ages ran' than
formerly: but to the inhabitant of a small state of Hellas the vision was
necessarily limited like the valley in which he dwelt. There was no remote
past on which his eye could rest, nor any future from which the veil was

partly lifted up by the analogy of history. The narrowness of view, which to ourselves appears so singular, was to him natural, if not unavoidable.

5. For the relation of the Republic to the Statesman and the Laws, and the two other works of Plato which directly treat of politics, see the Introductions to the two latter; a few general points of comparison may be touched upon in this place.

And first of the Laws.

(1) The Republic, though probably written at intervals, yet speaking generally and judging by the indications of thought and style, may be reasonably ascribed to the middle period of Plato's life: the Laws are certainly the work of his declining years, and some portions of them at any rate seem to have been written in extreme old age.

(2) The Republic is full of hope and aspiration: the Laws bear the stamp of failure and disappointment. The one is a finished work which received the last touches of the author: the other is imperfectly executed, and apparently unfinished. The one has the grace and beauty of youth: the other has lost the poetical form, but has more of the severity and knowledge of life which is characteristic of old age.

(3) The most conspicuous defect of the Laws is the failure of dramatic power, whereas the Republic is full of striking contrasts of ideas and oppositions of character.

(4) The Laws may be said to have more the nature of a sermon, the Republic of a poem; the one is more religious, the other more intellectual.

(5) Many theories of Plato, such as the doctrine of ideas, the government of the world by philosophers, are not found in the Laws; the immortality of the soul is first mentioned in xii; the person of Socrates has altogether disappeared. The community of women and children is renounced; the institution of common or public meals for women (Laws) is for the first time introduced (Ar. Pol.).

(6) There remains in the Laws the old enmity to the poets, who are ironically saluted in high-flown terms, and, at the same time, are peremptorily ordered out of the city, if they are not willing to submit their poems to the censorship of the magistrates (Rep.).

(7) Though the work is in most respects inferior, there are a few passages in the Laws, such as the honour due to the soul, the evils of licentious or unnatural love, the whole of Book x. (religion), the dishonesty of retail trade, and bequests, which come more home to us, and contain more of what may be termed the modern element in Plato than almost anything in the Republic.

The relation of the two works to one another is very well given:

(1) by Aristotle in the Politics from the side of the Laws:—

'The same, or nearly the same, objections apply to Plato's later work, the Laws, and therefore we had better examine briefly the constitution which is therein described. In the Republic, Socrates has definitely settled in all a few questions only; such as the community of women and children, the community of property, and the constitution of the state. The population is divided into two classes—one of husbandmen, and the other of warriors; from this latter is taken a third class of counsellors and rulers of the state. But Socrates has not determined whether the husbandmen and artists are to have a share in the government, and whether they too are to carry arms and share in military service or not. He certainly thinks that the women ought to share in the education of the guardians, and to fight by their side. The remainder of the work is filled up with digressions foreign to the main subject, and with discussions about the education of the guardians. In the Laws there is hardly anything but laws; not much is said about the constitution. This, which he had intended to make more of the ordinary type, he gradually brings round to the other or ideal form. For with the exception of the community of women and property, he supposes everything to be the same in both states; there is to be the same education; the citizens of both are to live free from servile occupations, and there are to be common meals in both. The only difference is that in the Laws the common meals are extended to women, and the warriors number about 5000, but in the Republic only 1000.'

(2) by Plato in the Laws (Book v.), from the side of the Republic:—

'The first and highest form of the state and of the government and of the law is that in which there prevails most widely the ancient saying that

"Friends have all things in common." Whether there is now, or ever will be, this communion of women and children and of property, in which the private and individual is altogether banished from life, and things which are by nature private, such as eyes and ears and hands, have become common, and all men express praise and blame, and feel joy and sorrow, on the same occasions, and the laws unite the city to the utmost,—whether all this is possible or not, I say that no man, acting upon any other principle, will ever constitute a state more exalted in virtue, or truer or better than this. Such a state, whether inhabited by Gods or sons of Gods, will make them blessed who dwell therein; and therefore to this we are to look for the pattern of the state, and to cling to this, and, as far as possible, to seek for one which is like this. The state which we have now in hand, when created, will be nearest to immortality and unity in the next degree; and after that, by the grace of God, we will complete the third one. And we will begin by speaking of the nature and origin of the second.'

The comparatively short work called the Statesman or Politicus in its style and manner is more akin to the Laws, while in its idealism it rather resembles the Republic. As far as we can judge by various indications of language and thought, it must be later than the one and of course earlier than the other. In both the Republic and Statesman a close connection is maintained between Politics and Dialectic. In the Statesman, enquiries into the principles of Method are interspersed with discussions about Politics. The comparative advantages of the rule of law and of a person are considered, and the decision given in favour of a person (Arist. Pol.). But much may be said on the other side, nor is the opposition necessary; for a person may rule by law, and law may be so applied as to be the living voice of the legislator. As in the Republic, there is a myth, describing, however, not a future, but a former existence of mankind. The question is asked, 'Whether the state of innocence which is described in the myth, or a state like our own which possesses art and science and distinguishes good from evil, is the preferable condition of man.' To this question of the comparative happiness of civilized and primitive life, which was so often discussed in the last century and in our own, no answer is given. The

Statesman, though less perfect in style than the Republic and of far less range, may justly be regarded as one of the greatest of Plato's dialogues.

6. Others as well as Plato have chosen an ideal Republic to be the vehicle of thoughts which they could not definitely express, or which went beyond their own age. The classical writing which approaches most nearly to the Republic of Plato is the 'De Republica' of Cicero; but neither in this nor in any other of his dialogues does he rival the art of Plato. The manners are clumsy and inferior; the hand of the rhetorician is apparent at every turn. Yet noble sentiments are constantly recurring: the true note of Roman patriotism—'We Romans are a great people'—resounds through the whole work. Like Socrates, Cicero turns away from the phenomena of the heavens to civil and political life. He would rather not discuss the 'two Suns' of which all Rome was talking, when he can converse about 'the two nations in one' which had divided Rome ever since the days of the Gracchi. Like Socrates again, speaking in the person of Scipio, he is afraid lest he should assume too much the character of a teacher, rather than of an equal who is discussing among friends the two sides of a question. He would confine the terms King or State to the rule of reason and justice, and he will not concede that title either to a democracy or to a monarchy. But under the rule of reason and justice he is willing to include the natural superior ruling over the natural inferior, which he compares to the soul ruling over the body. He prefers a mixture of forms of government to any single one. The two portraits of the just and the unjust, which occur in the second book of the Republic, are transferred to the state—Philus, one of the interlocutors, maintaining against his will the necessity of injustice as a principle of government, while the other, Laelius, supports the opposite thesis. His views of language and number are derived from Plato; like him he denounces the drama. He also declares that if his life were to be twice as long he would have no time to read the lyric poets. The picture of democracy is translated by him word for word, though he had hardly shown himself able to 'carry the jest' of Plato. He converts into a stately sentence the humorous fancy about the animals, who 'are so imbued with the spirit of democracy that they make the passers-by get out of their way.'

His description of the tyrant is imitated from Plato, but is far inferior. The second book is historical, and claims for the Roman constitution (which is to him the ideal) a foundation of fact such as Plato probably intended to have given to the Republic in the Critias. His most remarkable imitation of Plato is the adaptation of the vision of Er, which is converted by Cicero into the 'Somnium Scipionis'; he has 'romanized' the myth of the Republic, adding an argument for the immortality of the soul taken from the Phaedrus, and some other touches derived from the Phaedo and the Timaeus. Though a beautiful tale and containing splendid passages, the 'Somnium Scipionis; is very inferior to the vision of Er; it is only a dream, and hardly allows the reader to suppose that the writer believes in his own creation. Whether his dialogues were framed on the model of the lost dialogues of Aristotle, as he himself tells us, or of Plato, to which they bear many superficial resemblances, he is still the Roman orator; he is not conversing, but making speeches, and is never able to mould the intractable Latin to the grace and ease of the Greek Platonic dialogue. But if he is defective in form, much more is he inferior to the Greek in matter; he nowhere in his philosophical writings leaves upon our minds the impression of an original thinker.

Plato's Republic has been said to be a church and not a state; and such an ideal of a city in the heavens has always hovered over the Christian world, and is embodied in St. Augustine's 'De Civitate Dei,' which is suggested by the decay and fall of the Roman Empire, much in the same manner in which we may imagine the Republic of Plato to have been influenced by the decline of Greek politics in the writer's own age. The difference is that in the time of Plato the degeneracy, though certain, was gradual and insensible: whereas the taking of Rome by the Goths stirred like an earthquake the age of St. Augustine. Men were inclined to believe that the overthrow of the city was to be ascribed to the anger felt by the old Roman deities at the neglect of their worship. St. Augustine maintains the opposite thesis; he argues that the destruction of the Roman Empire is due, not to the rise of Christianity, but to the vices of Paganism. He wanders over Roman history, and over Greek philosophy and mythology, and finds everywhere crime, impiety and falsehood. He compares the worst parts of the Gentile religions with the best elements of the faith of Christ. He shows nothing of the spirit which led others of the early Christian Fathers to recognize in the writings of the Greek philosophers the power of the divine truth. He traces the parallel of the kingdom of God, that is, the history of the Jews, contained in their scriptures, and of the kingdoms of the world, which are found in gentile writers, and pursues them both into an ideal future. It need hardly be remarked that his use both of Greek and of Roman historians and of the sacred writings of the Jews is wholly uncritical. The heathen mythology, the Sybilline oracles, the myths of Plato, the dreams of Neo-Platonists are equally regarded by him as matter of fact. He must be acknowledged to be a strictly polemical or controversial writer who makes the best of everything on one side and the worst of everything on the other. He has no sympathy with the old Roman life as Plato has with Greek life, nor has he any idea of the ecclesiastical kingdom which was to arise out of the ruins of the Roman empire. He is not blind to the defects of the Christian Church, and looks forward to a time when Christian and Pagan shall be alike brought before the judgment-seat, and the true City of God shall appear...The work of St. Augustine is a curious repertory of antiquarian learning and quotations, deeply penetrated with Christian ethics, but showing little power of reasoning, and a slender knowledge of the Greek literature and language. He was a great genius, and a noble character, yet hardly capable of feeling or understanding anything external to his own theology. Of all the ancient philosophers he is most attracted by Plato, though he is very slightly acquainted with his writings. He is inclined to believe that the idea of creation in the Timaeus is derived from the narrative in Genesis; and he is strangely taken with the coincidence (?) of Plato's saying that 'the philosopher is the lover of God,' and the words of the Book of Exodus in which God reveals himself to Moses (Exod.) He dwells at length on miracles performed in his own day, of which the evidence is regarded by him as irresistible. He speaks in a very interesting manner of the beauty and utility of nature and of the human frame, which he conceives to afford a foretaste of the heavenly state and of the resurrection of the body. The book is not really what to most persons the title of it would imply, and belongs to an age which has passed away. But it contains many fine passages and thoughts which are for all time.

The short treatise de Monarchia of Dante is by far the most remarkable of mediaeval ideals, and bears the impress of the great genius in whom Italy and the Middle Ages are so vividly reflected. It is the vision of an Universal Empire, which is supposed to be the natural and necessary government of the world, having a divine authority distinct from the Papacy, yet coextensive with it. It is not 'the ghost of the dead Roman Empire sitting crowned upon the grave thereof,' but the legitimate heir and successor of it, justified by the ancient virtues of the Romans and the beneficence of their rule. Their right to be the governors of the world is also confirmed by the testimony of miracles, and acknowledged by St. Paul when he appealed to Caesar, and even more emphatically by Christ Himself, Who could not have made atonement for the sins of men if He had not been condemned by a divinely authorized tribunal. The necessity for the establishment of an Universal Empire is proved partly by a priori arguments such as the unity of God and the unity of the family or nation; partly by perversions of Scripture and history, by false analogies of nature, by misapplied quotations from the classics, and by odd scraps and commonplaces of logic, showing a familiar but by no means exact knowledge of Aristotle (of Plato there is none). But a more convincing argument still is the miserable state of the world, which he touchingly describes. He sees no hope of happiness or peace for mankind until all nations of the earth are comprehended in a single empire. The whole treatise shows how deeply the idea of the Roman Empire was fixed in the minds of his contemporaries. Not much argument was needed to maintain the truth of a theory which to his own contemporaries seemed so natural and congenial. He speaks, or rather preaches, from the point of view, not of the ecclesiastic, but of the layman, although, as a good Catholic, he is willing to acknowledge that in certain respects the Empire must submit to the Church. The beginning and end of all his noble reflections and of his arguments, good and bad, is the aspiration 'that in this little plot

of earth belonging to mortal man life may pass in freedom and peace.'
So inextricably is his vision of the future bound up with the beliefs and
circumstances of his own age.

The 'Utopia' of Sir Thomas More is a surprising monument of his
genius, and shows a reach of thought far beyond his contemporaries. The
book was written by him at the age of about 34 or 35, and is full of the
generous sentiments of youth. He brings the light of Plato to bear upon
the miserable state of his own country. Living not long after the Wars of the
Roses, and in the dregs of the Catholic Church in England, he is indignant
at the corruption of the clergy, at the luxury of the nobility and gentry,
at the sufferings of the poor, at the calamities caused by war. To the eye
of More the whole world was in dissolution and decay; and side by side
with the misery and oppression which he has described in the First Book of
the Utopia, he places in the Second Book the ideal state which by the help
of Plato he had constructed. The times were full of stir and intellectual
interest. The distant murmur of the Reformation was beginning to be
heard. To minds like More's, Greek literature was a revelation: there had
arisen an art of interpretation, and the New Testament was beginning
to be understood as it had never been before, and has not often been
since, in its natural sense. The life there depicted appeared to him wholly
unlike that of Christian commonwealths, in which 'he saw nothing but
a certain conspiracy of rich men procuring their own commodities under
the name and title of the Commonwealth.' He thought that Christ, like
Plato, 'instituted all things common,' for which reason, he tells us, the
citizens of Utopia were the more willing to receive his doctrines ('Howbeit,
I think this was no small help and furtherance in the matter, that they heard
us say that Christ instituted among his, all things common, and that the
same community doth yet remain in the rightest Christian communities'
(Utopia).). The community of property is a fixed idea with him, though
he is aware of the arguments which may be urged on the other side ('These
things (I say), when I consider with myself, I hold well with Plato, and do
nothing marvel that he would make no laws for them that refused those
laws, whereby all men should have and enjoy equal portions of riches and

commodities. For the wise men did easily foresee this to be the one and only way to the wealth of a community, if equality of all things should be brought in and established' (Utopia).). We wonder how in the reign of Henry VIII, though veiled in another language and published in a foreign country, such speculations could have been endured.

He is gifted with far greater dramatic invention than any one who succeeded him, with the exception of Swift. In the art of feigning he is a worthy disciple of Plato. Like him, starting from a small portion of fact, he founds his tale with admirable skill on a few lines in the Latin narrative of the voyages of Amerigo Vespucci. He is very precise about dates and facts, and has the power of making us believe that the narrator of the tale must have been an eyewitness. We are fairly puzzled by his manner of mixing up real and imaginary persons; his boy John Clement and Peter Giles, citizen of Antwerp, with whom he disputes about the precise words which are supposed to have been used by the (imaginary) Portuguese traveller, Raphael Hythloday. 'I have the more cause,' says Hythloday, 'to fear that my words shall not be believed, for that I know how difficultly and hardly I myself would have believed another man telling the same, if I had not myself seen it with mine own eyes.' Or again: 'If you had been with me in Utopia, and had presently seen their fashions and laws as I did which lived there five years and more, and would never have come thence, but only to make the new land known here,' etc. More greatly regrets that he forgot to ask Hythloday in what part of the world Utopia is situated; he 'would have spent no small sum of money rather than it should have escaped him,' and he begs Peter Giles to see Hythloday or write to him and obtain an answer to the question. After this we are not surprised to hear that a Professor of Divinity (perhaps 'a late famous vicar of Croydon in Surrey,' as the translator thinks) is desirous of being sent thither as a missionary by the High Bishop, 'yea, and that he may himself be made Bishop of Utopia, nothing doubting that he must obtain this Bishopric with suit; and he counteth that a godly suit which proceedeth not of the desire of honour or lucre, but only of a godly zeal.' The design may have failed through the disappearance of Hythloday, concerning whom we have 'very uncertain news' after his departure. There is no doubt, however, that he had told More and Giles the exact situation of the island, but unfortunately at the same moment More's attention, as he is reminded in a letter from Giles, was drawn off by a servant, and one of the company from a cold caught on shipboard coughed so loud as to prevent Giles from hearing. And 'the secret has perished' with him; to this day the place of Utopia remains unknown.

The words of Phaedrus, 'O Socrates, you can easily invent Egyptians or anything,' are recalled to our mind as we read this lifelike fiction. Yet the greater merit of the work is not the admirable art, but the originality of thought. More is as free as Plato from the prejudices of his age, and far more tolerant. The Utopians do not allow him who believes not in the immortality of the soul to share in the administration of the state (Laws), 'howbeit they put him to no punishment, because they be persuaded that it is in no man's power to believe what he list'; and 'no man is to be blamed for reasoning in support of his own religion ('One of our company in my presence was sharply punished. He, as soon as he was baptised, began, against our wills, with more earnest affection than wisdom, to reason of Christ's religion, and began to wax so hot in his matter, that he did not only prefer our religion before all other, but also did despise and condemn all other, calling them profane, and the followers of them wicked and devilish, and the children of everlasting damnation. When he had thus long reasoned the matter, they laid hold on him, accused him, and condemned him into exile, not as a despiser of religion, but as a seditious person and a raiser up of dissension among the people').' In the public services 'no prayers be used, but such as every man may boldly pronounce without giving offence to any sect.' He says significantly, 'There be that give worship to a man that was once of excellent virtue or of famous glory, not only as God, but also the chiefest and highest God. But the most and the wisest part, rejecting all these, believe that there is a certain godly power unknown, far above the capacity and reach of man's wit, dispersed throughout all the world, not in bigness, but in virtue and power. Him they call the Father of all. To Him alone they attribute the beginnings, the increasings, the proceedings, the changes, and the ends of all things. Neither give they any divine honours to any other than him.' So far was More from sharing the popular beliefs of his time. Yet at the end he reminds us that he does not in all respects agree with the customs and opinions of the Utopians which he describes. And we should let him have the benefit of this saving clause, and not rudely withdraw the veil behind which he has been pleased to conceal himself.

Nor is he less in advance of popular opinion in his political and moral speculations. He would like to bring military glory into contempt; he would set all sorts of idle people to profitable occupation, including in the same class, priests, women, noblemen, gentlemen, and 'sturdy and valiant beggars,' that the labour of all may be reduced to six hours a day. His dislike of capital punishment, and plans for the reformation of offenders; his detestation of priests and lawyers (Compare his satirical observation: 'They (the Utopians) have priests of exceeding holiness, and therefore very few.); his remark that 'although every one may hear of ravenous dogs and wolves and cruel man-eaters, it is not easy to find states that are well and wisely governed,' are curiously at variance with the notions of his age and indeed with his own life. There are many points in which he shows a modern feeling and a prophetic insight like Plato. He is a sanitary reformer; he maintains that civilized states have a right to the soil of waste countries; he is inclined to the opinion which places happiness in virtuous pleasures, but herein, as he thinks, not disagreeing from those other philosophers who define virtue to be a life according to nature. He extends the idea of happiness so as to include the happiness of others; and he argues ingeniously, 'All men agree that we ought to make others happy; but if others, how much more ourselves!' And still he thinks that there may be a more excellent way, but to this no man's reason can attain unless heaven should inspire him with a higher truth. His ceremonies before marriage; his humane proposal that war should be carried on by assassinating the leaders of the enemy, may be compared to some of the paradoxes of Plato. He has a charming fancy, like the affinities of Greeks and barbarians in the Timaeus, that the Utopians learnt the language of the Greeks with

the more readiness because they were originally of the same race with
them. He is penetrated with the spirit of Plato, and quotes or adapts
many thoughts both from the Republic and from the Timaeus. He prefers
public duties to private, and is somewhat impatient of the importunity of
relations. His citizens have no silver or gold of their own, but are ready
enough to pay them to their mercenaries. There is nothing of which he
is more contemptuous than the love of money. Gold is used for fetters
of criminals, and diamonds and pearls for children's necklaces (When the
ambassadors came arrayed in gold and peacocks' feathers 'to the eyes of all
the Utopians except very few, which had been in other countries for some
reasonable cause, all that gorgeousness of apparel seemed shameful and
reproachful. In so much that they most reverently saluted the vilest and
most abject of them for lords—passing over the ambassadors themselves
without any honour, judging them by their wearing of golden chains
to be bondmen. You should have seen children also, that had cast away
their pearls and precious stones, when they saw the like sticking upon the
ambassadors' caps, dig and push their mothers under the sides, saying thus
to them—"Look, though he were a little child still." But the mother; yea
and that also in good earnest: "Peace, son," saith she, "I think he be some
of the ambassadors' fools.'")

Like Plato he is full of satirical reflections on governments and princes;
on the state of the world and of knowledge. The hero of his discourse
(Hythloday) is very unwilling to become a minister of state, considering
that he would lose his independence and his advice would never be heeded
(Compare an exquisite passage, of which the conclusion is as follows: 'And
verily it is naturally given...suppressed and ended.') He ridicules the new
logic of his time; the Utopians could never be made to understand the
doctrine of Second Intentions ('For they have not devised one of all those
rules of restrictions, amplifications, and suppositions, very wittily invented
in the small Logicals, which here our children in every place do learn.
Furthermore, they were never yet able to find out the second intentions;
insomuch that none of them all could ever see man himself in common, as
they call him, though he be (as you know) bigger than was ever any giant,

yea, and pointed to of us even with our finger.') He is very severe on the sports of the gentry; the Utopians count 'hunting the lowest, the vilest, and the most abject part of butchery.' He quotes the words of the Republic in which the philosopher is described 'standing out of the way under a wall until the driving storm of sleet and rain be overpast,' which admit of a singular application to More's own fate; although, writing twenty years before (about the year 1514), he can hardly be supposed to have foreseen this. There is no touch of satire which strikes deeper than his quiet remark that the greater part of the precepts of Christ are more at variance with the lives of ordinary Christians than the discourse of Utopia ('And yet the most part of them is more dissident from the manners of the world now a days, than my communication was. But preachers, sly and wily men, following your counsel (as I suppose) because they saw men evil-willing to frame their manners to Christ's rule, they have wrested and wried his doctrine, and, like a rule of lead, have applied it to men's manners, that by some means at the least way, they might agree together.')

The 'New Atlantis' is only a fragment, and far inferior in merit to the 'Utopia.' The work is full of ingenuity, but wanting in creative fancy, and by no means impresses the reader with a sense of credibility. In some places Lord Bacon is characteristically different from Sir Thomas More, as, for example, in the external state which he attributes to the governor of Solomon's House, whose dress he minutely describes, while to Sir Thomas More such trappings appear simple ridiculous. Yet, after this programme of dress, Bacon adds the beautiful trait, 'that he had a look as though he pitied men.' Several things are borrowed by him from the Timaeus; but he has injured the unity of style by adding thoughts and passages which are taken from the Hebrew Scriptures.

The 'City of the Sun' written by Campanella (1568-1639), a Dominican friar, several years after the 'New Atlantis' of Bacon, has many resemblances to the Republic of Plato. The citizens have wives and children in common; their marriages are of the same temporary sort, and are arranged by the magistrates from time to time. They do not, however, adopt his system of lots, but bring together the best natures,

male and female, 'according to philosophical rules.' The infants until two
years of age are brought up by their mothers in public temples; and since
individuals for the most part educate their children badly, at the beginning
of their third year they are committed to the care of the State, and are
taught at first, not out of books, but from paintings of all kinds, which
are emblazoned on the walls of the city. The city has six interior circuits of
walls, and an outer wall which is the seventh. On this outer wall are painted
the figures of legislators and philosophers, and on each of the interior
walls the symbols or forms of some one of the sciences are delineated.
The women are, for the most part, trained, like the men, in warlike and
other exercises; but they have two special occupations of their own. After
a battle, they and the boys soothe and relieve the wounded warriors; also
they encourage them with embraces and pleasant words. Some elements
of the Christian or Catholic religion are preserved among them. The life
of the Apostles is greatly admired by this people because they had all
things in common; and the short prayer which Jesus Christ taught men
is used in their worship. It is a duty of the chief magistrates to pardon
sins, and therefore the whole people make secret confession of them to the
magistrates, and they to their chief, who is a sort of Rector Metaphysicus;
and by this means he is well informed of all that is going on in the minds of
men. After confession, absolution is granted to the citizens collectively, but
no one is mentioned by name. There also exists among them a practice of
perpetual prayer, performed by a succession of priests, who change every
hour. Their religion is a worship of God in Trinity, that is of Wisdom, Love
and Power, but without any distinction of persons. They behold in the sun
the reflection of His glory; mere graven images they reject, refusing to fall
under the 'tyranny' of idolatry.

Many details are given about their customs of eating and drinking, about
their mode of dressing, their employments, their wars. Campanella looks
forward to a new mode of education, which is to be a study of nature, and
not of Aristotle. He would not have his citizens waste their time in the
consideration of what he calls 'the dead signs of things.' He remarks that
he who knows one science only, does not really know that one any more

than the rest, and insists strongly on the necessity of a variety of knowledge. More scholars are turned out in the City of the Sun in one year than by contemporary methods in ten or fifteen. He evidently believes, like Bacon, that henceforward natural science will play a great part in education, a hope which seems hardly to have been realized, either in our own or in any former age; at any rate the fulfilment of it has been long deferred.

There is a good deal of ingenuity and even originality in this work, and a most enlightened spirit pervades it. But it has little or no charm of style, and falls very far short of the 'New Atlantis' of Bacon, and still more of the 'Utopia' of Sir Thomas More. It is full of inconsistencies, and though borrowed from Plato, shows but a superficial acquaintance with his writings. It is a work such as one might expect to have been written by a philosopher and man of genius who was also a friar, and who had spent twenty-seven years of his life in a prison of the Inquisition. The most interesting feature of the book, common to Plato and Sir Thomas More, is the deep feeling which is shown by the writer, of the misery and ignorance prevailing among the lower classes in his own time. Campanella takes note of Aristotle's answer to Plato's community of property, that in a society where all things are common, no individual would have any motive to work (Arist. Pol.): he replies, that his citizens being happy and contented in themselves (they are required to work only four hours a day), will have greater regard for their fellows than exists among men at present. He thinks, like Plato, that if he abolishes private feelings and interests, a great public feeling will take their place.

Other writings on ideal states, such as the 'Oceana' of Harrington, in which the Lord Archon, meaning Cromwell, is described, not as he was, but as he ought to have been; or the 'Argenis' of Barclay, which is an historical allegory of his own time, are too unlike Plato to be worth mentioning. More interesting than either of these, and far more Platonic in style and thought, is Sir John Eliot's 'Monarchy of Man,' in which the prisoner of the Tower, no longer able 'to be a politician in the land of his birth,' turns away from politics to view 'that other city which is within him,' and finds on the very threshold of the grave that the secret of human happiness is the mastery of self. The change of government in the time of the English Commonwealth set men thinking about first principles, and gave rise to many works of this class...The great original genius of Swift owes nothing to Plato; nor is there any trace in the conversation or in the works of Dr. Johnson of any acquaintance with his writings. He probably would have refuted Plato without reading him, in the same fashion in which he supposed himself to have refuted Bishop Berkeley's theory of the non-existence of matter. If we except the so-called English Platonists, or rather Neo-Platonists, who never understood their master, and the writings of Coleridge, who was to some extent a kindred spirit, Plato has left no permanent impression on English literature.

7. Human life and conduct are affected by ideals in the same way that they are affected by the examples of eminent men. Neither the one nor the other are immediately applicable to practice, but there is a virtue flowing from them which tends to raise individuals above the common routine of society or trade, and to elevate States above the mere interests of commerce or the necessities of self-defence. Like the ideals of art they are partly framed by the omission of particulars; they require to be viewed at a certain distance, and are apt to fade away if we attempt to approach them. They gain an imaginary distinctness when embodied in a State or in a system of philosophy, but they still remain the visions of 'a world unrealized.' More striking and obvious to the ordinary mind are the examples of great men, who have served their own generation and are remembered in another. Even in our own family circle there may have been some one, a woman, or even a child, in whose face has shone forth a goodness more than human. The ideal then approaches nearer to us, and we fondly cling to it. The ideal of the past, whether of our own past lives or of former states of society, has a singular fascination for the minds of many. Too late we learn that such ideals cannot be recalled, though the recollection of them may have a humanizing influence on other times. But the abstractions of philosophy are to most persons cold and vacant; they give light without warmth; they are like the full moon in the heavens when there are no stars appearing. Men cannot live by thought alone; the world of sense is always breaking

in upon them. They are for the most part confined to a corner of earth, and see but a little way beyond their own home or place of abode; they 'do not lift up their eyes to the hills'; they are not awake when the dawn appears. But in Plato we have reached a height from which a man may look into the distance and behold the future of the world and of philosophy. The ideal of the State and of the life of the philosopher; the ideal of an education continuing through life and extending equally to both sexes; the ideal of the unity and correlation of knowledge; the faith in good and immortality—are the vacant forms of light on which Plato is seeking to fix the eye of mankind.

8. Two other ideals, which never appeared above the horizon in Greek Philosophy, float before the minds of men in our own day: one seen more clearly than formerly, as though each year and each generation brought us nearer to some great change; the other almost in the same degree retiring from view behind the laws of nature, as if oppressed by them, but still remaining a silent hope of we know not what hidden in the heart of man. The first ideal is the future of the human race in this world; the second the future of the individual in another. The first is the more perfect realization of our own present life; the second, the abnegation of it: the one, limited by experience, the other, transcending it. Both of them have been and are powerful motives of action; there are a few in whom they have taken the place of all earthly interests. The hope of a future for the human race at first sight seems to be the more disinterested, the hope of individual existence the more egotistical, of the two motives. But when men have learned to resolve their hope of a future either for themselves or for the world into the will of God—'not my will but Thine,' the difference between them falls away; and they may be allowed to make either of them the basis of their lives, according to their own individual character or temperament. There is as much faith in the willingness to work for an unseen future in this world as in another. Neither is it inconceivable that some rare nature may feel his duty to another generation, or to another century, almost as strongly as to his own, or that living always in the presence of God, he may realize another world as vividly as he does this.

The greatest of all ideals may, or rather must be conceived by us under similitudes derived from human qualities; although sometimes, like the Jewish prophets, we may dash away these figures of speech and describe the nature of God only in negatives. These again by degrees acquire a positive meaning. It would be well, if when meditating on the higher truths either of philosophy or religion, we sometimes substituted one form of expression for another, lest through the necessities of language we should become the slaves of mere words.

There is a third ideal, not the same, but akin to these, which has a place in the home and heart of every believer in the religion of Christ, and in which men seem to find a nearer and more familiar truth, the Divine man, the Son of Man, the Saviour of mankind, Who is the first-born and head of the whole family in heaven and earth, in Whom the Divine and human, that which is without and that which is within the range of our earthly faculties, are indissolubly united. Neither is this divine form of goodness wholly separable from the ideal of the Christian Church, which is said in the New Testament to be 'His body,' or at variance with those other images of good which Plato sets before us. We see Him in a figure only, and of figures of speech we select but a few, and those the simplest, to be the expression of Him. We behold Him in a picture, but He is not there. We gather up the fragments of His discourses, but neither do they represent Him as He truly was. His dwelling is neither in heaven nor earth, but in the heart of man. This is that image which Plato saw dimly in the distance, which, when existing among men, he called, in the language of Homer, 'the likeness of God,' the likeness of a nature which in all ages men have felt to be greater and better than themselves, and which in endless forms, whether derived from Scripture or nature, from the witness of history or from the human heart, regarded as a person or not as a person, with or without parts or passions, existing in space or not in space, is and will always continue to be to mankind the Idea of Good.